D0848286

Elsie de Wolfe

Elsie de Wolfe

The Birth of Modern Interior Decoration

BY PENNY SPARKE

Edited by Mitchell Owens

ACANTHUS PRESS
New York : 2005

ACANTHUS PRESS LLC
48 West 22nd Street
New York, NY 10010
212-414-0108
www.acanthuspress.com

COPYRIGHT © 2005 PENNY SPARKE

Every reasonable attempt has been made to identify the owners of copyright.
Errors of omission will be corrected in subsequent printings of this work.

All rights reserved. This book may not be reproduced in whole or in any part
(except by reviewers for the public press) without written permission from the publisher.

Library of Congress Cataloging-in-Publication Data

Sparke, Penny.
  Elsie de Wolfe : the birth of modern interior decoration / by Penny Sparke ; edited by Mitchell Owens.
     p. cm.
  Includes bibliographical references and index.
  ISBN 0-926494-27-9 (hardcover : alk. paper)
  1. De Wolfe, Elsie, 1865-1950--Criticism and interpretation. 2. Interior decoration--United States--
History--20th century. I. Owens, Mitchell. II. Title.

  NK2004.3.D45S63 2005
  747'.092--dc22

                        2004030113

Frontispiece: Decoupage bureau in Elsie de Wolfe's bedroom at After All.
(Collection of the Elsie de Wolfe Foundation)

Book design by Jeanne Abboud

PRINTED IN CHINA

Contents

*I*nterior decoration, unlike architecture, is a medium that has failed to be respectfully examined by many scholars and historians. After all, rooms are composed of ephemeral ingredients: fabric, paint, passementerie. An interior's physical and visual pleasures may be great but its lifespan is short, subject more than architecture to the fancies of popular taste. But as one of the most personal expressions of design, and arguably its most interactive, interior decoration is a crucial mirror of popular culture, a touchstone of society's public aspirations and private desires, a portrait of who we were at a particular moment. The trouble is that once a room or a house is completed, often so little documentation survives. Unless a museum or an archive makes a request for preservation, the items that provide insight into many decorators' careers and lives—invoices, letters, journals, even cancelled checks—have been dispersed or discarded. Because of this, some of the most important decorators of the modern age, from Syrie Maugham of the 1920s to Billy Baldwin of the 1960s, are known to us largely by hearsay, rumor, and often innuendo.

With this volume about Elsie de Wolfe, the mother of modern interior decoration, we launch a series of monographs that will focus on the great designers of the 20th century— men and women whose work changed the way we live. The books will illustrate each individual designer's professional trajectory in a chronological presentation, from the youthful, enthusiastic statements of their early work to the influential expressions of style of their

Opposite: Living room in Cora Potter's London house, 1906. (Collection of the Elsie de Wolfe Foundation)

mature years. These will not be definitive studies. Documentation continues to surface, in many cases on a daily basis, enabling scholars of design to correct past errors and misinterpretations—in short, to begin rewriting the history of interior decoration as we know it. A room is more than a space filled with furniture and color and light: It is a work of societal artistry, and its story is that of the designer who created it, the clients who paid for it, and the people who lived in it.

As with so many interior designers, de Wolfe's business records have disappeared. Evidence of the majority of her commissions, from early designs for Broadway plays to her beloved home Villa Trianon, is largely restricted to often inaccurate commentary in contemporary magazines and newspapers or buried in obscure archives in hard-to-access sites. Much of what we do know about her business dealings, staff, showrooms, and clients, both major and minor, has been conjecture. And given the span of time, clients are no longer available to talk about what it was like to work with de Wolfe and her associates. But through the measured re-examination of known materials as well as the review of history-clarifying documents that have been overlooked or underused by previous de Wolfe enthusiasts, *Elsie de Wolfe: The Birth of Modern Interior Decoration* provides the foundation of a renewed interest in her groundbreaking career, her philosophy of design, and her belief that an atmosphere of beauty could cure a world of ills.

— MITCHELL OWENS

Introduction

"I am going in now for interior decoration. By that I mean supplying
objets d'art and giving advice regarding the decoration of their houses to wealthy
persons who do not have the time, inclination, nor culture to do such work
for themselves. It is nothing new. Women have done the same thing before."[1]

"We of the twentieth century can only add material comforts
and an expression of our personality."[2]

*E*lsie de Wolfe is a 20th-century legend. Her name is familiar to many who practice the art of interior design or who are linked to the fashionable world of taste making. Associated as it usually is, however, with social elitism and—anathema in a world in which less is more—with visual excess, a certain campiness, or even bad taste, mention of de Wolfe's name is often accompanied by a smile or, at worst, a pained grimace.

Time has been unfair, however. Repositioned within the era in which she worked, and judged by those standards, de Wolfe can be characterized as one of the most prominent interior decoratiors of the first half of the 20th century whose mission was to bring good taste into a world haunted by the spectre of Victorianism. She helped introduce light and air into a dark age, and although she earned her living by working for the wealthy, she sought through books, magazine articles, and radio broadcasts to convince women of modest means that they also had the power to remodel their homes and, in so doing, embrace modernity.

Elsie de Wolfe, as presented at Queen Victoria's court, 1885.
(*After All, 1935*)

Born Ella Anderson de Wolfe, on December 20, 1865, in New York City, Elsie played a key role in the formation of the modern American interior decorating profession, which provided appropriate settings for the new rich in the first half of the 20th century.[3] In the process, she also helped to shape the world's understanding of the modern domestic interior. She did not set out in life to undertake those tasks, however. An unmarried woman until the age of 60, with no inheritance, she simply followed her natural talents—a fashion sense, an appreciation of the finer things in life, and a steely determination to earn a living.

In developing her ideas as a decorator of interiors for the modern world, de Wolfe never aligned herself during her 45-year career with what was seen as the progressive face of modern architecture and design that was associated with the work of her European (predominatly male) contemporaries. Although her main home was in France after 1916, de Wolfe stood apart from the avant-garde activities of early modernist European architect-designers such as Otto Wagner and Josef Hoffmann in Vienna, Peter Behrens in Germany, and Henri Van de Velde in Belgium, men who sought to eradicate the influence of the past and formulate an entirely new visual language for the interior. Nor did she come into contact at any time with the subsequent generation that made that ambition a reality, the Germans Walter Gropius and Mies van der Rohe and the Swiss Le Corbusier among them.

De Wolfe pursued a parallel path that focused on the inside rather than on the outside of the house and that embraced a feminine rather than a masculine model of modernity. Aesthetically, her contributions were conservative and not at all dependent upon any new architectural vision. She valued the achievements of the past—especially those of 18th-century France—and trusted traditional judgments and conventions of beauty and taste.

Where de Wolfe's attitude toward the complex meanings and functions of the domestic interior was concerned, however, she was arguably every bit as modern as her male contemporaries. In certain ways she was perhaps even more radical. Her means of engaging with modernity was just not linked to the visual style with which she chose to express herself. Rather, her designs articulated a fundamentally modern belief in the intersection of the domestic interior with personal expression and individual identity. This connection had long been recognized and understood, but in the early 20th century it took on an enhanced significance for increasing numbers of people, particularly women, many of whom effectively were denied the opportunity to practice anything that could be defined as a profession. The only occupation many women had was the running of their homes, and de Wolfe encouraged them to take advantage of a golden opportunity that many understood only as a limitation. "You will," she wrote, "express yourself in your house, whether you want to or not."[4]

Perhaps more acutely than many of her male counterparts, de Wolfe understood the special social and psychological needs of women to develop aesthetic relationships with the environments in which they lived. She recognized the important links between a woman's understanding of her own identity, of her body, her dress, and her domestic interiors. "It is the personality of the mistress that the home expresses," de Wolfe maintained. "Men are forever guests in our homes, no matter how much happiness they may find there."[5] It was her mission to create a world in which femininity was celebrated in the material environment of everyday life—likely as an antidote to the male-dominated world she inhabited.

In addition to this strongly gendered view of the interior, doubtless developed because she found herself working for the most part with the wives of wealthy men rather than with the men themselves, her deeply rooted modernity also stemmed from an intuitive knowledge of, and ability to manipulate, the relationship between the domestic interior and social class. Her abilities in this area probably stemmed from the fact that she was determined to leave behind the uninspiring middle class into which she had been born. She knew how to provide the appropriate setting for people who were moving from one social position to another and who needed a material means of expressing their newly acquired identities. De Wolfe also anticipated a future era in which the interior would come to be linked to the other accessories of modern living and become an integral part of that elusive concept called "lifestyle." Above all, in an age before decorating had become a well-publicized

Elisabeth Marbury and Elsie de Wolfe, early 1900s.
(Mattie E. Hewitt, My Crystal Ball, *1923)*

professional activity, she was expert at harnessing the media in her effort to market taste.

De Wolfe's early years had a dramatic influence upon her later role as a decorator, if only because they made her realize that she was unable to tolerate mediocrity and ugliness and that she had a fundamental need to strive for beauty in her immediate environment. Her father, Stephen de Wolfe, was a doctor of French Huguenot descent whose family had moved to Connecticut from Nova Scotia. Her mother, Georgina Watt Copeland, had Scottish origins, although her family had moved to Nova Scotia in her childhood. Archibald Charteris, a member of her mother's family, was chaplain at Balmoral Castle for Queen Victoria and succeeded in getting the teenage de Wolfe presented to the monarch at court while the young New Yorker was staying in Britain in the 1880s. To be introduced to royalty was an experience she never forgot, and de Wolfe's subsequent decision to become part of international society seems to have originated at that moment.

Before her transformation, however, de Wolfe spent an unremarkable New York City childhood in a series of terraced brownstone houses with her parents and her brothers, Edgar, Harold, and Charteris. Her memory of those years was dominated by a hatred of the rooms in which she lived, as well as her sense of her own physical shortcomings. In 1901, at age 35, she recalled another lasting memory from her youth, from a day when she returned home from school eager to see the family sitting room, which had been redecorated that day. "I finally sobbed out," she remembered, "that the room was *ugly*—UGLY—and that 'my heart was breaking from the disappointment of it.' During that day I was inconsolable."[6] It was a turning point in her life. "I think," she went on to admit, "that this intense love of everything beautiful, and my equally intense resentment of the ugly, has been the dominant trait through all my life."

At age 69 she recalled a similar experience, this time concerning her childhood drawing room, which had been papered in what she described as "a Morris design of gray palm-leaves and splotches of bright red and green on a background of dull tan."[7] In response to what she remembered as being the epitome of bad taste, she "threw herself on the floor, kicking with stiffened legs, as [she] beat her hands on the carpet."[8] Another poignant recollection returned to her in 1935, related this time to her own appearance. Recalling that she had broken a tooth and that her father had exclaimed that she had ruined her only decent feature, the decorator explained, "Fortunately, I had an imagination which lifted me out of myself into a dream world where I was no longer ugly but some great lady I

had read about or some beautiful creature I had seen riding by in her carriage on Fifth Avenue."[9]

Thus were de Wolfe's social aspirations engendered, her campaign for beauty initiated, and her desire to create a new identity stimulated, initially leading her to a career as an actress. Later, as a decorator, she harnessed the ability to sense similar aspirations in other women, especially the undoubtedly insecure wives of the *nouveaux riches*.

In the context of de Wolfe's decorating career, these early domestic traumas can be equated to James Joyce's "epiphanies," moments of extreme clarity in which he saw his destiny laid out before him. De Wolfe's destiny lay in her enduring determination to imbue the environments that surrounded her—and anyone else who paid her enough—only with beauty. Beautiful atmospheres, she clearly believed, would make her beautiful by association, and creating them meant constructing new identities for herself and for her clients.

This determination to create beauty became an obsession that dominated de Wolfe's professional and personal lives, leaving little room for other emotions. Although she experienced a close companionship of 30 years with the pioneering theatrical manager and literary agent Elisabeth "Bessy" Marbury, and on March 10, 1926, at the age of 60, she married Sir Charles Mendl, a press attaché assigned to the British Embassy in Paris, her closest relationships throughout her life were with her homes. She was always the best articulator of her own sensibilities. "Probably when another woman would be dreaming of love affairs," she revealed in 1913, "I dream of the delightful houses I have lived in."[10] Seven years earlier, a newspaper journalist had already divined the important role that rooms played in de Wolfe's life: "I have the notion that Miss de Wolfe regards every room she beautifies as a beloved child that must be dressed for the duty or the delight of the day."[11] Whether children or lovers, the emotional role that her interiors played in her life was never seriously challenged.

De Wolfe took some time to realize that she was destined to be an interior decorator and spent her youth and early middle age on the stage. Encouraged by people she met in London—among them Cora Brown-Potter, a New York socialite turned actress—to participate in amateur dramatics, she discovered that this genteel profession provided a way for her to move into high society. Indeed, de Wolfe's first awareness of Bessy Marbury's existence occurred in 1887, while she was performing in *A Cup of Tea* at Tuxedo Park.[12] When de Wolfe's father died in 1890, leaving the family penniless, she was forced to become a professional, even though it meant moving down a rung or two of the social ladder; amateur acting was considered a ladylike amusement, whereas working on the professional stage

Elsie de Wolfe in a couture dress, c. 1900.
(Collection of the Elsie de Wolfe Foundation)

Elsie de Wolfe as Lady Teazle, 1891. (After All, 1935)

was deemed by society's most conservative leaders only slightly better than prostitution.[13]

Between 1891 and 1905, de Wolfe performed many roles, made possible through Marbury's work as her agent and as a literary representative of many European writers, including Oscar Wilde. De Wolfe's first professional role was as Fabienne Le Coultueux in Charles Frohman's American production of Victorien Sardou's *Thermidor*. Her part as a young girl engaged to a lieutenant of Napoleon's army was the first of many historical roles, including Lady Teazle in Sheridan's *The School for Scandal*; a maid in *The Marriage of Convenience*; and Lady Mildred Yester in *The Shades of the Night*, which played at the Lyceum Theater in 1901.

De Wolfe was a member of Frohman's Empire Theatre Stock Company for several years, and she appeared in a number of his productions, including *Joseph, The Bauble Shop, Sister Mary,* and *Judge*. She also created a number of sets for Frohman's company and

Elsie de Wolfe, c. 1900.
(Baron de Meyer, Collection of the Elsie de Wolfe Foundation)

advised on costumes. She also established her own company for a short period. It was not a success, but it gave her greater control over the design of the costumes and sets. One of the plays she produced, Clyde Fitch's *The Way of the World,* which was written for her and in which she played Mrs. Croyden, received special attention for its set. The actress had gone to great lengths to procure just the right antique tea table to ensure a high level of realism.[14]

Most accounts of de Wolfe's theatrical performances indicate that she was not a great actress. Even Marbury conceded that her graceful companion's acting talents were limited.[15] Nor was she considered a beauty, but it was generally recognized that de Wolfe's slim figure meant that she wore clothes very well. Indeed, she had French couturiers—Paquin, Doucet, and Worth among them—create outfits especially for her. As she was one of the fashion industry's best billboards, she

was given special prices. In the era before the catwalk fashion show, actresses like de Wolfe provided a means of bringing couture clothing to audiences and of stimulating consumer desire for them. While her perceived ugliness, the actress explained, required her to use the best makeup artists, her figure made her a natural fashion plate.[16] The setting for those clothes also was important, providing a frame that could significantly enhance them. Although in de Wolfe's early life that frame was provided by a stage set, it was soon to be exchanged for the domestic interior.

By the early 20th century, as her reviews got worse and as she grew older, it was clear to de Wolfe that she needed to change careers. She began to look into the possibility of earning a living through buying and selling antiques and decorating the houses of friends and acquaintances. A number of factors combined to make this a potentially viable way forward for her, including her well-known eye for couture outfits and objets d'art; her experience, on annual trips to France with Marbury, of purchasing antique furniture and art objects for their homes on East 17th Street in New York City and in Versailles, France; her successful redecoration of those homes in a clean, crisp style informed by 18th-century French interiors; and, from 1891, her relationship with Marbury, a forceful and effective promoter of de Wolfe's work. Most importantly, however, her experience in designing stage sets meant that she understood how to construct an expressive, emotional relationship between an environment and its inhabitants.

While de Wolfe had become extremely well known as an actress, much of the extensive press attention she received was directed less at her acting achievements than at her fabulous costumes and her stylish homes. In 1905, de Wolfe decided to make decorating the focus of her working life, and in that year she received what is said to be her first commission as a professional decorator. It was to decorate the so-called entertainment annex at the country house of Emily and John R. McLean, the publisher and majority owner of *The Washington Post.*

The details of some of her most important commissions, as well as those of the homes she created for herself, are contained in the pages of this book. The exact number of projects she and her firm worked on during the 32 years of its existence is unknown. Many of the projects involved the decoration of complete interiors, yet many more were partial refurbishments that focused on the private, feminine spaces of houses and apartments—bedrooms, boudoirs, dressing rooms, bathrooms. Although Elsie de Wolfe Inc.'s business records were destroyed when it went into liquidation in 1937, the number of commissions the firm had undertaken by that date undoubtedly numbered in the hundreds.

Elsie de Wolfe in her home at 123 East 55th Street, New York. (The House in Good Taste, *1913*)

Title page. (The House in Good Taste, *1913*)

Only 29 projects are described here in depth, while a number of others are listed at the back of this book. This list is not the last word on de Wolfe's career. Details of other projects will continue to emerge as her contribution to the modern domestic interior is increasingly understood and her oeuvre receives greater scholarly attention.

In 1905, de Wolfe received her life- and career-changing commission to create the interiors of the Colony Club in New York. It was designed by the architect Stanford White, who proved to be one of her most important mentors and champions. Other commissions came her way from across the United States—Detroit, Spokane, San Francisco, New York, St. Louis, Boston, Newport, Galveston, and elsewhere—and France. She and her staff were kept busy right through World War I.

Much of de Wolfe's best work was produced in the years between 1905 and 1916, most of it realized

Anne Vanderbilt. (Collection of Mitchell Owens)

in the French 18th-century style. It was also at this time that she developed her personal theory of interior decoration, which she—or rather her ghostwriter, Ruby Ross Goodnow, later the prominent decorator Ruby Ross Wood—articulated in her bestselling book of 1913, *The House in Good Taste.* Those ideas broadly underpinned everything she did from that moment onward, though, inevitably, her visual language of interior decoration changed over the years.

Her early projects were undertaken in a period of enormous optimism, enthusiasm, and wealth, one in which a new class of Americans—including de Wolfe herself—sought both to construct and express themselves through their homes. De Wolfe was available to supply the necessary props and ideas to make that possible. As she became increasingly wealthy and famous and could afford to live out her childhood dreams, de Wolfe's own life changed beyond recognition. She

entertained, socialized with, and created interiors for society women and an impressive range of cultural figures, from the bandleader John Philip Sousa to the writer Henry Adams. She took on new offices, employed more staff, purchased designer clothes, and furnished a new home for herself and Marbury in New York City, as well as one in Versailles, Villa Trianon, which they acquired in 1906. Along with Anne Morgan, a daughter of J. Pierpont Morgan and who soon would become extremely close to Bessy Marbury, the two women spent their summers in France driving in expensive automobiles, hosting dinners, and shopping for antiques and high fashion. In 1908, ever keen to participate in the achievements of the modern world, de Wolfe became one of the first women to ride in an airplane.

There was another side to this tasteful, fashion-conscious, free-living woman, however. She participated in the suffrage movement, albeit at the margins, marching with the militant socialite Alva Belmont in 1912. She also involved herself in the fundraising and charity work embraced by her close friends. During World War I she spent nearly two years in France, nursing badly burned soldiers, for which she was awarded the Croix de Guerre and the Legion d'Honneur.

At heart de Wolfe was a society decorator, however. Following the war and the gradual demise of her relationship with Bessy Marbury, she spent increasing amounts of time in France, eventually making it her main home and running her New York business from there. In her postwar life in Paris and Versailles, de Wolfe designed interiors for herself, close friends like Marbury, Morgan, and Anne Vanderbilt, and rich clients, and she returned annually to America to oversee the activities of the office. Following her marriage to Sir Charles Mendl in 1926, however, she assumed a new role as Lady Mendl, well-known hostess, holding parties at her flat in Paris or at her villa in Versailles. A natural extension of her career as a lifestyle pioneer, de Wolfe's hostessing was performed in an equally professional capacity, and she regularly introduced wealthy Americans to Parisian antiques dealers, couturiers, jewelers, and decorators, receiving favors in kind.

As Jane S. Smith pointed out in her biography of de Wolfe, the social group de Wolfe maintained in the years after her marriage consisted for the most part of wealthy Europeans and Americans and people from the entertainment and film industries.[17] Several were also decorating clients. De Wolfe also worked very hard at entertaining members of the European aristocracy and artistic community at her Versailles house and socializing with them during summers in the south of France. Her close relationship with Condé Nast, the publisher of *Vogue* from the pre–World War I days into the interwar years, ensured her continued visibility as a member of the beau monde, a consumer of couture fashion and expensive jewels, and her position as trendsetter. De Wolfe was among the first women, for example, to dye her hair pale blue, reportedly to match an aquamarine tiara, undergo frequent facelifts, and be injected with goat-cell serum, while in later life de Wolfe's strings of pearls and her custom-made kid gloves—the left with a hole cut out at the wrist so she could see the face of her watch—were widely emulated.

Elsie de Wolfe, interior decorator, however, continued to exist alongside Lady Mendl, socialite, although she allowed the New York office, which was managed for a period of time by her brother Edgar and his second wife, Winifred, to function autonomously while she continued to work directly with friends and the most important clients. So important was the Elsie de Wolfe name to the operation of the firm, however, that she maintained a sufficient professional presence to ensure its continued success.

The New York firm ceased to exist in 1937 (although de Wolfe reportedly had not had a role in its activities for a year), but she continued to decorate. Surprisingly, some of her most innovative work was undertaken over the next decade and a half. De Wolfe's return to the United States, not long after the outbreak of World War II, and the few years she spent on the West Coast in her last home, After All—the title of her 1935 autobiography—brought her life full circle, from the footlights of Broadway to the sound stages of Hollywood. She moved back to France in 1946 to restore her beloved Villa Trianon. On July 12, 1950, de Wolfe died there, at age 84.

In addition to her deep understanding of the importance of the relationship of the domestic interior to the construction and expression of gender and class, de Wolfe made many original contributions to the art of modern interior decoration. Stylistically, and to some extent philosophically, she owed an enormous debt to Edith Wharton and Ogden Codman. Their jointly authored book, *The Decoration of Houses,* was published in 1897, the year in which de Wolfe transformed her Irving Place home. Although Codman claimed with some authority that he taught de Wolfe everything she knew, de Wolfe added the important concepts of comfort, livability, and intimacy to his and Wharton's more lofty, formal preoccupations.[18] She echoed their commitment to 18th-century European neoclassicism as a counterpoint to excessive Victorianism and their belief in the principles of suitability, simplicity, and proportion—de Wolfe's creed was "suitability, suitability, suitability." Unlike Wharton and Codman, who aimed their ideas at a social elite, de Wolfe made hers relevant to a much larger audience. It is difficult to imagine Wharton promulgating her decorating ideas in popular ladies' magazines like *The Delineator, Good Housekeeping,* and *McCall's,* but de Wolfe understood the importance of these mass-market publications to the average woman, who was not rich, but who appreciated beautiful things and wanted a comfortable, appropriate home.

Also in her favor, de Wolfe worked at a time that represented a transitional moment for American architecture. The buildings displayed in Chicago at the World's Columbian Exposition of 1893 had heralded a neoclassical revival that would be called Beaux Arts. In her understanding of the close psychological identification of inhabitants with their interiors, especially of women, however, de Wolfe advocated a much simpler, more private, and deeply personal interior than those created by the neo-neoclassical architects, such as the firm of McKim, Mead & White. The architectural frame of the interior was less important to de Wolfe than the psychological setting of the internal domestic arena, which could draw on theatrical illusion as much as it could on material reality. In acquiring furnishings, for instance, de Wolfe bought antiques, contemporary objects, or she had items custom-made as required. She could dismiss the fact that a Louis XVI console was made in the early 20th century, provided that the required effect was achieved. She even designed simple objects, including a kidney-shaped side table and a metal bed, and used them in numerous projects. Several accessories—a three-branch candlestick among them and a wall sconce with a ram's-head motif—appeared over and again in de Wolfe's personal decorating language.

In understanding and expertly manipulating the expressive function of the domestic interior, Elsie de Wolfe belonged unequivocally to the 20th century, and she took interior decorating into a new era. While only the wealthy could afford to actually employ her on multi-room commissions, through her writings and the widespread publication and emulation of her work, she addressed her message to all women, whether they lived in neo-Renaissance palaces, small city apartments, or suburban cottages. By 1913, when *The House in Good Taste* was published, all of the decorator's important aesthetic strategies were in place. Seeing each room as an individual unit, she created entire living environments based on the broad-brush concept that life would go on in them. She attended to every last detail, which might include the introduction of small props, such as a pen and paper on the surface of a desk, to make that life livable.

In the years prior to World War I, de Wolfe favored paneled walls painted in shades of gray, white, or ivory; the use of plain or flowered glazed chintz; antique wall sconces (usually adapted to electricity but often candle-powered for atmosphere); simple furniture embellished with painted rococo patterns; a mix of antique (usually 18th-century French) and reproduction furnishings; marble fireplaces; as many big mirrors as she could possibly include, and trelliswork. It was an overtly feminine aesthetic, intended primarily as an accompaniment to women's lives—men and children were ignored, for the most part—that aimed to eliminate Victorian gloom and to introduce light and air.

After World War I, de Wolfe's palette and stylistic preferences suddenly changed, and contemporary features began to enter her interiors, including animal skins—real or artificial—and murals painted in modern, albeit neoclassically inspired styles. Another apparent volte-face occurred in the late 1930s and early 1940s when she embraced a style she called Modern Regency (an idiom that had been in vogue in England since the 1920s) and took a liking to dark green walls, chintz printed with green fern fronds, and the inclusion of numerous small decorative objects, usually crystal animal figurines. There also were important periods of interior schemes dominated by beige or black and white. Given the length of de Wolfe's career, of course, it would have been surprising if her taste had not evolved. The photographer Cecil Beaton explained, "Elsie de Wolfe passed through a number of fashion periods, yet each phase found her picking the creative vibrations of esoteric people and exploiting them commercially with great flair."[19] Strikingly, unlike many creative artists, the older she got, the less conservative de Wolfe became.

In spite of these shifts, de Wolfe maintained a high level of continuity, manifested in her repeated use of certain features, among them green and white stripes, mirrors, Louis XVI chairs, handy small tables, footstools, chintz upholstery, and plenty of flowers, whether in vases, printed on fabric, or painted on furniture. Above all, the maxim of livability stayed with her throughout her life, ensuring that her rooms were always eminently inhabitable.

De Wolfe pushed the notion of the domestic interior into an era that was characterized by an emphasis on individualism. Her preoccupation with the concept of taste and its social and psychological implications aided the emergence of independent-minded women wanting to take charge of their own interior worlds and, by extension, their own lives. She also offered a model of a new kind of aesthetic professional, combining a new combination of services for a new market. Before de Wolfe entered the scene, wealthy clients would have sought interior schemes from architects, or they would have gone to an elite furnishing firm, such as Herter Brothers or Tiffany Studios, to supply everything from furniture to wallpaper, or they would have worked directly with antiques dealers or a range of specialist tradesmen. By the early 20th century, exclusive European decorators, such as Alavoine et cie and the London-based White, Allom & Co., were establishing New York offices, but they worked only for the cream of American society.

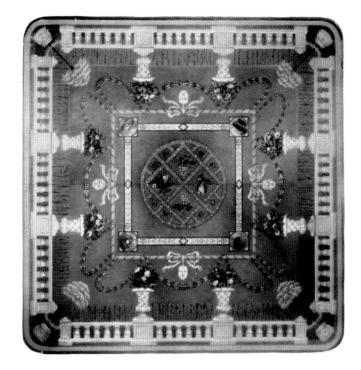

Mrs. James Warren Lane's table.
(The House in Good Taste, *1913*)

De Wolfe offered something new and different, and she offered it to a different clientele. With enviable precision, she was able to walk through a room or set of rooms and suggest an aesthetic ensemble that would suit the taste and lifestyle of the client in question.[20] Usually she dealt with the female head of the household, discovering her taste and aligning it with the decorator's own, so that the final scheme subtly reflected both. She also was able to provide everything needed to create complete interiors, down to the smallest bibelot. Although she was not the first to offer such a service—many firms had been doing so for several years before de Wolfe arrived on the scene—she made it appeal to a new audience of nouveau-riche clients who saw in the acquisition of a de Wolfe interior a chance to climb the social ladder and proclaim their entry into the fashionable world.

Her clients were seldom the cream of American society but more commonly the next tier down, the second generation of moneyed Americans whose fortunes had been made in the industrial economic boom years of the late 19th century. As the years went on, the second generation of nouveaux riches who constituted the core of her clientele gradually were supplemented by others from the entertainment industry. Most of her clients, both American and European, needed a de Wolfe interior to facilitate their entrée into society.

Given the fact that de Wolfe imbued every interior she created with her own identity to some extent, it is impossible to separate the decorator's personality, and the rich and fascinating life she led, from her work. There is no doubt that she was a snob and a social climber and was breathlessly self-absorbed—*Me* was the title of an album of photographs she kept of herself. Because many of her clients were very like her in some of those respects, the decorator had an insight into their needs.

Unable to accept anything less than beautiful, de Wolfe was as obsessed with her own appearance as she was with her interiors. As she got older, she kept a vegetarian diet under the supervision of celebrity nutritionist Gayelord Hauser. She undertook grueling exercises, bought youthful clothes from favored couturiers and jewels from Cartier. She wore necklaces, bracelets, and brooches, but not earrings, which she thought barbaric. Also, she chose her friends, among them the Duke and Duchess of Windsor and countless French counts and princesses, very carefully. She was photographed over the years by the world's leading photographers, from Baron de Meyer to Cecil Beaton, and she adopted white gloves when her hands became crabbed from arthritis. A picture emerges of a vain and egotistical woman, which she undoubtedly was. As de Wolfe was always on duty, however, a living example of what the possession of taste could accomplish, it is difficult to know if this is the whole picture. Her sophisticated, self-generated publicity machine—formed in

part through her close relationship with Condé Nast and his magazines *Vogue* and *House and Garden*—was never at rest. There were, at moments, glimpses of another woman in her generosity to her close friends, in her voluntary and charitable activities during both world wars, and in her adoration for the series of Pekingeses, chows, and miniature poodles she owned throughout her life. Whatever de Wolfe was really like, she expressed herself as the woman she aspired to be, through her work and her environments. From her own homes a portrait emerges of a well-mannered, tasteful, fastidious, flirtatious, feminine woman who never ceased to be optimistic or lose her faith in the possibility of continual self-improvement.

So successful was de Wolfe's assessment of the marketplace and her ability to fulfill its needs that many others followed the path she had established. By the interwar years, the female interior decorator had become a significant phenomenon, especially in the United States. The leading women who emulated her professional role in America included Ruby Ross Wood, Dorothy Draper, Rose Cumming, and Frances Elkins. Decorators less well known today were also part of this early movement, among them Gertrude Gheen, Agnes Foster Wright, Elsie Cobb Wilson, and Alice M. Swift.

By the end of World War II, however, the industry had changed dramatically. Female decorators continued to follow the professional model established by de Wolfe, but male-dominated modernism ascended as the dominant aesthetic ideology, eclipsing and undermining the achievements of de Wolfe and her disciples. As part of this new moment, the more professional-sounding term *interior designer*—used perhaps because it was less sexually suspect and implied a level of higher education and professional training—began to displace the more old-fashioned *interior decorator.*

As the concept of interior decoration became marginalized by doctrinaire modernism and its supporters, a number of critics and designers began to distance themselves from de Wolfe's oeuvre. In his 1944 book *Goodbye, Mr. Chippendale,* the designer T. H. Robsjohn-Gibbings, for example, blamed de Wolfe for everything he thought was wrong with the contemporary American interior, especially its dependence on historical styles. "Decoratively speaking," he explained, "American women live in the shadow of Elsie de Wolfe and if it was the Chicago World's Fair that held American architecture back fifty years, it was she who did the same thing for American furniture design. Should this suggestion make you writhe in your *bergere* chair, or wince under the *couvre-pieds* of your chaise-longue, or pale against your *boiserie,* I hasten to spread out on the Aubusson rug some blossoms gathered from the parterres of Miss de Wolfe's garden of décor."[21]

The dramatic social and cultural transformations of the post–World War II years moved the focus away from the interior decorator as a seminal figure within polite society and turned the spotlight on the democratic possibilities of modernism. The reign of the modernist architect-designer as the arbiter of taste and style had moved from the periphery to the center of the picture. The interior designer had come to be seen as both morally and aesthetically superior to the snobbish, largely self-taught—and therefore, somehow unprofessional—interior decorator. Interior design was democratic, masculine, in tune with modern architecture, and, above all, did not look to the past for inspiration. Traditional decorators suddenly became the enemies, perpetrators of the joint crimes of elitism and historicism.

Only now, as the grip of modernism has loosened and we have come to inhabit a more eclectic and inclusive world, can we see that things are more complex than the modernist ideology implied. People do not necessarily want what they are told is good for them. The cycle of fashion dictates that people often aspire to things not easily available to them, and often through the exercise of imagination and the assistance of a pot of paint and a yard of fabric, models of beauty can be created by large numbers of people.

Today the austerity that modernism engendered has lost much of its appeal and there are many people who, in the early 21st century, seek a more human, more comfortable approach to decorating their private spaces. Above all, the need for people to express or change their identities through material goods and their homes has never been greater. In this context, de Wolfe's philosophy of interior decoration remains highly relevant. The moment to revisit the subtle workings of her "house in good taste," nearly a century after its formulation, has arrived.

Staircase in the Bayard Thayer house.
(The House in Good Taste, *1913*)

1892–1910

Elsie de Wolfe–Elisabeth Marbury Residence
122 East 17th Street
New York City

"A regular Rip Van Winkle of a house"[1]

Elsie de Wolfe and her theatrical manager and companion, Elisabeth Marbury, lived together in New York in a small rented house on the corner of East 17th Street and Irving Place for 18 years.[2] They moved there in 1892, five years into their close friendship, two years after the death of de Wolfe's father, and a year after the actress had turned professional.

For the first few years of their cohabitation, the women's careers involved them in a great deal of traveling and they had very little time in which to establish a shared domestic life. By the mid-1890s, however, their circumstances had changed, and together they began to build a home life that was to remain in place for more than a decade. The house at 122 East 17th Street played a crucial role in the women's changing lives: it provided an aesthetic and a functional backcloth for both women, allowing them to grow professionally and personally. Most significantly, it offered de Wolfe an opportunity to exercise her growing talent as a decorating artist and to develop ideas and strategies that would underpin her 45-year career in the field of interior decorating.

In 1911, Elsie de Wolfe described the way she went about decorating, explaining that just as an actress prepares to play a new role by getting inside the persona of the character she is to enact, so when she began a new interior project, her first step was to study the people who lived in the house in which she was to work.[3] Her years of experience on the stage had

Opposite: Redecorated drawing room with the Nattier portrait above the marble mantel, early 1900s.
(The House in Good Taste, 1913)

led her to understand the close relationship between a domestic interior and its inhabitants, and she recognized the power that a decorator possesses to form character. The characters she was forming in 122 East 17th Street were those of herself and her companion.

The Union Square area was a vibrant environment in which to live in the 1890s. The house was on the same block as the Irving Place Theater and approximately two blocks from the Academy of Music. Marbury's family home was two blocks away in Irving Place. In her 1902 book *Eminent Actors in Their Homes,* the writer Margherita Arlina Hamm deemed the area highly suitable for de Wolfe, stating, "No neighbourhood is more appropriate as the home of a famous actress."[4] The streets around Union Square exuded a bohemian atmosphere, and the two women had a number of illustrious neighbors, who were also friends, among them architect Stanford White and the Hewitt sisters, Sarah and Eleanor (known to their friends as "Sallie" and "Nellie"). The sisters, who founded the Cooper-Hewitt Museum, had been childhood friends of Marbury.[5]

The house on East 17th Street had allegedly been lived in by the well-known writer Washington Irving. Although it has now been established that he did not live there (although at least one member of his family had done so), Marbury and de Wolfe subscribed to the myth that the famous writer had lived in their house, and they fantasized about him being able to look across to the river from the first-floor veranda. By the time of their purchase, that view was already blocked by the numerous buildings that stood between the house and the river.

Built in the 1840s, 122 East 17th Street had a very simple brownstone exterior. It consisted of three floors, as well as a basement and an attic, and its only distinguishing exterior features were a veranda, a bay window, and a box window. The entrance was on East 17th Street beside the bay window, whereas the veranda looked out over Irving Place. Decorative cast-iron metalwork surrounded the entrance. The first floor comprised a long drawing room and a dining room. There were two bedrooms on the second floor, and above them, a library. The rest of the interior space, including the basement and the attic, was given over to the utility areas of the house and to the servants.[6]

De Wolfe conceived her redecoration of the interior as an act of restoration, likening it to "reviving an old garden."[7] As one might with a garden that had not been nurtured for many years, however, she experienced a level of resistance from this little house, which she described as "petulant and querulous."[8]

For the first five years of their time there, the two women managed to live with the cluttered high Victorian character of the rooms, which were overwhelmingly gloomy and ornamented. Photographs from 1896 depict flowered wallpaper in the style of the English designer William Morris, textured velvet upholstery, patterned cushions, dark varnished wood, decorative jardinières containing potted palms, suspended chandeliers, and fabrics draped across every available surface. A Turkish "cozy corner," made up of numerous cushions placed on a raised plinth, bore witness to the contemporary interest in Orientalism. The Victorian emphasis on exotic items was an aspect of the "house beautiful" approach, which, influenced by the ideas of the English tastemakers Charles Eastlake and Oscar Wilde, had dominated fashionable American interiors from the 1870s onward.

Perhaps the only surprising addition to the otherwise familiar setting in the 17th Street home was the inclusion of a number of 18th-century French furnishings that had been purchased by Marbury and de Wolfe on their annual summer trips to France.

De Wolfe's house on the southwest corner of Irving Place and East 17th Street, undated.
(Byron Collection, The Museum of the City of New York)

Except for numerous photos and personal mementos, there were no other signs of the women's desire, at that early date, to introduce a more individual note into their otherwise remarkably conventional late-19th-century interior.

Between the second half of 1897 and the first half of 1898, Elsie de Wolfe set about transforming the house on East 17th Street. She was inspired, undoubtedly, by the highly influential book *The Decoration of Houses,* written by Edith Wharton and Ogden Codman and published in 1897, which advocated the use of French furniture and interior

detailing as a means of achieving a new level of simplicity. De Wolfe, albeit in a much more modest interior than those illustrated by Wharton and Codman, set about replacing the high Victorianism of her own domestic interior with the modern look they advocated.[9] The result was an utterly changed set of spaces that introduced many of the decorating ideas and themes that would characterize de Wolfe's work for the next half-century.

Several descriptions of the interior of 122 East 17th Street at the end of the 19th century and the early years of the 20th century appeared in the popular press at the time.[10] The enormous interest that had already been expressed in the actress's elegant gowns, which she brought back from Paris to inspire theater audiences, was now transferred to the elegant home she had created. Her collection of antique shoes, her dolls from around the world (which she used for her research into theatrical costumes), and her paintings and furnishings also were subjected to a great deal of press attention, and several articles pointed out that many of the items de Wolfe and Marbury had bought for very little money on their summer vacations had come to be valuable. Their 18th-century painting of the Duchess of Châteauroux by Jean-Marc Nattier, for example, which hung over the fireplace in the drawing room, received frequent mention, as did the items of antique French furniture. The mantelpiece itself was an 18th-century French addition to the interior, made of strongly veined marble, probably rose and white.

Although de Wolfe was clearly aware of the public interest in her home, she probably decorated it for two other reasons. The first was undoubtedly personal: she wanted to create a comfortable home for herself and Marbury. The second reason was likely to have been the fact that their home was increasingly becoming a site for fashionable entertaining, especially on Sunday afternoons, when numerous well-known figures from the worlds of theater, literature, art, philosophy, business, and politics squeezed into the small house and sat on the stairs and elsewhere to eat sandwiches and salad, drink tea, coffee, and punch, and engage in stimulating

Elsie de Wolfe in the Turkish corner, before redecoration, 1896. (Byron Collection, The Museum of the City of New York)

conversation. Over the years, visitors to 122 East 17th Street included such prominent figures as Sarah Bernhardt, Sir Henry Irving, Ellen Terry, Dame Nellie Melba, Count Robert de Montesquiou, Oscar Wilde, Cora Potter, Henry Adams, and Isabella Stewart Gardner. De Wolfe undoubtedly had these visitors in mind when, in 1897, she set about reviving her home and introducing a radically new aesthetic into it.

The results of de Wolfe's efforts were dramatic. Without losing a commitment to the values of the past, she succeeded in introducing a new, lighter palette, a much simpler look, more light and air, a feeling of spaciousness, and a sense of modernity. In so doing, she developed a language and a philosophy of the domestic interior that were to remain the baselines of her oeuvre for the next half-century.

The narrowness of the entrance hall and stairwell in 122 East 17th Street provided the decorator with her first challenge. She replaced the mural decorations and tapestries that had embellished the walls when she and Marbury had moved in and, in order to create a greater sense of space, introduced green-and-white vertically

*View from drawing room to the dining room, early 1900s. (*The House in Good Taste, *1913)*

Dining room before redecoration, 1896. (Byron Collection, The Museum of the City of New York)

striped wallpaper and woodwork painted light gray-green. To finish off the hall and stairwell, de Wolfe hung a sequence of French 18th-century costume prints on the walls at eye level.

The main space on the first floor consisted of a long drawing room that led into the dining room at one end. Two yellow marble Corinthian pillars flanked an arch that originally broke the space visually into a double parlor. In 1901, Edith Wharton's coauthor, well-known architect and decorator Ogden Codman, was invited to undertake some work in the drawing room. Codman's brief was to create a "salon" that exuded a "mellowed atmosphere of French society."[11] His intervention involved adding panel moldings, painting the walls ivory, dressing the doors with mirrors to create an illusion of additional space, and introducing a niche into one wall,

in which a statue of a small girl was positioned. Ivy was added to trail around it.

Although de Wolfe needed Codman's assistance in order to realize her vision for her home, she had achieved many of the changes of 1897–98 on her own. It was she, for example, who decided to eliminate the cozy corner and add a small conservatory in the bay window. By placing a piece of white marble in the bay behind a raised area that concealed a drainpipe, she was able to transform a 17th-century marble baptismal font into a fountain and have six ornamental goldfish swimming in its water.

Rose pink upholstery was used on much of the drawing room furniture, while other pieces were covered with tapestry and embroidered fabric. Sheer white muslin hung against the windows, behind the inner

Dining room after redecoration, 1896. (Byron Collection, The Museum of the City of New York)

curtains, and the Nattier portrait was mounted into the woodwork over the fireplace. Next to it de Wolfe placed a small glass case covering a wax figurine. The finished room confirmed the decorator's belief in the values of "light, air and comfort" and represented a dramatic shift from the Victorian aesthetic that had previously dominated it.[12]

The most dramatic transformation of all, however, took place in the dining room, an octagonal room with wooden cupboards positioned across the four corners. Two stages of renovation took place here, the first in 1897–98 and the second a few years later. The initial work involved removing the clutter in the room, painting the woodwork white, and introducing a gray, white, and ivory color scheme. A mirror was hung over the fireplace, on which a bust of Marie-Antoinette was

carefully positioned, flanked by small shaded candlesticks. The original heavy chairs were replaced by painted cane-backed French chairs, and the table was covered with a sheet of protective glass. Mirror-backed wall sconces, purchased in France, replaced the overhead lighting, helping to create a mellow atmosphere.

The subsequent refurbishment of the dining room took things further, with the decorator adding mirrored panels around the cupboard doors and hanging on the walls a series of Monnoyer grisailles, described by her as "India-ink sketches." The window seat, framed by two more brown marble Corinthian columns, was covered with yellow velvet to match the numerous footstools that were included in the interior, either for the comfort of diners' feet or to accommodate guests on crowded Sunday afternoons when there weren't enough proper

Dining room after the addition of the Monnoyer grisailles, early 1900s. (The House in Good Taste, *1913)*

seats to go around. A rose-colored Chinese carpet, covered with blue and yellow medallions, completed the striking decor achieved by de Wolfe. The result was a light, simple, utilitarian space that exuded an air of historical elegance but was eminently modern nonetheless.

Whereas the public first-floor rooms were decorated in a formal manner, the two upstairs bedrooms were treated in a much more intimate way. Indeed, de Wolfe explained that she thought of her bedroom as a kind of "secret garden" that she wanted to be as "simple as a convent cell."[13] The privacy of the decorator's own bedroom—a comfortable, lived-in space

where she spent much of her time and that also served as a reading and writing room—was reinforced by the inclusion of a canopied mahogany Breton bed, which she had obtained from a French chateau. The bed could completely enclose its sleeper, and de Wolfe installed mirrors inside it and hung it with embroidered rose-colored silk. That this was de Wolfe's main living area was confirmed by the presence of a little wicker bed next to the fireplace for her small dog. Unlike the stage-set interiors downstairs, this room, which housed many of her books and other personal possessions, was more cluttered and homely.

Elsie de Wolfe's bedroom, early 1900s. (The House in Good Taste, *1913*)

Based on the work she undertook at this time in 122 East 17th Street, de Wolfe later went on to develop what she described as a "creed of comfort" for her bedrooms, which she achieved by including a set of key items: a little table at the head of the bed, complete with a well-positioned reading light, a clock, and a telephone to summon servants; a daybed for an afternoon nap; and a writing table equipped with a number of small, useful accessories such as pincushions (often covered in a fabric that blended with the interior scheme) and a small bowl for clips or other necessary items.

Attention to detail was an important aspect of de Wolfe's approach to decorating. She combined her commitment to a harmonious whole with an interest in the smallest components of a scheme. Most importantly, she wanted to make her spaces workable as well as beautiful.

De Wolfe's scheme for 122 East 17th Street had to work for two busy career women who needed privacy and a suitable environment for their very full lives. In the 1897–98 bedroom refurbishment, de Wolfe used a striking floral chintz for her curtains and her dressing table, combining it with a matching wallpaper. A few years later, she introduced a calmer scheme into the same room but retained what she described as the "[soft] carnation pink silk" used for her bedding and cushions, the dye for which, she explained, could be acquired only in the French department store Bon Marché.[14] A magazine article explained the trouble she took to store and look after her clothing, explaining that the arrangement of her garments in their drawers was reminiscent of the efficient storage to be found in a department store.[15]

The bedroom for the Catholic Marbury also went through a couple of transformations in the capable hands of her companion. In 1898 it was distinguished by a large crucifix, a prie-dieu, and a reliquary. It was transformed later, however, with a blue and white scheme, although it was less obviously filled by the personality of its occupant than was de Wolfe's bedroom. Marbury's bedroom was given a bird-of-paradise-patterned chintz that de Wolfe used for a neat fitted cover for the box spring and matching bolster cushion, a long sofa, a small bedside chair, an elegant screen that separated the sleeping and sitting areas of the room, and a dressing table. Plain ivory-white walls and sconces replaced elaborate patterned wallpaper. The furniture,

made of white-enamel-painted wood, reinforced the cleanliness and clarity that defined the room's decor after de Wolfe had worked on it. Sparseness was avoided, however, by hanging on the walls 18th-century French prints and paintings of landscapes and ladies.

With the exception of the servants' quarters and the more functional areas in the basement and the attic, the only other room in the house was the library, located on the third floor. It was a simple, comfortable room filled with books, personal mementos and photographs, and a small number of utilitarian furnishings, including a desk and a fireside chair. It also contained de Wolfe's antique shoe collection, displayed in a glass case.

The decorator's love of collecting, which was visible throughout the house, reflected her commitment to objects as markers of the richness of human culture.

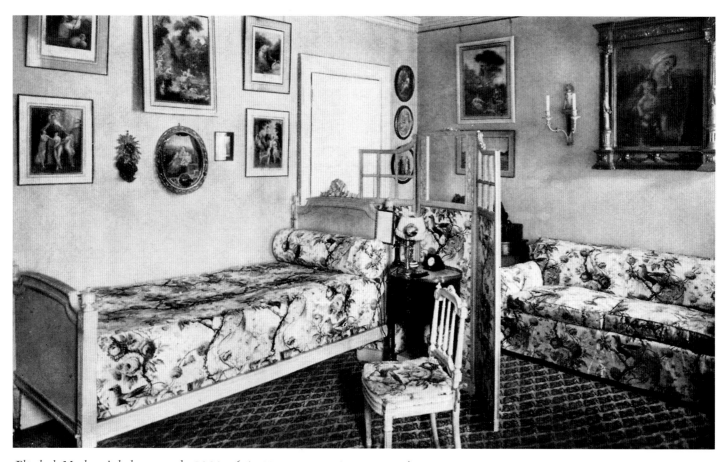

Elisabeth Marbury's bedroom, early 1900s. (The House in Good Taste, *1913*)

Indeed, her complex attitude toward material objects was to become an important part of her decorating philosophy, as was her interest in the interior defined as an expression of its inhabitant. "A person's environment should speak for that person's life," she explained in 1911.[16] Her collections—including her shoes, her dolls from many countries, and her books—played a practical part in her life. Like her dolls, her books (mostly on the subject of French and English court life) contained the information she needed to draw upon in order to create historical theater sets and costumes. Many of the plays in which she performed through the 1890s and early 20th century were set in 18th-century France and, as a result of creating sets and costumes, she became highly knowledgeable about the material culture of that period. From 1897 onward, she also took lessons on the subject from Pierre de Nolhac, the curator of the château of Versailles. She also appreciated the craftsmanship that went into the fabrication of many artifacts and described her collection of little carved figures, displayed in the drawing room of East 17th Street, as "labors of love."[17]

With the exception of Villa Trianon, her French home from 1906 until her death in 1950, de Wolfe's work on the house at 122 East 17th Street was the most intense and personally meaningful of all the interior projects she worked on in her 45 years as a professional interior decorator. She undertook the work as an amateur, however, and, inasmuch as she lived in the house, the project could never be finished. In a magazine article of 1901, she explained this sense of continual change, following the vagaries of her emotions: "Here in my own house I move the furniture to suit my mood. If I have been irritated I get out my new draperies or rehang my pictures to restore my good humor. I put on now one gown, now another, as I am

cheerful or sad."[18] She exhibited a considerable level of conscious understanding about the way in which she used her clothes and her material accessories as means of both constructing and expressing her personality. This understanding, applied to her clients, informed all the projects she was to undertake as a professional decorator from 1905 onward.

De Wolfe also described her approach to interior decoration as being one of emphasizing a room's best features, a process that she said she had learned to do with her own limited physical attributes.

Elsie de Wolfe found her decorating voice in 122 East 17th Street. She had time there to experiment, to be able to alter and re-alter things until she got them right—and, of course, she knew the people who lived there better than anyone else. It was an ideal training ground, and, although modest in scale, it offered her the opportunity to develop and test a number of the ideas that she had brought to interior decoration from the worlds of theater and haute couture.

When, in 1905, de Wolfe was given the opportunity to try out her ideas in a professional arena, and on a much larger scale, in her work for the interior of Stanford White's Colony Club, she was ready for the challenge. The move into the public sphere of professional life did not mean that de Wolfe ceased to work in the capacity of an amateur on her own homes, however. On the contrary, arguably the most successful interiors she created between 1905 and 1950 were those she constructed for herself. The decoration of her own homes also may have rewarded her most richly. Everything she knew about color, light, proportion, texture, decoration, comfort, function, mood, personal identity and expression, privacy, hospitality, history, and manners she had learned by turning 122 East 17th Street into a home for herself and Elisabeth Marbury.

1905-08

The Colony Club
120–124 Madison Avenue
New York City

"Elsie de Wolfe was like a witch sweeping
the cobwebs out of the sky." [1]

In abandoning her stage career, Elsie de Wolfe feared that she had lost her celebrity status. "[I felt] . . . the mediocrity of which I had always had a horror . . . closing in on me."[2] To alleviate this growing anxiety, she quickly sent out business cards to show people that she had not retired but had simply settled on a new career: interior decoration.

Several friends and acquaintances already had sought her advice in the refurbishment of their houses, and through her work with Charles Frohman and her own theater company, and the time she spent in France with Count Robert de Montesquiou, Pierre de Nolhac, and other aesthetes, she had acquired an extensive knowledge of French historical styles and antiques. By 1905 de Wolfe was in demand as a professional decorator. A newspaper article of that year explained that she had "contracts for important work" in Newport, Boston, Pittsfield, Washington, D.C., and Philadelphia.[3] Her first reported paid project was undertaken for a sum of $10,000 for Emily and John Roll McLean, the publisher of *The Washington Post,* who hired de Wolfe to decorate the so-called "entertainment annex" of their country house, Friendship, on the outskirts of Washington, D.C.[4] The finished product was described as a "pink taffeta house," decorated in "a manner that is beyond criticism by the most captious" and "reminiscent of one of those little 'pavilions' so popular in France during the reign of the Grand Monarch."[5] According to the same newspaper article, the decorator was also fulfilling several unidentified assignments in Paris, confirming that her

Opposite: 120-124 Madison Avenue, c. 1907. (New York Public Library)

success in this new arena had come about quickly. Once again, de Wolfe had moved from amateur to professional almost overnight.

A project that was to consolidate her role as a professional decorator came to her attention around 1902, shortly before she embarked on her new career. Elisabeth Marbury played a key role in providing de Wolfe with this opportunity to prove her worth by championing her abilities to the organizers of the nascent Colony Club, the first women's club in New York.

The idea for a women's club, which would have a social and a leisure role as well as provide a place for professional women to stay, had been conceived in 1902 by Daisy Harriman (née Florence Jaffray Hurst), a farsighted society matron who was married to the banker J. Borden Harriman.[6] With the help of several friends, including Marbury, Anne Morgan (the youngest child of financier J. Pierpont Morgan), and Helen Barney (daughter of Charles Tracy Barney, the former president of the Knickerbocker Trust Company), in the following year Harriman secured a plot of land on lower Madison Avenue and, to design the club building, the services of Stanford White, a partner in the highly successful New York architectural practice McKim, Mead &White. He already had designed some of the best men's clubs in Manhattan so was well aware of the required amenities. For this new venture he decided to work in the Federal Revival style and to base his design on the 1809 Nathaniel Russell House in Charleston.

In 1903 Harriman became the club's first president, a position she held for the next 13 years before moving into political life in Washington, where she became, among other things, a major force behind the establishment of the Woman's National Democratic Club. In her 1923 autobiography, Harriman described the widespread resistance to the idea of a women's club in early-20th-century New York. "Women shouldn't have clubs," one old gentleman had protested. "They'll only use them as addresses for clandestine letters."[7] Despite such opposition, Harriman and her friends remained convinced that the time was right, but when the Colony Club opened its doors in 1907 it continued to be denounced as a threat to the family and an encouragement for women to drink and smoke.[8] Many contemporary female commentators, on the other hand, pledged their support, among them the writer Olivia Howard Dunbar.[9] She wrote enthusiastically, "Women upon whom the knowledge has burst that they enjoy their homes more if they are not always

Elisabeth Marbury, early 1900s. (My Crystal Ball, 1923)

imprisoned in them, and professional women who per-force spend much of their time in the uncomforting glare of public places, unquestioningly need, when they league together, though they have not long realised it, a roof and walls for shelter."[10]

An organizing committee of 40 women was formed in 1903, numbering among its members prominent society women such as Lucy Clews, the wife of investment banker Henry Clews; Helen Hastings, the wife of the architect Thomas Hastings of the firm Carrère & Hastings; Helen Whitney, the poet wife of millionaire Payne Whitney; Josephine Canfield, the widow of yachtsman A. Cass Canfield; the writer Margaret Terry Chanler, who was married to the sportsman Winthrop Astor Chanler; Ava Astor, first wife of John Jacob Astor IV; Ruth Morgan, a feminist, peace advocate, and later a vice president of the National League of Women Voters; and Mary Irvin, widow of the banker Richard Irvin.

The club started to become a reality by 1905, and a team of governors was elected, Marbury among them, to serve for a period of four years. According to Harriman, "Bessie [sic] Marbury worked like a steam-engine and brought all her business experience into our service as Chairman of the House Committee."[11] The club's officers—including Harriman, Astor (second vice president), Morgan (assistant treasurer), and the only male member of the team, Julian Gerard (treasurer)—did most of the work needed to get it off the ground. A men's advisory committee, including J. Pierpont Morgan, was considered a necessary adjunct, perhaps to overcome continuing opposition to the project within the more conservative quarters of New York society while raising money and providing insights into the details of running of a club from their own experience.

De Wolfe was selected as the club's "interior coordinator" in 1905, with strong support from

Lounging room, c. 1907. (New York Public Library)

Marbury and White, who was a frequent visitor to the Sunday-afternoon social events hosted by the couple in their home on East 17th Street. There was, not sur-prisingly, a certain amount of resistance to the idea of employing an ex-actress turned (newly minted) deco-rator, but by the summer of 1905, de Wolfe was trav-eling in Europe with $5,000 to buy furnishings for the club. The decoration lasted nearly two years. The club opened in March 1907, although the roof garden was not completed until the following January.[12]

The parameters of de Wolfe's involvement shifted significantly through the project, and her role continu-ally redefined itself. In a characteristic desire for clarity and efficiency, she wrote to Mary Irvin, chairman of the house furnishing committee, at the outset of the project: "It is understood that the Club is given to me with all the floors laid, all mantel pieces in, cornices and plastered wall, ranges, grates, brick floors on the veranda, and all the electric light connections made."[13] Her main responsibility was to supply all furnishings, including light fittings and wallpaper. "We have nothing to do," explained a member of the architectural firm a little later, "with the selection of any of the

Trellis room, c. 1907. (The House in Good Taste, 1913)

household furnishings."[14] Despite de Wolfe's letter to Irving, however, the decorator's task proved wide-ranging, and she ended up supplying a number of the fireplace surrounds (she even went to the New York Customs House herself on one occasion to ensure that they reached the club in time). She advised on cornices and wall treatments and insisted that electrical outlets be positioned to facilitate her lighting schemes and floor plans. She also designed blue and buff uniforms for the Colony Club staff. On a number of occasions she pressured the architects to decide on the positioning of stair-cases and mantels, and to show her their plans so that she would be able to complete her work by the necessary

deadline. In a letter written the day after Christmas 1906, for example, she pleaded, "Will you let me know please if I am to get into the reading room and the bed-rooms on next Saturday, the 29th, as promised?"

White's murder the previous June—he was shot dead by an ex-lover's husband—considerably compli-cated the project.[15] De Wolfe was devastated. "Owing to the dreadful tragedy of Mr. White's death I will find it difficult to work with anyone else," she wrote to the architect's office. "He so thoroughly understood what I meant to do in the Club."[16]

The Colony Club was a six-floor building con-structed of pale pink bricks laid with the narrow end, or header, facing out; the windows and doors were trimmed with discreet amounts of white marble. (Stanford White approvingly described his design as "simple and severe.") The shallow front veranda and balcony above were supported by slender iron Corinthian columns (all this was removed several years later when Madison Avenue was widened). The double front doors opened to a long, narrow hall—lined with the same green-and-white wallcovering that the decorator had used in the entrance hall of her house on East 17th Street—that led into a spacious lounging room, or lobby, anchored by a massive fireplace. This de Wolfe said she wanted to resemble the cozy entrance hall of a Virginia plantation house. It was invitingly arranged with a wide range of seating, some button-tufted and covered in green-and-white-striped glazed chintz, others William and Mary in style and upholstered in green leather. All stood on a spring green broadloom carpet. The fresh, cheerful simplicity of the space and its feathery potted palms contrasted sharply with the gloomy entrance halls of most men's clubs of the era. Inexpensive glazed chintz, with its rural connotations, was considered particularly daring when used in an urban American context. Many members were shocked to see it in such a luxurious setting, but de Wolfe maintained that chintz was "as much at home in the New York drawing room as in the country cottage."[17] A vogue for the fabric rapidly developed, and de Wolfe quickly became known as the "Chintz Lady."

A resting room, reading room, reception room, and glassed-in veranda or winter garden made up the rest of the ground floor, along with a pantry, wine room, office, bathroom, coat room, a waiting room for visitors, and the kitchen—not to mention the elevators and telephone booths.[18]

Complementing the lounging room's country-house air was the decor of the 40-foot-long-by-20-foot-wide veranda next door, which de Wolfe spectacularly

Tea room leading into card room, c. 1907. (New York Public Library)

turned into what came to be known as the trellis room, one of the country's most influential interiors. Green-painted trelliswork was mounted floor-to-ceiling on the east, west, and south walls of roughly finished white plaster—the north wall was largely glass—and around light wood tables were gathered straw-backed wood dining chairs of de Wolfe's own design, also painted the same specially mixed Colonial Trianon green used on the trelliswork, window frames, tables, and French doors. The floor was paved with glazed earth-red tiles. At one end of the room, which was used as a tea room or winter garden, stood a white marble fountain banked with ferns and flanked by matching urns on plinths.

The use of trellis was "as old as architecture itself," having been found "in Japan, China, Arabia, Egypt, Italy, and Spain." De Wolfe claimed that its use in America was relatively unusual. As a result, she said she found it difficult to locate workmen to undertake the necessary task of "crossing and recrossing little strips of green wood" and shaping it into dramatic architectural elements complete with cornices, dadoes, arches, and friezes."[19]

Her frustration, however, was not supported by facts. Stanford White, in 1903, had placed a domed trelliswork ceiling in the breakfast room of the New York City mansion of newspaper publisher Joseph Pulitzer and in 1906 added a trelliswork conservatory to the country house of socialite James L. Breese. Ogden Codman, Jr. had designed exquisite trelliswork for the terrace and gardens of Edith Wharton's house in Newport in the 1890s and created a trelliswork ballroom for another client around 1900. During the construction of the Colony Club, the architects Little & Brown were putting trelliswork accents in a mirrored hall at diplomat Larz Anderson's mansion in Brookline, near Boston. Presumably, trained workmen were available, though perhaps not quickly enough to meet de Wolfe's pressing deadlines.

So well publicized was the Colony Club project and so refreshing the decor of the veranda—"[the] room has positively a refrigerated look," a reporter for *The New York Times* explained—trelliswork rapidly became a feature of fashionable decoration in the first decade of the century.[20] Along with chintz and

Reading room, c. 1907. (New York Public Library)

Colonial Trianon green, it was a leitmotif of fashionable interiors across the country.[21] Capitalizing on its popularity and likely asserting her claim to popularizing the trend, in 1913, de Wolfe (or more likely, her ghostwriter, Ruby Ross Goodnow) wrote "The Art of Treillage" for *Good Housekeeping*, describing its ancient origins and its architectural function.[22]

The reading room, an east-facing space next to the lounging room, was a much more English affair centered on an Adam mantelpiece. Across the plain blue-green broadloom carpet was furniture in a cozy range of traditional styles and patterned fabrics that blended rather than matched—from modern side chairs in a bird-and-vine-pattern chintz to green-leather sofas to Marlborough chairs in English needlework. Large sheets of mirror set into the applied moldings on the plaster walls gave the effect of paneling. At the center of the room was a large table loaded with the latest magazines and newspapers.[23]

The sumptuous white marble swimming pool could be found in the basement; probably it was the work of White rather than de Wolfe, but its outfitting came under her purview.[24] Encased by mirrored walls, the pool was illuminated by ceiling lights in the form of bunches of pink grapes ripening in a leafy arbor. Statues, columns, marble benches, and boxes of greenery completed the Alma-Tadema-in-Manhattan effect. Members could follow their swim with therapies and beauty treatments, including electric, Russian, Turkish, and Nauheim baths, massages of various kinds, and manicures.[25]

The club's second and third floors were largely taken up by the assembly room, high-ceilinged, painted brilliant azalea pink, and with a majestic Van Dyck painting above one of its two fireplaces. A gymnasium with a cork running track—an amenity championed by

Bedroom, c. 1907. (The House in Good Taste, 1913)

Anne Morgan—as well as lavatories and dressing rooms, could also be found across the hall, and courts for squash and basketball were located nearby.

Ten bedrooms for members staying overnight occupied most of the fourth floor. (Rooms for the members' maids were located on the top floor, near the roof garden.) De Wolfe treated each to a different scheme. Most were American Colonial in style, though one exotic chamber had black-and-gold furniture set against leafy wallpaper swarming with parakeets and birds of paradise; the decorator had the furniture made to match a chair she found at an auction.[26]

Several bedrooms contained furniture painted with flowery 18th-century decorations by de Wolfe's protégé Everett Shinn, later a member of the gritty Ashcan school of painting.[27]

On the fifth floor were the members' dining room, kitchens, and pantries, as well as what was described as the strangers' dining room, where the ladies of the club could bring guests. Here, applied moldings divided the "yellowy tan" walls into long panels lined with pale gray paper that Shinn had enlivened with exuberant Louis XV–style designs of flowers, ribbons, and arabesques in Pompadour colors:

Bedroom, c. 1907. (The House in Good Taste, *1913*)

relieved by chairs of tightly woven split rattan from Canton, China. In two corners stood tall green ceramic wood-burning stoves that de Wolfe found in Italy.[30] From the glass-and-metal ceiling dangled lights made to resemble masses of wisteria blossoms, and the front wall, also glass, opened to a plein-air wood pergola and terrace whose street edge was planted with a three-foot-high box hedge.[31] Here was an assortment of white tables and green chairs where members sipped "cold fizzes … until the midnight hour."[32]

Admired and condemned in equal measure, the Colony Club was a great success, as a vehicle of women's liberation and as a professional triumph. It also was a daunting project for a decorator who had undertaken very little professional decorating. De Wolfe had the advantage, though, of possessing not only technical know-how, thanks to her experience on the stage, but also an intimate knowledge of society women, their

snuff and sepia browns, pale beiges, yellow cooled with a hint of pink.[28] Beneath a central skylight curtained in the same rose-pink as the plain broadloom carpet stood a table and chairs painted pink and gray and upholstered in striped rose brocade. De Wolfe was especially pleased with her camouflage of the two radiators, hiding them behind wood cabinets, their iron grilles painted to mimic woven wicker and backed with gently gathered lengths of rose-pink silk; the flared tray tops of the radiator covers were designed to hold potted plants. Far more conservative than this fanciful space were the mahogany furniture, gray walls, and green carpet of the members' dining room on the same floor.

On the roof was another winter garden, an Arcadian refuge of potted topiary bay trees and ivy clambering up white trellis laid over red brick walls.[29] Long sofas and capacious armchairs covered in grapevine-patterned chintz were arranged into intimate conversation groups, their overstuffed silhouettes

Strangers' dining room in the Colony Club, c. 1907. (The House in Good Taste, *1913*)

Rooftop winter garden, c. 1907. (New York Public Library)

dreams, and their requirements. During the winter of 1906–07, she took up full-time residence in the club building for a number of months. Arguably, in decorating the club's interior she was fulfilling her own needs as much as those of its nearly 600 members.

The club's rapidly expanding membership soon outgrew the building.[33] By 1916 it had moved to a new building at East 62nd Street and Park Avenue, designed by the architects Delano & Aldrich.[34] A few items from the original headquarters, including the furnishings of the strangers' dining room, survived the relocation, but most of the contents remained behind when the building eventually was sold.[35]

After its opening, and the rapturous comments that were made about it in the press nationwide, the Colony Club brought more work in de Wolfe's direction. Several members became clients, among them

Ethel Crocker (the club's San Francisco regional representative), Lolita Armour (who held the same position for Chicago), and actress Ethel Barrymore (de Wolfe's former understudy). Its size and complexity also prepared her for work on interiors not part of the domestic sphere; over the next few years, she would rely on lessons learned at the Colony Club to design a dormitory building for Barnard College, a men's club in San Francisco, and a hostel for working women in New York City.

More important, the club project honed all of the skills she needed as a professional interior decorator: working to a tight deadline and a strict budget; coordinating contractors, artisans, and artists; collaborating with architects: and, most importantly, learning how to juggle dozens of projects, large and small, in the same instant. As a result of the Colony Club commission, in 1906 the busy de Wolfe moved her office from her house on East 17th Street to a recently converted town house at 4 West 40th Street. It was now the official headquarters of the most talked-about decorator in America.

Assembly room with musicians' gallery, c. 1907. (New York Public Library)

1907

Ethel and William H. Crocker Residence
New Place
Burlingame, California

"Her beautiful new home

in Burlingame" [1]

The Colony Club started me on my way, in which I can think of my business only as a small snowball suddenly achieving the stature and shape of a giant snowman," de Wolfe said.[2] Seemingly overnight, wealthy women across the United States wanted her new, light and airy, feminine decorating style in their own homes.

The Colony Club needed to attract members nationwide, so a number of women were elected to represent the key cities. Ethel Crocker, the wife of banker and railroad millionaire William H. Crocker, and Edith Grant, the wife of landowner Joseph D. Grant, were put forward to represent San Francisco. The former became de Wolfe's first "big private client."[3] The decorator described how she "went west" with Crocker to advise her on the interior decoration of the mansion called New Place.

A press cutting from the period described the forceful and professional way in which de Wolfe purchased items for the Crockers' house near San Francisco, explaining how, for example, leaving Crocker and her daughter Helen outside in the car, she "entered various establishments, dickered with their managers, dictated orders and generally manipulated the world."[4]

A daughter of a prominent Stockton flour merchant, Crocker (née Ethel Willard Sperry, 1863–1934) was an eminently suitable client for de Wolfe. For one, she was among the leaders of San Francisco society, a woman known for her "cold, strict, and austere" demeanor as well

Opposite: Main entrance, 1906–07. (Burlingame Country Club)

Rear facade showing landscaping by Bruce Porter, 1906–07. (Burlingame Country Club)

as her aristocratic connections (her sister was married to a Polish prince), her travels abroad (the Crockers had a house in France), and her appreciation of haute couture (Lucile and Callot Soeurs were favorites).[5] For another, she was the mistress of a newly built $500,000 mansion that was one of the grandest houses on the San Francisco Peninsula, built after the family's home on Nob Hill was destroyed by the earthquake of 1906— hence the name New Place. Furthermore, Crocker and

her husband would be giving de Wolfe a free hand with their fine period furniture, their tapestries, and an impressive collection of paintings, including examples by Millet, Corot, Rousseau, Cezanne, and Monet. De Wolfe explained that the project involved "composing a picture around them," an experience she found both "delightful and satisfying."[6]

The Crocker family was a prime example of the second-generation nouveau riche clients whom de

Wolfe was to work with over the next decade. William Henry Crocker (1861–1937) was the son of robber baron Charles Crocker, who had played a major role in the construction of the Central Pacific railroad and was described as a "banker and civic leader." He also was involved with a number of business ventures and the building of landmark edifices, such as Grace Cathedral in San Francisco, which stood on the site of the burned Crocker mansion and was designed, like New Place, by Crocker's cousin by marriage, Lewis Parsons Hobart (1873–1954).[7] William H. Crocker was a member of a generation of rich Americans who had not made their own fortunes but who were intent on establishing a position in society for themselves and their families.

When the former Crocker residence of 1888 at 1105 California Street burned to the ground, Crocker, the founder of Crocker National Bank, remarked, "I may say, however, [it] is almost a certainty that we will replace our home with another equally good."[8] A number of Ethel Crocker's paintings had been destroyed in the conflagration, among them *The Holy Family* by Rubens and work by Degas.

New Place was completed in 1907. Set in an estate of 700 acres, the house was loosely modeled on a villa at Caen, France, with a few Italian influences mixed in, and fronted by an elaborate glass-and-iron marquee that spread above the entrance like a peacock's tail. The formal Italianate gardens, created by a local painter and designer of stained glass, Bruce Porter, were an elegant landscape of planned vistas interrupted by fountains, large urns, pools, low walls, and stone steps, reminiscent of Porter's later work at Filoli, the home of Agnes and William Bowers Bourn II, in nearby Woodside. Rows of cypress trees punctuated the scenery, and from a company in Rome, the Crockers purchased a copy of Bernini's 17th-century Fountain of the Tortoises.

De Wolfe explained that her role in the creation of the new interiors was one of making "suggestions," but from the results it was clear that they were readily adopted. The massive house was furnished mainly with 18th-century French furniture, and the main rooms had a high level of grandeur and elegance. De Wolfe's hand was especially obvious in the sunroom, or loggia, which was added to the west side of the house soon after the home's initial construction, along with the ballroom. Three sides of the sunroom were made of glass, and its white marble floor was bordered with green and black. Both the ceiling and the woodwork were painted "warm gray."[9] It was furnished with wicker chairs and embellished with Chinese paintings and pieces of porcelain. A 1915 text described the room as "gay with an abundance of blossoming plants," adding, "the whole effect is one of airiness and sunlight."[10]

Hung with large crystal chandeliers, the sunny, spacious drawing room, called the Gold Room, was hung with ornate French mirrors—all identical, so likely copies of 18th-century originals—that reflected 18th-century French furniture upholstered in elegant flowered fabrics and de Wolfe's favorite rose-colored silk. A painted screen, of the kind frequently used by de Wolfe and decorated by Everett Shinn in the French rococo style, created a division between the furniture gathered around the fireplace and the entrance to the room. A kidney-shaped wood side table, which de Wolfe designed and which appeared in several of her interiors around this time, was also used here.

The dining room was a heavier, oak-lined room with Renaissance-style chairs upholstered in dark velvet. The large ballroom had marble walls and floor, with an English-style carved wooden ceiling. No attempt at precise historical reproduction was made, however, so that New Place was described as "a home that is lived in."[11] The Chinese rugs used in the ballroom had equivalents

Drawing room, 1907. (Burlingame Country Club)

Drawing room, 1907. (Burlingame Country Club)

Ballroom, 1907. (Burlingame Country Club)

Library, 1907. (Burlingame Country Club)

Guest room, 1907. (Burlingame Country Club)

Guest room, 1907. (Burlingame Country Club)

Guest room, 1907. (Burlingame Country Club)

Guest room, 1907. (Burlingame Country Club)

in several other de Wolfe interiors of this period. Many of Ethel Crocker's finest paintings, including a Rousseau, a Monet, Millet's *The Man with a Hoe,* and one of three family portraits by the fashionable society painter Boldini, who had put de Wolfe's own likeness to canvas, were displayed in the wood-lined library. The room was described as being "at once dignified and intimate."[12]

With their daybeds, small folding screens, well-lighted desks, mirrors, and assortment of small Persian rugs, the guest rooms conformed to the by-now familiar de Wolfe formula for these private spaces. One contained an 18th-century English fireplace surround, recalling the one de Wolfe had installed in the library of the Colony Club. With their painted, plainly paneled walls, a mixture of 18th-century French antiques and reproductions, cheerful chintzes, and wall-hung bookshelves, the bedrooms also were highly reminiscent of other de Wolfe interiors created at this point in her career.

In her 1913 publication *The House in Good Taste,* the decorator illustrated and described a bed that she had created for one of the Crockers' young daughters, either Ethel Mary or Helen Victoria, who were 16 and 11 at the time de Wolfe was working on New Place. "I am showing," she wrote, "a photograph of a bedroom in the Crocker house in Burlingame, California, where I used a small draped bed with charming effect."[13] She went on to explain that she had placed the bed against the wall, like a sofa, as she had done in Bessy Marbury's room on East 17th Street. De Wolfe created similar draped beds for a number of other clients, among them Lillie Havemeyer and Helen Whitney. The Louis XVI–style bed for the Crocker daughter was made of gray painted wood, and the hangings were of "blue and cream chintz lined with blue taffeta."[14] The tightly fitting bedcovers and

cushions resembled those the decorator had created for Marbury's bedroom.

Working closely with Ethel Crocker, the decorator turned a grand house into a livable one, its brand-new interiors managing to look as if they had evolved over time. The muted colors, and the attempt to bring the outside indoors through flowered fabrics and lightly constructed curtains, resulted in rooms that were notable in turn-of-the-century California for their unforced charm and sophisticated air.

Miss Crocker's Louis XVI bed, 1907.
(The House in Good Taste, *1913*)

1907

Brooks Hall, Barnard College
116th Street and Broadway
New York City

Although many of the commissions de Wolfe received in the first decade of her professional life as an interior decorator were for individual clients' domestic spaces, she also was offered a number of projects, both small and large, that were not located within private single-family homes.

At one end of this spectrum, for example, in 1905–06 de Wolfe redecorated financier J. Pierpont Morgan's opera box at the Metropolitan Opera House. "The walls are of handsome dull red silk brocade, and so are the chairs and settees," a newspaper article of the day described de Wolfe's work. "They are framed, like the mirror upon the wall of the box, in gold laid in straight lines with wreaths and ribbons in relief. An engraving in colors, by Jeannet . . . lends a bit of fine color to the deep-toned walls. The frame of this exquisite picture is in the Louis XV style as are the entire furnishings of the box."[1]

At the other end of the spectrum was a New York project offered to de Wolfe in 1907: the decoration of Brooks Hall, a new dormitory building that was being created for New York's first women's college, Barnard College. Inasmuch as the assignment required the decoration and furnishing of multiple bedrooms and shared areas for a community of women, it resembled the Colony Club. The Barnard project, however, was completed in only a few months, from May to September 1907, and its success depended upon several decisions that had already been reached by the decorator in the context of the Colony Club.[2]

Opposite: Brooks Hall, Barnard College, 1907. (Barnard College Archives)

Brooks Hall marked de Wolfe's first professional involvement with a group of women who were not the rich wives of first- and second-generation robber barons, her principal clients to date, and it forced her to think very carefully about the requirements of young single women living and working together in a communal environment. (Six years later, de Wolfe was asked to design the interiors of the Vacation Savings Association's headquarters at 38 West 39th Street, a New York residence for working women, and once again was to find herself confronted by a space dedicated to communal dwelling.)

When it opened in the spring of 1907, the Colony Club attracted the attention of, among many others, Lucretia Perry Osborn, the chairman of the buildings and grounds committee of Barnard College, an all-women's college created in 1889 and linked to Columbia University.[3] From the 1830s onward, women had very slowly begun to be admitted to institutes of higher learning, and by the mid-1880s, Oberlin, Vassar, Smith, Wellesley, the University of Michigan, Boston University, Cornell University, Harvard, and Bryn Mawr all catered to female students. There was, however, still no New York equivalent. Barnard College started out as a concept, rather than as a gift of land or buildings.[4] The idea of educating women within Columbia University had first been voiced by Frederick Augustus Porter Barnard, a Yale science and mathematics graduate and president of Columbia College (before it became a university), who was very committed to the idea of coeducation. Through the 1880s, Columbia had tried to incorporate women into its system in a number of ways, including allowing them to join the men at lectures, but it had been decided in that end that the best approach was to educate women in a "safe, isolated atmosphere."[5] Following a great deal of active campaigning

on the part of a number of women, a new school, Barnard College, was proposed, the academic control of which would lie with Columbia College, with the condition that the trustees of the school should acquire a building, without financial support from Columbia, that would be for instruction only.

The school opened on Monday, October 7, 1889, at 343 Madison Avenue, an ordinary brownstone town house, with 14 liberal arts students enrolled to study for degrees. The interior of the house was spartan compared with other colleges, where girls were "often enveloped in a Victorian array of statuary, stained glass, oil paintings, and even Wedgwood tableware in a determined effort to surround (not to say smother) them with culture."[6]

By the early 1890s, however, the Madison Avenue building was becoming crowded, and the trustees began to look for funds with which to expand In 1896 they acquired a block of land in the neighborhood known as Morningside Heights, opposite Columbia University, on Broadway between 119th and 120th streets. There Brinkerhoff Hall was built in the style of Henry II, by Charles Alonzo Rich of the New York architecture firm Lamb & Rich, which had designed numerous buildings for the campus of Dartmouth College. The following year saw work begin on Milbank Hall, its construction costs partially covered by philanthropist Elizabeth Milbank Anderson, and 1898 brought the inauguration of another building, Fiske Hall. Both were executed in the same style as Brinkerhoff Hall, again to designs by Rich. Fiske Hall served as a dormitory for nearly a hundred girls for four years until it was converted back into an academic building. In the same year, the undergraduates vacated their Madison Avenue base. Yet more space was needed as the college continued to expand, however, and when Laura Drake Gill became dean in

Dean Laura Drake Gill, c. 1905.
(A. Tennyson Beals, Barnard College Archives)

May 1901, she focused her energies on finding funds to enable Barnard to grow further.[7] In 1903 Anderson donated another three and a half acres of land, located on the southern side of the three existing buildings and bounded by Broadway and 116th and 117th streets.[8] The architecture firm of McKim, Mead & White had been invited to sketch a master plan of the area, but ultimately they were not selected to design what was to be Barnard College's new dormitory. Instead Charles Rich was given the responsibility for the project, doubtless because of his long association with Elizabeth Anderson, for

whose family he designed more than a dozen buildings, including the family mausoleum, her father's house in Greenwich, Connecticut, and her own homes in New York City and Santa Monica, California. Rich also was the architect of Sagamore Hill, the great Shingle Style country house created for Teddy Roosevelt, a close friend of Anderson's husband. The steel-framed building he created for Barnard offered 97 rooms for students, who were to be housed in spaces ranging from single rooms to multi-room private suites, roommates being thought an unnecessary burden on privacy and study habits.

Rented accommodations had been available in the city for out-of-town students, but this was not considered an ideal situation. Gill knew that the only way of easing parents' worries about their daughters coming to study in a New York City college was to provide respectable dormitory accommodations. State-of-the-art housing, she felt, would be an attractive selling point to both parents and students. It also would facilitate supervision and encourage sociability.[9] One of Barnard's tenets was its sense of integration, where "the obscure, poor, self-denying, hard-working girl meets on terms not only of equality, but of cordiality with the girl whose family has been distinguished for generations."[10] Aware of the issues, Anderson donated another $150,000 for the construction of a permanent dormitory for Barnard College. In September 1907, 56 young women moved into their new rooms in Brooks Hall, which was named after Reverend Arthur Brooks, an original member of Barnard's board of trustees and a well-known champion of the cause of women's education.

The interiors of the building were designed by Elsie de Wolfe. A Barnard College *Bulletin* of September 1907, the month of the dormitory's opening, did not name her specifically but praised her

Students eating in the dining room, Brooks Hall, 1907. (Brown Bros., Barnard College Archives)

work. "The furnishing of the whole building was done by a New York firm who have certainly equipped it to perfection in every detail—from turret to foundation stone."[11] Unlike Rich's other three buildings, Brooks Hall's neoclassical-style, redbrick facade, with its ground-floor colonnades and two stacks of north-facing bay windows, did not shout excessively of historicism, and its structure and internal services utilized the latest contemporary technology; the building was considered more modern than the other Barnard halls. The building was lit by electricity and heated by steam, de Wolfe's bête noire, who found radiators unappealing; each room had a sink with hot and cold running water, and there was elevator service. It was also conveniently positioned next to a subway line for downtown shopping and theatrical excursions. Above all, Brooks Hall had none "of the gingerbread details and gimcrack trimmings, either inside or out, which are irritating to our modern eyes in some buildings of that era."[12] In her 1907 dean's report, Gill wrote that Brooks "is in every way modern in its equipment and design, representing in so far as can be interpreted from the new hotel construction, the increasing demand among Americans for greater physical conveniences with diminished display."[13]

The first floor of the building contained a double-height reception room, a dining room, three small parlors—these later would be called beau parlors

Parlor, Brooks Hall, 1907. (White Studio, Barnard College Archives)

by students who could be courted in them only in the presence of a chaperone—and a large parlor that looked onto 116th Street and was separated by a long, thin corridor from a series of offices. The second, or mezzanine, floor housed bedrooms, a couple of communal sitting rooms, a small kitchen, and bathrooms, as did the third, fourth, fifth, sixth, and seventh floors. The attic contained an infirmary, a nurse's room, a large linen closet, storerooms, and servants' quarters, while all the services and the physical plant were in the basement along with a pantry, the main kitchen, and a cold-storage room.

De Wolfe characteristically wanted to be very clear about what was expected of her at Brooks Hall, especially as she was given only a few months in which to complete the project. She was working on it alongside the Colony Club and other projects in what must have been, at that time, a very busy office. The decorator expressed a sense of urgency in a letter of May 25, 1907, sent from her West 40th Street office, in which she wrote to Gill, "I think it is of vital importance that we should meet for a few moments in regard to the decoration of Brooks Hall before I leave as I am more or less working in the dark. I have only seen Mrs. Osborn for a few moments, and merely know from her that I can have $35,000 dollars to cover all the furnishings, electric lights, kitchen utensils, china, glass, linen, &c. This does not include anything of the

A Brooks Hall apartment, c. 1935.
(Wendell MacRae, Barnard College Archives)

kitchen fitments, ranges, plumbing, tubs, &c., with which I prefer to have nothing to do."[14] This need for clarity was reiterated in an undated, handwritten letter, which probably followed immediately afterward, in which de Wolfe wrote again to Gill, "I do not wish to undertake any kitchen fitments, plumbing or stationery [*sic*] woodwork. I feel that the *batterie des cuisine* comes under my contract. I would be glad if I can have some definite statement by tomorrow as really I am working night/day on this layout as I am sailing [for England] next week and it must all be laid out before I go."[15] By May 28, everything had been clarified and de Wolfe confirmed to Osborn, "It is understood that I am to undertake the decoration and furnishing of Brooks Hall, Barnard College, for the sum of $3,000."[16] The completion date was set as September 20.

It was evident that, from her experience at the Colony Club, de Wolfe had learned what her professional limits should be at Brooks Hall. She was responsible for the decor of all the rooms—the parlor, the reception room, the dining room, and all the 97 bedroom suites, as well as all the movable equipment in the other rooms. It was up to her to find appropriate furniture and furnishings, whether antique or reproduction, and to develop a complete decorative scheme for the building. Brooks Hall was a much more modest project than the Colony Club, although the intention was clearly to make the interior as comfortable as possible within the given constraints, and Barnard College would not have employed de Wolfe, knowing her reputation, without expecting her to make a significant impact.

As she did for the Colony Club, de Wolfe approached the task from aesthetic and functional perspectives simultaneously. The challenge was to create a modern environment for modern young women who wanted to combine privacy with a level of communality, a balancing act that required de Wolfe to think carefully about the conflicting roles of individualization and standardization in the interior.

To balance these potentially conflicting ends, de Wolfe used both standardized and individualized approaches. There was already considerable variety among the bedrooms. Some had bathrooms attached; others didn't. Some had bay windows suitable for cozy corners, while corner rooms had fireplaces. Some were suites of two or three rooms; some were single rooms. Whatever the combination, however, all the individual spaces were approximately 16 feet long by nine feet wide.

De Wolfe provided each study-bedroom with an identical set of items of basic equipment, the formula with which she had experimented at 122 East 17th Street and subsequently applied at the Colony Club. Each contained "a rug, a couch bed, a bureau, a study table, one straight chair, one easy chair, one screen, one towel rack, one glass shelf."[17] In addition, each room had "chintz curtains of varied light patterns and a cover for couch and chair of the same."[18] While a level of individuality was provided through the use of

Two students sharing a book in an apartment, Brooks Hall, 1912. (Brown Bros., Barnard College Archives)

different patterned chintzes, the decorator made sure that the curtains had the same cream-colored linings "so that all the windows may present the same appearance from the street."[19]

All the rooms combined a high level of comfort with a sense of the lifestyle needs of a female student who might want to work alone at times and, at others, to entertain a friend in a light, modern space with none of the elaborate decor that characterized the interiors of other women's colleges established earlier in the century. There was no attempt to smother the inhabitants with culture, but rather an effort was made to provide

them with functional, attractive interiors in which they could create their own lives as emerging young women in an era of female emancipation.

Mirrors, pictures, cushions, ceramic tea sets, footstools, vases of flowers, framed photographs, and standard lamps all helped to bring life into the study-bedrooms in Brooks Hall, and the presence of fireplaces imparted a warm, domestic focus. Storage was in plain wardrobes and chests of drawers. Whereas de Wolfe had used mahogany extensively in the Colony Club to convey a sense of opulence, in Brooks Hall she utilized oak to give a more casual, homey feel to the interior. The furniture selected was simple and robust, some of it conforming to the contemporary taste for Mission or Arts and Crafts furniture, but Thonet bentwood chairs, cane-seated chairs, wicker furniture, Windsor chairs, solid Victorian desks, adjustable metal tables, and a range of modern, upholstered armchairs, complete with ottomans, also made an appearance, as did framed mirrors and wall-mounted bookcases. Unsurprisingly, there was no sign of de Wolfe's beloved French taste. It would have been out of the price range of the budget and inappropriate for the lifestyle of the inhabitants, who were more concerned with educating themselves than with social display and aspiration.[20]

Historian Andrew S. Dolkart has written that de Wolfe was attempting "to create traditional interiors where the women from elite families who could afford the cost of room and board, would presumably feel at home."[21] While this was undoubtedly true to some extent, Barnard's mission was much more egalitarian and forward-thinking, and the simplicity and overt functionality of these rooms created an ambiance of modernity, as Gill explained. In *The House in Good Taste*, de Wolfe dedicated several pages to a description of the modern apartment, especially those destined for inhabitants of modest means, suggesting that they should be equipped with simple furniture, including Windsor chairs, cane chairs, and oak gate-leg tables.[22] The students' rooms in Brooks Hall can be seen as prototypes for the modern apartment envisaged later by de Wolfe. Much discussion had been taking place in architectural magazines and elsewhere on the subject of the so-called bachelor apartment, and de Wolfe's rooms for Barnard College students could, in some ways, be seen as its feminine equivalent. "Like bachelors, college women were expected to receive and entertain guests but were not expected to cook."[23]

De Wolfe employed a novel color-coding system as a means of differentiating between the five identically laid-out floors. "The rooms on the 8th floor were finished in blue, those on the 7th in pink, on the 6th in green and so on," explained a writer in the *Bulletin*.[24] The article went on to explain that this had been done "so that when the doors are all open the effect from the hall is that of one large room rather than a row of band-boxes."[25] It was a basic but highly effective visual strategy. Another very successful touch was the decorator's decision to line doors between adjoining rooms with mirrors to create a sense of spaciousness and provide the students with full-length mirrors for dressing.

Scholar Jessica Dawson has made the point that the public and private divide was very clear in Brooks Hall, as it would have been in any contemporary single-family home.[26] The color scheme for the ground floor was a combination of cream and oak, the walls of the parlor being painted a deeper shade of cream to create a subtle variety of ambiences. Each of the 15 tables in the dining room, which seated eight, four, or two women, had an oak candlestick on it with a cream shade. A decorative touch was provided on the otherwise bare walls by the addition of neoclassical-style, custom-made metal wall sconces fitted with electric candles. There was no central ceiling light. The parlor, where there was often dancing after dinner, was a large, long room with a brown mottled carpet, effective at hiding stains and other wear and tear, two large, comfortable sofas upholstered in glazed striped chintz (probably English in origin), two armchairs with floral upholstery, an old mahogany table that the designer or her staff found in Baltimore, a stained mahogany carved fireplace surround with a mirror above it, Colonial-style cabinets, and a borne upholstered in blue-and-white striped linen around a support column. Floral-patterned chintz curtains hung at the arched

Two students taking afternoon tea in an apartment, Brooks Hall, 1912. (Brown Bros., Barnard College Archives)

windows. The overall effect was of a comfortable drawing room in an English country house, right down to the piano.

It took a little while for Brooks Hall to be fully occupied—the first students moved in while the building was still under construction—but by 1911 Barnard College was once again unable to provide housing for all the students who requested it. Rich and de Wolfe's dormitory allowed the young women sufficient levels of privacy, comfort, and communality

to be able to lead a pleasant student life. They were both part of Manhattan and simultaneously protected from it. Rituals such as afternoon tea were encouraged, and the girls experienced a lifestyle that permitted them to retain old values while becoming modern, educated women ready to participate in 20th-century urban life. The practical, logical, and sensitively furnished interiors provided by de Wolfe undoubtedly played an important part in allowing that transition to happen.

circa *1907–08*

Lolita and J. Ogden Armour Residence
Mellody Farm
Lake Forest, Illinois

"The most beautiful house between
New York and San Francisco."[1]

The second major commission to decorate a domestic interior that Elsie de Wolfe received following the rapturous reception of the Colony Club was from another of the organization's out-of-town members, Lolita Armour. Along with Bertha Palmer—the doyenne for whom de Wolfe designed an armchair—Armour was one of Chicago's two representatives at the club. And like the Colony Club's San Francisco representative, Ethel Crocker, Armour was so impressed by de Wolfe's work that she wanted some of it herself.[2]

In her autobiography, de Wolfe suggested that she had more of a free hand in the Armour house than she had at the Crocker residence in San Francisco.[3] "It was," she explained, "entirely of my planning."[4] Not only did it appear that Lolita Armour left her free to develop her own ideas for the estate, it also seems, thanks to the Armour family's meat-packing millions, that de Wolfe was able to work with an exceptionally generous budget. "Once I had inspired confidence," she wrote with satisfaction, "no limit was put on the expenditure."[5] Thanks to a personal taste that had been canonized by the popular press across the country, de Wolfe and her interior decorating philosophy clearly carried enough prestige for wealthy women—often married to the sons of self-made men—to seek her advice when furnishing their homes and thereby establish the perfect backdrop for their social positions. A trendsetting former actress who had become a member of high society, elevating herself

Opposite: Main hall. (Architectural Record, Feb. 1916, courtesy of the Art Institute of Chicago)

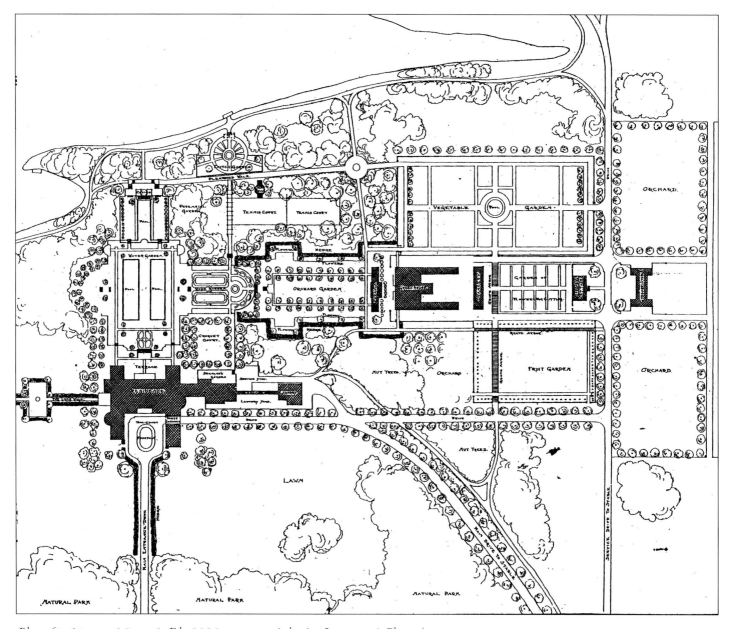

Plan. (Architectural Record, Feb. 1916, courtesy of the Art Institute of Chicago)

from parvenu to posh in barely a decade, she was in the perfect position to understand the dreams and requirements of newly minted hostesses. And de Wolfe had the contacts and the aesthetic skills to ensure that any interior commission she accepted not only would be appropriate but admired and envied. Indeed, as western and midwestern socialites, Crocker and Armour undoubtedly looked upon this prominent, prosperous, well-traveled, and socially adept New Yorker as essential to the

maintenance of their self-images as their Paris dressmakers and their London jewelers.

The lavish interiors that de Wolfe created for Lolita and Ogden Armour's mansion in Lake Forest, a suburb of Chicago on Lake Michigan, represented an early example of the professional decorator working with a wealthy client on a brand-new house, on a substantial financial scale, and with an open brief. The results were widely praised at the time and received

*Rear facade. (*Architectural Record, *Feb. 1916, courtesy of the Art Institute of Chicago)*

considerable local attention, although de Wolfe's name was missing from some accounts.[6] When the *Architectural Record* published a lengthy article about Mellody Farm in 1916, for example, all credit for the house and its interiors was given to architect Arthur Heun.[7] In 1918, however, *Harper's Bazaar* acknowledged de Wolfe's contribution to the Armour interiors, noting that she gave the sprawling building "an atmosphere of domesticity and warmth, often lacking in houses of its size."[8]

De Wolfe worked on the Armour house for a period of about three years. She bought furniture for it in Europe and New York City, sometimes with Lolita Armour at her side. She created schemes for its huge rooms, both upstairs and downstairs. She oversaw the work of artisans in the installation of aspects of the interior. She coordinated the craftsmen and upholsterers, and she supported Lolita Armour in her quest for an impressive family home, a family seat that would

Entrance porch. (Architectural Record, Feb. 1916, courtesy of the Art Institute of Chicago)

solidify the Armours' position among Chicago's slaughterhouse elite. It is not known how closely de Wolfe worked with Heun in the planning of Mellody Farm, though she already was aware of his talents, having installed a fountain in another Heun-designed Chicago house, that of industrialist James Deering. The period of overlap with Heun on the Armour project was probably only about a year, as work on Mellody Farm had begun in 1904, before de Wolfe's decision to become a decorator, and the home was completed and inhabited by the Armour family in May 1908. Most of the rooms were furnished after the architectural work had been done.

Mellody Farm, which was to be the Armours' home for 19 years, was presented to Lolita Armour as a surprise from her husband. Like Ethel Crocker, Lolita Armour was a woman admired for her taste, which included her Parisian couture and her Hispano-Suiza town car. Like many other wealthy matrons of the era, she spent much of her life working as a patron of the arts, and she also left a collection of antique shoes to the Art Institute of Chicago on her death in 1953. (Whether there was any link to de Wolfe's own historical shoe collection is unknown, although they both included French 18th-century items.)[9] Armour also was noted for her award-winning roses, which she cultivated in Mellody Farm's extensive gardens; one of the roses grown there, an orange-and-red variety bred in 1919, was named for her daughter.[10] The house, many people reported, was constantly filled with flowers: roses, zinnias, snapdragons, stock, and marigolds.

Born in Connecticut, Lolita Sheldon had married Jonathan Ogden Armour in 1891. Five years later, their only child, also named Lolita, was born with a dislocated hip that eventually was cured by a Viennese surgeon in a series of controversial operations that made national headlines. Perhaps due to this ongoing health issue, the family was very close, and the child famously spoiled. (Lolita Armour's widowed mother also lived in the house.) The life the Armours led in Lake Forest in the years leading up to World War I was one of great luxury. Picnics were worthy of Versailles, the staff "setting up a board with a damask tablecloth on the *tapis vert* 50 yards from her front door and served on the second-best Meissen by the butler and the footman."[11] At parties, guests arriving by train were met by carriages driven by uniformed, cockaded men. It perhaps comes as no surprise to hear that when Lolita Armour entertained, her husband often went to his club to play cards. Curiously, his bedroom at

Mellody Farm was not connected to his wife's. Armour also had a private suite connected to his ground-floor office, an observer once wrote, "where he could entertain special guests without the bother of announcing to the rest of the household they were there."[12]

Ogden Armour's wealth came from his role as the head of the multimillion-dollar meatpacking business Armour and Company, which he took over in 1901 on the death of its founder, his father, Philip D. Armour. He inherited a fortune but also took the company to new financial heights by investing in railroads, elevators, refrigerators, and street railways. The bubble burst in the early 1920s, however, and after losing more than $150 million in an economic downturn, Armour suddenly died in 1927. Debts forced his widow to sell Mellody Farm the following year—a consortium of rich Chicago men bought it with the intention of turning it in to a country club—and move to a more modest nine-room house on 20 acres of land that she had retained from the sale.

At the turn of the century, however, Ogden Armour was a very rich man. In 1904 he purchased the farm from Martin Mellody and commissioned a new house from Heun, then one of Chicago's younger architects, known for his innovative work. He had experimented with the Prairie style, but for the Armours, who were not particularly adventuresome, he created a handsome Italianate mansion with arched windows and two towers set amid formal gardens. Although the idiom of Mellody Farm—if anyone left out one "l," Armour became irritated—was clearly Italian, it was not a historical re-creation. "Superficial observers only have called it an Italian villa, which it is not," wrote Peter Wight, an observer, in 1916. "It is only a rational rendition of a plan and materials which the architect decided to use, and its beauty, which no reasonable person can deny, is due

to the discreet use of these materials and the absence of all striving for effect."[13]

Mellody Farm cost $10 million—inclusive of the landscaped gardens by Jens Jensen, who also landscaped the Michigan estate of Henry Ford—and was surrounded by 1,000 acres of land. It had its own water and power sources, and orchards, greenhouses, an orangerie, stables, a carriage house with a clock tower, and an icehouse. Armour created a private spur of the Chicago, Milwaukee, St. Paul and Pacific Railroad in order to bring the large pieces of marble needed for the floors, the wooden staircases, and the 15 marble mantelpieces close to the building site. The roughly H-shaped house was made of concrete and brick and supported by steel beams. Its roof was fashioned of red tiles, made in Ohio, and a pinkish wash was applied to the walls, emphasizing its Italian countenance.

The pillared entrance, designed as a loggia with three tall arches, led to an entrance hall measuring a stupendous 20 feet wide by 112 feet long that connected the left wing to the right wing of the house. The left wing contained a music room at the front of the house, a library in the middle, and a living room at the back. The right wing contained a drawing room at the front, a dining room in the middle, and a breakfast room at the back. Between the living room and the dining room was a grand curved stairway of rose and green marble with bronze railings, designed, it was claimed at the time, for young Lolita Armour to make an entrance on her eventual wedding day. Perhaps there is some truth to the story, since Heun was invited back to create the decorations for the heiress' wedding to John J. Mitchell Jr.

Other important rooms on this floor were Armour's study, with a private stair leading to his bedroom above, and, situated behind the main hall, a huge

Music room. (Architectural Record, Feb. 1916, courtesy of the Art Institute of Chicago)

winter garden. Measuring 55½ feet long by 24 feet wide, its five arched glass doors opened at the rear of the house to the west terrace and gardens punctuated by topiary and water features.

Antique and reproduction furniture, primarily 18th-century French in style, was deployed throughout most of the Armours' rooms, and decorative tapestries added a regal air. The rooms were sunny, comfortable but not overfurnished, and there was a fully realized atmosphere of grace and refinement, undoubtedly

pleasing Lolita Armour and underscoring her position near the apex of Chicago society. Displaying tapestries against warm white walls, the entrance hall was furnished with long, low benches, giant porcelain jardinières, marble-topped 18th-century consoles, and a Chinese lacquer cabinet on a gilt-wood stand. The mauve dining room initially was decorated with tapestries, too, but Lolita Armour removed them at a later date and had an Italian artist create a lavishly veined *faux-marbre* finish on the plain plaster walls.

Dining room. (After All, 1935)

The applied panels of the room were filled with large scenes of 18th-century ladies and gentlemen in wooded landscapes. The reproduction Régence-style chairs had canework backs, and a console with extraordinarily attenuated cabriole legs was positioned at one end of the room, its surface displaying flowers in porcelain cachepots and other ornamental ceramics. The oak parquet floor was inlaid with a border of black and varicolored marble. Adjacent to this was a black-and-gold breakfast room.

The green music room was executed in neoclassical French taste, and at one end stood the obligatory instrument of the era, an Aeolian pipe organ. Here could be found a number of de Wolfe hallmarks, including several groupings of Louis XVI chairs and small sofas; Chinese jars made into table lamps and topped by shirred silk shades; a marble fireplace surround topped by an inset sheet of mirror; multi-armed cast-bronze sconces; lightly painted neoclassical-style paneling, and an Aubusson carpet. In many ways it was

Winter garden. (Architectural Record, *Feb. 1916, courtesy of the Art Institute of Chicago*)

a more spacious version of the living room at 122 East 17th Street, right down to the potted palm.

The library was a darker room, also wood paneled and decorated in green, as was the living room, which had a walnut background and carvings by the 18th-century master woodworker Grinling Gibbons. De Wolfe used blue as the main color in this room, contrasting it with red petit-point chairs and sofas. After de Wolfe had finished working on Mellody Farm,

Lolita Armour purchased a complete Georgian room in London and had Heun fit it into the living room. He did so reluctantly, as he did not feel that it suited the rest of the house.

The most impressive room in the Armour house was the winter garden, a feature as common to the mansions of the wealthy at this time as a ballroom. The architect provided a dramatic pastoral plaster frieze depicting animals and birds, below which de Wolfe positioned panels of trelliswork. In his account of the room in *Architectural Record,* Peter Wight described the treatment of the lower walls as "an intimation that we are approaching what surpasses all that art may be," revealing a profound admiration for this space, which openly recalled features of the Colony Club—both the tea room and the roof garden—but found new ways of expressing similar ideas. As in the trellis tea room in New York City, a fountain was placed at one end of the Armours' winter garden and the trelliswork panels were lighted by floral-theme metal sconces, here in the form of two thorny long-stemmed roses suspended by bows and ribbons. Caryatid pedestals held pots of azaleas aloft in front of the pilasters on the long inside wall, while Chinese porcelain cachepots, planted with specimen ferns, stood between the glass doors to the garden. A prime example of de Wolfe's ease at mixing periods, the room was furnished with a variety of styles and periods of furniture arranged for multiple uses and encounters. French Provençal ladderback chairs surrounded a painted Louis XVI–style round table, ready for luncheon or a game of bridge. Mismatched Louis XV–style chairs were gathered around a modern upholstered sofa, while alongside a Provençal-style sofa cushioned with button-tufted chintz stood a Colonial-style tripod table and a Louis XVI chair. The winter garden's atmosphere embodied casual elegance, aristocratic ease, and a refreshing and highly persuasive mixture of traditionalism and modernity, spiced with accents both whimsical (a white-ceramic elephant planter) and classical (a statue of the goddess Diana).

In *The House in Good Taste,* de Wolfe described a jardinière table—an object that had been popular in Biedermeier interiors—in the Armours' winter garden, which combined the function of a desk with that of a plant holder. "The desk, or table, is painted gray, with

Electric lighting fixture in the winter garden. (Author's photograph)

faint green decorations. At each end of the long top there is a sunken, zinc-lined box to hold growing plants. Between the flower boxes there is the usual arrangement of the desk outfit, blotter pad, paper rack, ink pots, and so forth. The spaces beneath the flower boxes are filled with shelves for books and magazines." Ever anxious to bring the rarefied world of decoration down to the less privileged masses and conscious of her role as a professional with sound ideas as well as decorative conceits,

Bedroom. (New York Public Library)

de Wolfe continued, "The idea is so thoroughly practicable for any garden room, and is so simple that it could be constructed by any man who knows how to use tools."[14]

An article in *Good Housekeeping* in April 1913 illustrated the table that de Wolfe designed for the Armours. The decorator adapted the same idea to other furniture she created for the winter garden. "The sofas were eight feet long," she recalled in her autobiography. "Their covers, especially woven, were of white velvet striped in a design of green leaves. At each end was a zinc-lined receptacle holding flowering plants. The tables were of green and black and white marble to match the floors and mantel."[15] She was openly pleased with her design for the winter garden, calling the space "the perfection of beauty."[16]

The upstairs bedrooms at Mellody Farm conformed to the layout that she liked best, each having its own sitting room, or boudoir, attached. A later commentary on the house pointed out that one of its notable features was the use of floral-patterned "chintz and block linen fabric" on bedroom walls as well as for the curtains and the covers of daybeds and side chairs, another example of de Wolfe's en-suite approach to fabric and patterns at this period in her career. Lolita Armour's bedroom had a two-tone walnut parquet floor; the paneled walls were painted cream picked out in de Wolfe's favorite shade of rose, a color that was repeated in the upholstery of the French furniture. Her dressing room walls were

Mrs. Ogden Armour's Chinese-paper screen.
(The House in Good Taste, *1913*)

covered in green, gold, and red-striped satin. The bedroom of the Armours' young daughter was decorated in pink-and-white toile de Jouy; at its heart was a Louis XVI bed resembling the one de Wolfe created for one of the Crocker daughters at Burlingame.

Ogden Armour's bedroom in this part of the house was, in contrast, decorated in American Beauty red, a dark, brilliant shade named for the popular rose variety of the day, and mahogany Chippendale.[17] Another bedroom was fully paneled in wood and featured a four-poster bed whose undulating canopy was dressed with a bird-of-paradise fabric; a William and Mary bench stood at its foot. A particularly delightful de Wolfe creation used elsewhere in the house was a three-panel folding screen for Lolita Armour, decorated with images of exotic tropical birds.

Mellody Farm was one de Wolfe's most ambitious domestic projects undertaken in the years following the completion of the Colony Club. As they were realized according to de Wolfe's vision, the interiors of this house represented the decorator's ideas in action in pure, untrammeled form. Such was the wealth and commitment of the Armours that de Wolfe was able to work without the constraints she had experienced at the Colony Club; no compromises were made. The winter garden and the public rooms, although grand in scale, had a simplicity of execution and a humanity of materials—colorful chintzes and linens, low-key gilding, warm woods—that distinguished them from many of their more conspicuous equivalents in other large houses of the era. At Mellody Farm, de Wolfe succeeded in demonstrating that a leading position in American society could be maintained without the overtly luxurious displays of the recent past but rather through the application of a discriminating eye, a feeling for refinement and subtlety, and, above all, the expression of good taste.

1910

Show House
131 East 71st Street
New York City

At the height of her success as an interior decorator, de Wolfe decided to ally her celebrity and talent to the solution of the spatial and aesthetic problems of the Victorian town houses that dominated the streets of New York. These were the very buildings whose chocolate-dark ugliness had offended her as a child and sparked her quest for beauty. It was a challenge for which she now had sufficient time and funds. "By 1910 the snowball that was my career had bounded ahead with such rapidity that it no longer needed even a tap to help it on its way," she wrote in her autobiography. "With enough money to warrant my making the experiment, I bought one of these houses on East 71st Street, and Ogden Codman, the distinguished architect, and I waved the divining rod which brought its latent graces to the surface."[1]

De Wolfe's real reasons for undertaking this project were more pragmatic that her blithe tone would indicate. Turning a dark and dismal house into a light and cheery home would provide the decorator with an ideal showcase for her talents, generate a great deal of publicity, and hopefully realize a handsome profit when the smartly renovated house would be sold.[2]

Alteration of the five-story house was undertaken without the constraints that came from working for clients, so it could embody, literally, all the decorator's deeply felt beliefs about interior decoration at that time. A real-estate column in *The New York Times* of March 23, 1910, noted that "Elsie De Wolfe, who recently purchased the four-story dwelling at 122 [sic] East Seventy-first Street from Douglas Elliman, through Albert B. Ashworth, filed plans yesterday for altering the dwelling at a cost of about $15,000."[3]

Opposite: The entrance hall to the model house on East 71st Street. (The House in Good Taste, *1913)*

Codman was an inspired as well as a comfortable choice for the project. De Wolfe had worked successfully with him on refurbishments at 122 East 17th Street, and his archives indicate unspecified work planned, if not executed, for de Wolfe and Marbury at 103 East 35th Street.[4] Elsie also had consulted him about fitting antique boiserie from Minna Anglesey's Versailles house into the salon of Villa Trianon.[5] In 1912, she worked with Codman again on the decoration of the Bayard Thayer house in Boston as well as the interiors of a house in Newport for the John Whipple Slaters. It is probable that the two collaborated in some fashion on even more projects, given the tightly knitted social community they shared. Additionally, Codman was an obvious choice to renovate the house on East 71st Street, since the architect had been making alterations to New York brownstones for more than a decade, adding "decorative plasterwork and paneled moldings in the French style" to numerous clients' homes.[6] Helping them determine the interior schemes here was de Wolfe's associate Paul Chalfin.[7]

The house on East 71st Street was typically narrow, taking up much of a lot measuring 17 feet wide by 102.2 feet deep. De Wolfe's purchase price is not known, but the house had been sold to its previous owner in 1902 for $14,000.[8] The decorator and the architect chose to alter it in a number of ways—structurally and decoratively—in order to maximize the effects of light and space. First, they removed the high stoop and moved the entrance from the second to the first floor and shifted its position from the side of the facade to its center. This gave the house neoclassical-style symmetry uncommon on the Manhattan streetscape. The square of land between the house and the sidewalk was turned into a welcoming courtyard outfitted with "an iron railing and grille, and rows of formal box-trees against the iron rail," a gesture that recalled elegant town houses in London and Paris.[9] The front door was painted a dark glossy green to coordinate with the plants and was accented by a huge bronze knob. Above the door, Codman added an iron balcony, and beneath the windows were mounted flower boxes thick with green ivy.

One of the most influential features of the renovation, given the usual darkness of this area in conventional New York brownstones, was the spacious entrance hall, newly floored with a checkerboard of black and white marble squares, which the architect considered "more suitable, not to say stylish."[10] In *The House in Good Taste*, de Wolfe dedicated a section to halls and wrote about her preference for formal halls that "afford the visitor a few moments of rest and calm after the crowded streets of the city."[11] By moving the staircase from its position at one side of the house to the heart of the building, de Wolfe and Codman were left with enough room to devote the entire front half of the first floor to a spacious interval between the noise outside and the quietude upstairs. It was a generosity of square footage rarely seen in middle-class town houses in Manhattan, and the panel-molded room's dominant feature was a full-length arched niche, centered on the east wall and nestling a tall, glazed porcelain stove that provided the glow of warmth on chilly days. De Wolfe first used traditional wood-burning European stoves like this on the roof terrace of the Colony Club, and she was surely aware that in *The Decoration of Houses*, Wharton and Codman had suggested that an old-fashioned faience stove was a suitable addition to a modern hall.[12] On either side of the stove, de Wolfe positioned a pedestal of carved and gilded gray-toned wood, each topped with a "quaint French" ornament in the shape of a footed bowl filled with fruit.[13] A large panel on the opposite wall was filled with a tight grid of small square mirrors that reflected the snow-white stove and pedestals and

The drawing room in the model house on East 71st Street. (The House in Good Taste, *1913*)

increased the room's perceived size. Befitting its purpose as a conduit rather than a room to live in, the space was lightly furnished. Box shrubs in Versailles-style wood tubs flanked the front door: two simple French chairs were available for visitors waiting to be admitted upstairs; a marble-topped iron table held the Edwardian hostess' all-important visitors book; and positioned next to the door was a handy iron stand for canes, parasols, and umbrellas. Dress curtains of cream linen hung over undercurtains of pale muslin. The effect was light, restful, clean, and practical, a space de Wolfe described as "cool, stately."[14]

Key structural changes to the East 71st Street house included the positioning of an elegant enclosed spiral staircase at its heart and the construction, in what had been the garden, of a wing to house the servants' quarters, laundry, and pantry. Relegating the "below stairs" functions to a separate area allowed the main body of the house to be given over entirely to living spaces. Above the entrance hall was a drawing room; the dining room was on the same floor, placed behind the stair. Codman designed neoclassical panels for both rooms, which de Wolfe furnished in a subdued French style, though it was observed that "No especial period has been carried out. . . ."[15] The drawing room she later would describe as a "friendly, pleasant place, full of quiet color."[16] As in the drawing room at 17th Street, the primary color was rose, the color derived from the room's Savonnerie carpet, used against cream-painted walls and soft white woodwork. Codman's imposition of mirrors to expand space was exhibited here as well, with one set over the fireplace surround of white marble veined with gray and another set into the facing wall, resulting in rose-pink rooms reflected to infinity. Long sheets of mirror were fixed between the three windows, which looked out over the front

A Chinese cabinet in the drawing room.
(The House in Good Taste, *1913*)

courtyard. De Wolfe hung these with rose-and-yellow shot silk over white muslin undercurtains, which were used throughout the house to create unity from outside, as at Brooks Hall.

Though de Wolfe had become known for her preference for 18th-century French decor, she made a deliberate attempt to create a sense of unpretentious warmth throughout the house. In the drawing room she assembled an eclectic array of furniture that looked as if it had been collected over years or by inheritance.[17] Thanks to the carefully controlled color scheme and attention to the tones of painted and natural wood, "all [was] in harmony."[18] "The strongest, the most intense feeling I have about decoration is my love of color," de Wolfe explained in 1912, recalling for some readers, perhaps, her well-dressed appearances on stage, when the actress would coordinate the colors of her gowns to the tenor of her character. "It is an emotional matter with me, as is music with many women. I have felt as intimate satisfaction at St. Mark's [Piazza San Marco in Venice] at twilight as I ever felt at any opera, and I love music."[19] That signature shade of rose showed up in the brocade used on some chairs as well as the needlework covering the neoclassical-style sofa. Hanging from picture moldings was an assortment of decorative etchings and prints, the suspension wires camouflaged by braided rose-colored silk ribbons, an effect greatly praised by a reporter from *The New York Times.* "Miles of wire stretching over a tinted wall have always been an obstacle to beauty, and this ingenious method of solving the problem will be received with gratitude."[20] Adding a backbone of strength to the soft, feminine palette was a mahogany writing desk, its darkness repeated in a cabinet of black Chinese lacquer that de Wolfe—whose stage costumes often included black details, enough for the press to comment on this as a hallmark of the actress' fashion sense—ever conscious

*Third-floor front bedroom—sitting room. (*The House in Good Taste, *1913)*

to mood and special effects, had positioned "so the light [from the windows] catches its gilded mounts."[21]

The palette of the dining room—yellow, blue, black, and cream—again was inspired by a carpet, a decorating strategy that was to become another hall-mark of the de Wolfe oeuvre. Following the lead of the medallion-patterned yellow Chinese carpet, de Wolfe installed curtains of blue "taffeta, lined with felt and tinted to give an impression of deep and light gold," and she placed blue-and-dull-yellow-striped velvet on the seats of cream-painted chairs she had custom made

for the house. It was a refined, gently colorful interior that must have made a strong impression on visitors who came to the house at its grand opening the first week of January 1911, doubtless imagining the space as the perfect setting for women in pastel gowns and men in black tie.[22]

The decorator developed some of her most striking color schemes to date in the bedroom suites on the third and fourth floors. As at East 17th Street, the Colony Club, and Brooks Hall—and as de Wolfe was to do for Anne Morgan in her family's mansion on

Third-floor rear bed–sitting room. (The House in Good Taste, *1913*)

Madison Avenue at around the same time—the most interesting ideas were found in the most private spaces.

The large front bedroom on the third floor was conceived as a joint bedroom–sitting room, although, as de Wolfe herself proclaimed, "you would never suspect [this multipurpose use], so delightfully quaint is the furniture."[23] This time the chromatic cue was derived from a set of Chinese ceramic jars and vases destined for the mantel. She described them as "the oddest things . . . a sort of turquoise blue-green, and mauve and mulberry,

with flecks of black, on a cream porcelain ground."[24] Chalfin, an admirer of Asian decorative arts, may have been the source of these. The challenge was to create an interior with this unusual color combination, which was familiar enough in Chinese porcelain made for the Western market in the 19th century, but less so for domestic interiors. What resulted was dramatic and stimulating. Pale blue-green paint was used on the walls—the woodwork, again, was white—while a mauve chintz patterned with roses and peacocks was used for the curtains, chair covers, mattress, and box spring. Shades for both the double-branch wall sconces and the green-painted urn-shaped table lamps were made of a gently shirred silk of solid mauve, and the room-size rug was a velvety mauve broadloom. The diminutive wood chest of drawers was painted pale gray-green and decorated with neoclassical-style, multicolored swags of flowers applied to its four drawers. This piece was probably painted by Everett Shinn. The selection of mauve as the dominant color in the scheme surely reminded worldly visitors of one of the decade's most admired mauve rooms, the boudoir of Empress Alexandra of Russia, and de Wolfe's own well-known appreciation of the color, which was often commented on in descriptions of her costumes in the theatrical press. These connections would have not escaped de Wolfe, who always was skillful at exploiting popular fashions and effectively broadcasting them to a wide audience.

Apparently appropriate furnishings that would work with the mauve-and-blue-green scheme were difficult to find, so de Wolfe had carpenters and painters create them, including a version of the kidney-shaped side table that was used in the Crocker house in California and simple green-painted bookshelves. The room seemed minimally furnished, because of its lack of tabletop clutter and limited artwork, but it had the requisite necessities: a well-appointed desk draped with a heavy piece of green damask, the chest of drawers, lightweight side tables that could be easily moved when needed elsewhere in the room. There also was an engaging assortment of seating: a Provençal-style ladderback side chair, a high-back armchair, and a modern upholstered armchair. The sofa, painted to match the chest of drawers, was a generous 42 inches deep, de Wolfe pointed out, so it could be pressed into service as a bed at night, making the room an inspiration for homeowners with limited space. The only notes of

whimsy were the shining bronze andirons in the fireplace, each in the shape of a life-size cat.

In a further attempt to show how democratic and easily applied to any budget her ideas were—a theme that would dominate her 1913 book *The House in Good Taste*—de Wolfe remarked, optimistically, "Any woman who is skillful with her brush could decorate this furniture, and I dare say many women could build it."[25]

The other suite of private rooms on the third floor was decorated in red, white, and blue. Anchored by a lit à la polonaise and a mantel of Siena marble, the cream-walled, white-trimmed space was decorated en suite with

Chest of drawers decorated by Everett Shinn in the third-floor front bedroom–sitting room. (The House in Good Taste, *1913*)

*Third-floor front bedroom—sitting room. (*The House in Good Taste, *1913)*

Third-floor rear bed–sitting room. (The House in Good Taste, *1913*)

Third-floor dressing room in the rear suite. (The House in Good Taste, *1913*)

a brilliant glazed chintz printed with medallions of rosy flowers and dull blue ribbons that was used for the curtains, upholstery, and bed hangings (these also were trimmed with red fringe). The room-size broadloom carpet was rose red with a discreet tone-on-tone diamond pattern similar to the carpet used in Marbury's bedroom on East 17th Street, and the familiar kidney table—de Wolfe placed one in every room of the house—made yet another appearance. It was made of mahogany, as was the little Colonial-style desk, which was placed at a right angle between the two windows. They were accompanied by a Louis XVI–style armchair dressed in chintz, a little Pilgrim-style stool covered in fringed blue velvet, and an inexpensive wastebasket of woven wicker. Next to this bedroom was a dressing room with mirrored walls. Here, another bold chintz was used for curtains and upholstery, this time depicting colorful parrots and green foliage on a black ground. To provide sufficient light, the dressing table was placed in front of the double window, the triple mirror was flanked by candlestick lamps, and overhead was a ceiling fixture with a fringed ruche-silk shade. As the decorator once said, women like to dress by electric light but be seen by candlelight.

The final bedroom, located on the floor above, had a chinoiserie atmosphere, with "quaint water green" curtains and the wallpaper—also used in the dressing room—was printed with thousands of tiny Japanese fans.[26] The rear wing contained the servants' quarters and storage, areas the decorator considered to be crucial elements of modern living and not to be neglected. The servants' rooms were chaste but thoughtfully equipped with beds painted with white enamel (probably the patented metal model de Wolfe used at the Colony Club), upholstery and curtains of crisp glazed chintz (probably a plain color rather than printed), natural wicker armchairs (doubtless similar to

the Canton ones used in the roof garden of the Colony Club), and humble, easy-to-clean rag rugs.

Much publicized in the local and national newspapers and magazines, the East 71st Street venture apparently was a great success. "When it was finished Ogden Codman and I gave a reception to which all of New York flocked, and went away applauding this perfect solution of transmuting an unattractive house into a stylish dwelling-place. Soon the process of bringing it to a second blooming was copied not only in New York, but throughout the country in cities so overburdened with the dull and heavy facades of the mid-Victorian relics."[27] *The New York Times,* for example, praised the renovation's inventiveness, declaring it "very clever" and a repository of "taste and ingenuity." [28]

Although the house was a business proposition, its decor depended on de Wolfe's emotional engagement. Presented to the public as a smart solution to an architectural problem, it also was an idealized, romantic home, a feminine fantasy wrapped within in a hard-nosed reconstruction project. So perhaps it is not surprising that de Wolfe used it as the working model for the home she would remodel in 1911 for herself and Bessy Marbury 16 blocks south.

Fourth-floor bedroom. (The House in Good Taste, *1913*)

Elsie de Wolfe–Elisabeth Marbury Residence

123 East 55th Street

New York City

"As perfect a city house as the
two of us could have had."[1]

Shortly after opening the show house on East 71st Street, de Wolfe and Bessy Marbury signed a long lease on a similar building on East 55th Street and once again called on the help of Ogden Codman. The women were fast outgrowing the small rooms of East 17th Street, and the decorator—her fame increasing and her New York clientele based largely on the tony Upper East Side—realized it was time to move to a more fashionable neighborhood farther north.

The rented house was another "grimy, four-story, high-stooped brownstone."[2] Built in around 1860 when, according to one writer, "American domestic architecture was at a low ebb," it presented de Wolfe with an irresistible challenge.[3] "It pursued me in my mind, pleading to be given a chance, and I just had to listen to it," she said.[4] Their landlord, Stuyvesant Wainwright, agreed to the couple's plans to remodel the building into "a five-story American basement house."[5]

As with the East 71st house, de Wolfe explained, "I tore away the ugly street stairs and centered the entrance door in a little stone-paved courtyard, framed with a big iron railing, bordered with box trees."[6] Codman rusticated the ground floor of the house, added an iron demilune balcony to the pedimented window above the front door, and

*Opposite: Front facade. (*The House in Good Taste, *1913)*

Entrance hall. (The House in Good Taste, *1913*)

flanked it with full-length French doors set with low decorative iron grilles. Once again the entrance hall was given a black-and-white marble floor, but there were two arched niches this time, each with an 18th-century French statue of a draped female figure on a plinth. De Wolfe furnished this space more fully than she did at East 71st Street, installing a Louis XVI white marble wall fountain, positioned against a large mirror, and a small reservoir of water in which goldfish swam, just as in the little bay window fountain in East 17th Street. At the foot of the fountain she placed containers of plants bearing flowers in shades of white and orange.[7] A polished wood desk stood at the ready with writing equipment. "How often have I been in people's houses," de Wolfe explained, "when it was necessary to send a message, or to record an address, when the whole household began scurrying around to find a pencil and paper!"[8] Black silk curtains sparkling with silver and gold trim were threaded onto rods at the windows, and in emulation of grand French houses, de Wolfe placed a hooded porter's chair against one wall, giving the appearance if not the reality of a fully staffed aristocratic household.

Drawing room. (The House in Good Taste, *1913*)

Codman introduced a central spiral staircase into the house once again, and a similar back extension, this one five stories in height, was built to house the servants' quarters and physical plant.[9] As in the show house, the drawing room was placed at the front of the second floor, with the dining room located at the rear. The second-floor drawing room, with its wall of full-length French doors opening to the balcony and a courtyard view, was one of de Wolfe's most admired interiors. There she created a tranquil, evocative space, dominated by one of her favorite colors during this period, rose. The room was overtly created "for conversation, for hospitality."[10] This was achieved, de Wolfe claimed, by not being "too careful."[11] In describing this room she articulated what had become the baseline for her decorating philosophy. "I believe," she wrote, "in plenty of optimism and white paint, comfortable chairs with lights beside them, open fires on the hearth and flowers wherever they 'belong,' mirrors and sunshine in all rooms."[12] No one was more aware, though, than de Wolfe of the dangers of sticking to the rules, however good they were, and in the drawing room at East 55th Street, she wanted to experiment. "Somehow the feeling of homey-ness is

*Drawing room view showing mirror placed between the windows. (*The House in Good Taste, *1913)*

lost when the decorator is too careful," she explained.[13] As a result, unlike the staged, uninhabited drawing room at East 71st Street—a house where, upon close inspection of the contemporary photographs, the etchings and other pictures don't appear to actually be framed, only matted and hung to give the impression of habitation—this room was truly lived-in and loved.

As de Wolfe described it, "In the center of the mantel was a terra-cotta group by [Augustin] Pajou. On the ends there were always little white flowers, preferably roses and lilies" arranged in footed crystal bowls or plain glass vases.[14] A gilt-wood Louis XVI sofa stood against one long wall, accompanied by a pair of painted Louis XV armchairs upholstered in a bird-and-flower chintz. Over it was displayed the Nattier portrait of the Duchess of Châteauroux. A pair of Louis XVI armchairs covered in Aubusson or Beauvais tapestry stood before the fireplace on the opposite wall, joined by a cane-backed Régence armchair and a gutsy gilded rococo stool with a worn

Drawing room showing the Nattier painting. (The House in Good Taste, *1913*)

velvet seat that had been used in the drawing room at 121 East 17th Street. To the right of the fireplace stood a cozy sofa in deep rose damask and a tall gilt pedestal holding a shell-shaped ceramic bowl aloft; all three items were formerly used in the drawing room at 17th Street. The walls, divided into Louis XV–style panels with applied moldings, were painted a rich, dark cream and stippled to achieve a dull, mottled effect. Paintings of 18th-century ladies in moody landscapes were mounted above the doors, and small watercolors and paintings of flowers and landscapes in crisply gilded frames were arranged into symmetrical groups. A trumeau mirror from an old French house—its painted finish doubtless led to the wall color de Wolfe eventually used—was installed over the heavily veined marble mantel, and on the shelf above the mirror stood the three Chinese jars and two vases from the mauve bedroom in the East 71st Street show house. The lighting was a combination of electrified Chinese jars and vases with shirred silk shades and

Porcelain flower sconce alongside the marble mantel in the drawing room. (The House in Good Taste, *1913*)

Drawing room detail showing de Wolfe's framed collection of miniatures. (The House in Good Taste, 1913)

silver candlesticks (20 candles in total). The sconces in the room, possibly 18th-century antiques, took the form of ribbon-tied bouquets of striped roses, their blossoms made of porcelain, probably Sèvres. From the ceiling was suspended a small crystal chandelier, its cord disguised by a braided rope and tassel. The delicacy of the objects in the room, combined with the soft lighting, the dull glitter of the gilded furniture, and the blushing color scheme, resulted in one of the warmest and most elegant interiors de Wolfe ever created and one that was greatly admired.[15] Completing

the intimate, highly individual, and decorative nature of the room was a collection of miniatures, watches, and fans, grouped into a gilded frame above a small writing desk.

The dining room at East 55th Street was more refined than its predecessor at East 17th Street, and de Wolfe and Marbury reinforced this refinement by employing a "young and thoroughly competent" French cook with the "best foreign training."[16] The grisailles found a new place there, set into raised panel moldings. The color scheme, again similar to the dining

*Dining room. (*The House in Good Taste*, 1913)*

room of the East 71st Street show house, was dominated by soft gray, taken from the carpet, which also contained rose and dull yellow, complemented by the blue-and-yellow-striped velvet upholstery and the yellow damask table covering, itself covered with a protective sheet of glass. At night two sliding mirrored panels were drawn over the windows, a trick introduced by de Wolfe—and doubtless copied from the Hall of Mirrors at Versailles—to make the room seem more spacious and increase the illumination of the candles. The frequent use of space-enhancing mirrors

throughout the house—the panels of the curved stairwell were paved with squares of mirror as well—led de Wolfe to call it the Little House of Many Mirrors.

The third floor was dedicated to the decorator's private quarters and the fourth to Marbury's suite, as with the arrangement of the upper floors of the show house at East 71st Street, and reinforced the success of the latter project's remodeling. As their interests began to diverge, Marbury and de Wolfe began to lead increasingly separate lives under the same roof, and they needed rooms in which they

*Elsie de Wolfe's sitting room—boudoir—library. (*The House in Good Taste, *1913)*

could entertain and work independently. (Both had electric buzzers that connected directly to each other's rooms, however.) In *The House in Good Taste,* de Wolfe described her rooms in East 55th Street as if they constituted a small apartment, suggesting this arrangement as a model for others to emulate.[17] These spaces, although realized more modestly, were similar to Anne Morgan's suite of rooms in her family house at 219 Madison Avenue.

De Wolfe's apartment consisted of a combined boudoir, sitting room, and library, and a separate

bedroom. The first room, its applied-molding boiserie painted in pale eggshell, blue-green, and white, acted as an office in the morning and as a refuge in the evening. It contained a large Louis XV daybed, a writing table (which de Wolfe preferred to a desk) placed at a right angle to the window, lots of bookshelves, and an old secretary that held the decorator's collection of porcelain figurines. Comfortable chairs were readily at hand, including a Louis XVI armchair covered with Gobelins-style tapestry of ribbons, roses, and medallions. Yet another of her kidney-shaped occasional tables was

Elsie de Wolfe's writing table in her sitting room—boudoir—library. (The House in Good Taste, *1913*)

included, tall enough to be pulled up while sitting in a chair or in the chaise longue, and a variety of prints, paintings, and photographs—landscapes, portraits of 18th-century ladies, fashion illustrations, a photograph of an infant de Wolfe held by her mother—decorated the walls and tables, as did black-and-gold metal sconces ornamented with oval Wedgwood plaques and galloon-trimmed silk shades.[18] As had become habitual in de Wolfe's interiors, the wood floor was covered with a low-pile broadloom carpet, the plain expanse broken up by a flowery Persian rug.

The sitting room was described as a "delightfully intimate room, full of personal souvenirs, where one loves to linger." This strongly personal space also housed an aquarium for a fan-tailed goldfish; an old Chinese lacquer box, complete with little gold bells, for de Wolfe's dog of the moment, a Pekingese called Wee Toi; and a birdcage for a bullfinch.[19] Where Marbury's pet, a prize-winning French bulldog, slept was unmentioned.

As it had been in the East 17th Street house, de Wolfe's bedroom was filled with numerous personal

*Elsie de Wolfe's bedroom. (*The House in Good Taste, *1913)*

artifacts. The mirrored Breton bed from East 17th Street dominated the space, and de Wolfe decorated the room around it. Beside the fireplace stood the obligatory chaise longue, slipcovered in flowered chintz, and small tables were pulled up to comfortable chairs. That signature shade of rose once again was in evidence. As in every room in this house, mirrors were included, two full-length sheets of mirror on the window wall, magnifying the light as well as causing the windows to seem larger and providing de Wolfe with a multitude of mirrors to dress by. Also making

an appearance here were the decorator's favorite metal wall sconces with rams' heads, later to appear in several of her other interiors, including those created for Anne Morgan and Nell Pruyn Cunningham.

Marbury's bedroom, with gray-blue painted walls, was on the floor above and was described as a "sunshiny place of much rose and blue and cream." A glass-topped, chintz-hung dressing table was positioned between the windows, themselves framed by tailored curtains of lightly fringed blue linen. The theatrical agent's adjacent sitting room was decidedly more moody

Elsie de Wolfe's bedroom. (The House in Good Taste, *1913*)

than de Wolfe's light, feminine one, outfitted with a glazed chintz of flowers printed on a dramatic coal-black ground. The chaise longue had a slipcover of plain black chintz, the walls were painted dove gray, and the broadloom carpet was "old blue," Marbury's favorite color. Several cages of birds were suspended in the room's center window, and everywhere were mirrors and books and decorative French prints. The quarters were as cozy and disheveled as de Wolfe's own equally accessorized sitting room was quintessentially feminine.

Ruby Ross Goodnow, the ghostwriter for *The House in Good Taste,* left in her unpublished diaries a

vivid impression of life in the Marbury–de Wolfe home on East 55th Street, commenting on its inhabitants' "different ideas of comfort and luxury." The decorator, she wrote, occupied her rooms like a latter-day Pompadour, dressed in a "silk and lace tea gown, embroidered mules, working on [a] piece of needlework, French maid brushing her hair, lying on [the] daybed." In her suite upstairs, Marbury sat in a "felt wrapper, gored like morning glory, red felt bedroom slippers, shiny dark pompadour over rat, working on [an] ugly piece of knitting." Goodnow added, "They could afford the same things, but they wanted different things."[20] It was an observation with which Marbury would not have argued. As she once said, "I don't care for dresses and I don't care for jewels, but I'm mad on the subject of anything artistic."[21]

Although she offered affectionate recollections of both the East 17th Street house and Villa Trianon in her 1923 autobiography, Marbury did not mention the house on East 55th Street. One senses, in fact, that she actually spent very little time in it or perhaps recognized that the Little House of Many Mirrors was really de Wolfe's home, philosophically and emotionally. Marbury only spent six months a year in New York in any case, and two each in London, Paris, and Berlin, where her literary agency had branch offices that annually sifted through some 5,000 manuscripts—she herself read a half dozen new plays per day.[22]

For de Wolfe, however, the East 55th Street house provided her, as decorator and as client, with everything she needed. In her own words, "in its proportions, balance, arrangements, furnishings, objets d'art, atmosphere, and suitability of purpose, it was as perfect a city house as the two of us could have had."[23] Ironically, because of her war work and increased focus on Villa Trianon and life in France, de Wolfe spent only a few winters there, and the documentary evidence suggests that Marbury did not completely commit herself to living in the house either. Nonetheless, the Little House of Many Mirrors was widely documented in popular consumer magazines, including *Good Housekeeping, American Homes and Gardens,* and *Harper's Bazaar.* It also inspired much of the content of *The House in Good Taste,* and it clearly offered an ideal that many women wanted to follow. "This house is an especially interesting study to those who are interested in house planning and in problems of interior decoration as it embodies many features of importance."[24]

Elisabeth Marbury's bedroom.
(The House in Good Taste, *1913)*

When Marbury moved to Sutton Place in 1920, some of the contents of the East 55th house followed her across town; others likely were sold at auction or to clients. The dining room grisailles ended up in Condé Nast's penthouse. The idyllic domestic setting that de Wolfe had begun to create in 1911 was fully realized but never fully occupied. Yet 123 East 55th Street served as a significant opportunity for de Wolfe to thoroughly develop her decorating ideas in the context of her own home, without the spatial and stylistic restrictions of the poky house on East 17th Street.

1910–11

Mary and Charles W. Harkness Residence
Mirador
Madison, New Jersey

"The height of good taste."[1]

*M*irador (or "Golden View" as it was subsequently named) was the Madison, New Jersey, home of Mary and Charles William Harkness.[2] It was constructed on Madison Avenue in 1909–10 on a piece of land that Harkness had purchased four years earlier. The existing house was knocked down, and up went an elegant red-brick-and-limestone country manor in the English Georgian style that cost half a million dollars.

Stephen V. Harkness had amassed a fortune in the 1870s through his involvement with the oil refinery business and died in 1888, leaving an estate of $150 million. His eldest son, Charles Harkness (1860–1916), followed his father into the same business. In 1896, he wed a Philadelphia woman, Mary Warden (1864–1916). They settled in New York in a town house at 685 Fifth Avenue, which they bought from railroad magnate Henry Flagler. They later moved to 2 East 54th Street, and they also maintained homes in Ohio and Florida. The couple's search for a site for a country place took them across the Hudson River to suburban New Jersey, where they found an ideal tract of land near Morristown. The area was being transformed from modest farmland into estate country by the arrival of rich New Yorkers like the Harknesses and banker Otto Kahn. And as John W. Rae noted in 1979, thanks to Harkness and his ilk, Madison Avenue, also known as Millionaires' Row, soon came to be called "The Great White Way of Morris County's Gilded Age."[3] Mirador was demolished in

Opposite: Mrs. C. W. Harkness' cabinet for objets d'art. (The House in Good Taste, *1913*)

Elsie de Wolfe, c. 1910.
(Collection of the Elsie de Wolfe Foundation)

1978, and little information about it has survived. However, enough documentation exists to indicate that it was an exceptionally grand residence with handsome, sophisticated furnishings, many likely acquired and arranged by de Wolfe. One commentator from 1917 remarked, "One can hardly imagine a noise about the place. Its tone seems to have been created for rest, study and quiet enjoyment."[4]

Building didn't start on the house until 1909. A contemporary newspaper report noted that on June 25 of that year, "Work on the Harkness estate, next to the James estate on Madison Avenue, is progressing fine—Dempsey and Cooney, masons, have the basement and first story up, and John T. Ritter has stone roads built, excepting a small section—a handsome mansion and barn of brick, iron and stone will be erected."[5] The landscaping of the 240-acre estate, undertaken by John R. Brimley, followed the English approach, with a beautiful eight-acre lawn. A large linden, imported from Germany, was positioned in front of the house, which was hidden from the road by artfully contrived woodland. As at the Armour estate in Lake Forest, the Harknesses' lifestyle required numerous outbuildings, including a large garage with rooms and baths overhead for the chauffeurs and their families, a gardener's house, several greenhouses, spacious stables, and a large barn. There also was a generating plant to ensure a constant supply of electricity. As for the main house, it contained more than 50 rooms. There were seven rooms on the ground floor, with a wide veranda outside. The second floor consisted of five bedrooms with baths and two dressing rooms, while on the third floor there were four more bedrooms, baths, a sitting room, and a cedar storage room. The servants' wing contained another 20 rooms.

Only a handful of images of the interiors of Mirador have survived, including two of the living room, which was illustrated and briefly mentioned in de Wolfe's *The House in Good Taste*. Loosely designed in the English Renaissance style, the drawing room was half-paneled in mellow English oak and crowned by an ornate plaster high-relief ceiling. To suit the dramatic scale of the space, de Wolfe had introduced substantial high-backed seating—including generous Georgian arm chairs and a couple of tall wing chairs—and wood furniture with sturdy silhouettes, including a carved Italian table piled with books, newspapers, tall silver

Approach to Mirador. (Madison Public Library)

candlesticks, and vases of flowers. Three- and four-branch metal sconces, footstools with cabriole legs ending in claw-and-ball feet, plain curtains drawn back to reveal French doors, and Chinese ceramic table lamps completed the warm, Anglo-American setting. The floor was covered in a modern broadloom carpet. "There are chairs and tables of all sizes, from the huge Italian table to the little table especially made to hold a few flower pots," de Wolfe explained. "Wherever there is a large table there is a long sofa or a few large chairs; wherever there is a lone chair there is a small table to hold a reading-light, or flowers, or what-not. The great size of the room, the fine English ceiling of modeled

Front facade. (Madison Public Library)

Rear facade. (Madison Public Library)

plaster, the generous fireplace with its paneled over-mantel, the groups of windows, all these architectural details go far toward making the room a success. The comfortable chairs and sofas and the ever useful tables do the rest."[6] The other illustration in *The House in Good Taste* relating to Mirador was of Mary Harkness' gently concave glass-front "cabinet for *objets d'art.*" This delicate hand-painted object, probably an 18th-century-style reproduction made especially for the Harkness house and containing a collection of small porcelain figures and miniature vases of artificial flowers, was much more feminine in appearance than the furnishings of the living room and undoubtedly belonged to the private quarters, possibly Mary Harkness' upstairs sitting room.

As with the Armour house, the family did not enjoy Mirador for long. Charles Harkness died of apoplexy in 1916, at age 56, leaving an estate estimated between $60 million and $150 million. He was fol-lowed seven months later by his widow, who died the day her husband's estate had been settled, which was to have given her more than $12 million. Mirador was

Living room. (The House in Good Taste, *1913*)

sold fully furnished, the following year. A photograph of the living room, dating from the 1930s, showed that very little in this stately interior had changed despite the house's change in ownership.

Although not much is known about Mirador and de Wolfe's involvement with it, the house represented a moment in the decorator's career when she had the confidence to work in whatever style was needed—here a relaxed English country house mode rather than her usual urbane Francophile aesthetic—and to find ways of injecting her own decorating philosophy into the

project. The Harknesses' living room fully subscribed to the decorator's belief that a living room, as opposed to a drawing room, should be "Big and restful, making for comfort first and always; a little shabby here and there, perhaps, but all the more satisfactory for that— like an old shoe that goes on easily."[7] Above all, she was continuing to play an important role in what a newspaper reporter described in 1917 as "the culture, ideals and ambitions that make the traditions of race [nationality] which are yearly making Americans more content to stay at home."[8]

1910–11

Anne Morgan's Rooms

J. Pierpont Morgan Residence, 219 Madison Avenue
New York City

"Comfort, practicality and beauty . . ."[1]

*F*rom the moment the Colony Club opened in 1907 until the outbreak of World War I, Elsie de Wolfe was in enormous demand across the United States. Partly as a result of Bessy Marbury's expert public relations techniques, and partly because de Wolfe had become so fashionable that hiring her was an invitation to instant refinement, the decorator and her growing staff were able to take on numerous projects in these years and earn de Wolfe a small fortune as a result. Information about many of these interiors is scant, while others probably were not recorded at all and have avoided scrutiny. The domestic work largely fell into three main areas: interiors and individual pieces of custom-made furniture for friends and society women in New York City; interiors for the country houses of businessmen and their families in New Jersey, Connecticut, and Long Island; and interiors for wealthy clients living in major cities across the country, including Chicago and San Francisco.

The majority of the New York City projects were undertaken between 1906 and 1913, when de Wolfe published *The House in Good Taste.* These projects included interiors for Ethel Barrymore, the actress who served as de Wolfe's understudy in *The Bauble Shop;* Henrietta Guinness, an English society hostess living at 8 Washington Square North; Daisy Harriman, the founder of the Colony Club, who lived at 128 East 36th Street; and Anne Morgan, the youngest child of financier J. Pierpont Morgan. Anne had a suite of rooms at her parents'

Opposite: Main sitting room. (Collection of The New-York Historical Society)

Portrait of Anne Morgan. (My Crystal Ball, *1923*)

house at 219 Madison Avenue and East 36th Street, in the Murray Hill neighborhood of Manhattan.

Anne Morgan (1873–1932) entered the lives of Marbury and de Wolfe in 1901, through an introduction by Odgen Codman Jr., who had been pursuing the young heiress unsuccessfully for some time.[2] The intense friendship between Marbury and Morgan, whose level of intimacy was the subject of much speculation, grew stronger over the next few years, threatening at several moments to disrupt Marbury and de Wolfe's own relationship. Soon Morgan was joining the other two women on their French summer holidays and moved into Villa Trianon. By 1908 the three had become known as the "Versailles Triumvirate." Although they were suspicious of each other, de Wolfe and Morgan clearly managed to coexist amicably for a

number of years, and the decorator executed two residential projects for Morgan—one in her parents' Manhattan home and later at her own home at 3 Sutton Place. She had also decorated a box at the Metropolitan Opera for Morgan's father. J. Pierpont Morgan had bought the family's large brownstone mansion in 1880. It was one of a block of three built in the 1850s by the Phelps family and had little aesthetic distinction, commodiousness being its signal attribute.[3] Frederick Allen Lewis explained that Morgan, who did not aspire to the showy Fifth Avenue palaces of his contemporaries, had "no wish to add to the architectural monstrosities corrupting our skyline."[4] He did, however, hire the fashionable and artistic Herter Brothers decorating company to renovate and refurbish the house soon after its purchase. The financier's relationship with his second wife, Frances Tracy Morgan, was not strong—he maintained a long-time liaison with Adelaide Douglas—and he devoted much attention to his bright but shy daughter.

Anne was educated at home, along with Daisy Harriman and Ruth Morgan, women with whom she was to retain close friendships for the rest of her life and who would join her in the creation of the Colony Club. Like Harriman, Morgan became intensely involved with the lives of working women and spent much of her time campaigning on their behalf. She was an active member of the women's department of the National Civic Federation, and her charity work included the establishment of a temperance restaurant in the Brooklyn Navy Yard. She supported the shirtwaist workers' strike of 1910, but like Marbury and unlike de Wolfe, she was never pro-suffrage.[5] She dedicated her whole life to social welfare, and after World War I, during which she was involved in civilian war relief operations, Morgan focused most of her energy on the establishment and running of the Museum of

Elsie de Wolfe, c. 1910.
(Collection of the Elsie de Wolfe Foundation)

Franco-American Friendship and Cooperation in Blérancourt, France.

The heiress, who never married, chose to live in her parents' home until 1921. She clearly had all she needed there, including a squash court. She had her own suite of rooms within the large house, and at some time in the early years of the century de Wolfe decorated it.

The sitting room, where "so many welfare and service committees have held interesting meetings," was a striking chamber decorated in black, white, and red.[6]

The large black carpet was bordered by a band of ruby red—similar to the one in the men's room in the Ormond G. Smith house—and the same jewel-like color was used for taffeta curtains that hung "between the net curtains and the over-draperies."[7] A large sheet of mirror, framed in red lacquer, was set into an ivory-painted boiserie above the marble fireplace surround. A button-tufted armchair and a deep chesterfield sofa were upholstered with black-and-white cut velvet in a Jacobean-style graphic floral pattern, while another armchair was covered with a deep rose brocade woven with an even larger-scaled pattern of stylized flowers and foliage. A plain velour, likely rose-colored, was used on a slipper chair set by the fireside.[8] Two tall inset cupboards with arched glass-paned doors, positioned on either side of the fireplace, were lined with red, black, and gold lacquer depicting exotic chinoiserie trees and contained Morgan's collection of rare pieces of porcelain. The cupboards were reminiscent of Mary Harkness' lacquered "cabinet for objets d'art," illustrated in *The House in Good Taste*.[9] The sitting room also contained a painted Chinese birdcage, one of de Wolfe's multipurpose kidney-shaped side tables—here used as a platform for several vases of flowers—and the decorator's favorite ram's head wall sconces.[10]

Describing Morgan's adjacent bedroom-boudoir, which was illustrated in *The Delineator*, de Wolfe wrote, "This is a small sitting room in a New York house of average proportions, treated with Louis XVI moldings and mantel. The armchair is modern, but it does not seem out of place in this period room. The screen, the bust on the mantelshelf, the old portrait, and the several small furnishings are also French and of the Louis XVI period but the rug is Persian, and the chest of drawers is English mahogany."[11] The room demonstrated the decorator's ease in mixing old with new and pieces from different periods. When

Library. (Collection of The New-York Historical Society)

de Wolfe illustrated the same room again in her 1913 book, the chintz-covered modern armchair had been removed and replaced by a Louis XVI side chair and two armchairs of the same period.[12] Other alterations included the addition of paintings and the removal of a rather unattractive fire screen. Another view of the same room illustrated a Louis XVI *lit de repos* piled with chintz pillows, and the obligatory leather-topped ladies' desk covered with all the usual accessories that de Wolfe deemed both practical and decorative.

The text in *The Delineator* described the room of this "woman of many interests" in more detail, indicating, among other features, the colors.[13] The walls, it explained, were cream, and the carvings and moldings picked out in blue. The daybed, some of the chairs, and the chest of drawers were made of soft brown walnut.

New items mingled with old, the new chintz of the daybed complementing presumably antique tapestries used to cover some of the chairs. *The House in Good Taste* also emphasized the presence of a portrait of a lady, hung by wires that were covered with a gathered length of blue silk, a trick that de Wolfe would use to some acclaim at the show house she and Ogden Codman created on East 71st Street. As the author explained, "the whole room might have been inspired by the lady of the portrait, so essentially is it the room of a fastidious woman."[14]

The House in Good Taste also illustrated Morgan's dressing room. Although small, this space was a highly characteristic de Wolfe installation that demonstrated the decorator's commitment to beauty and the need for a private space in which that beauty could be realized. "Dressing-rooms and closets should be necessities, not luxuries," de Wolfe explained with feeling, "but alas! our architects' ideas of the importance of large bedrooms have made it almost impossible to incorporate the proper closets and dressing-places a woman really requires!"[15] Rather than providing all a woman's needs in a single bedroom, de Wolfe preferred an antechamber, a sitting room or boudoir, a sleeping room, a dressing room, and a bathroom. Anne Morgan's suite was designed to de Wolfe's ideal, separated into a series of spaces with discrete functions.

The dressing room was the most private of spaces, the one in which the woman of the house constructed her public persona on a daily basis. Lined with mirror-covered cabinets and painted boiserie, Morgan could see herself as others did, from all sides. De Wolfe stressed the need for practicality in such spaces and wrote that she wanted "mirrors and then more mirrors and then more mirrors . . . so that one may see oneself from hat to boots."[16] Other necessities included a

Anne Morgan's boudoir. (Collection of The New-York Historical Society)

chaise longue with loose chintz covers that could be removed for easy washing, and a dressing table, placed against the windows to maximize illumination. Morgan's dressing table, draped with a chintz skirt that matched the upholstery of the room's two arm-chairs, was fitted into a deep window recess; its glass

Anne Morgan's boudoir. (Collection of The New-York Historical Society)

top protected the dressing table's fabric from corrosive perfumes and cosmetic stains. Two small tripod tables on either side of it had an electric light and a hand mirror on their respective surfaces, and underneath was laid a Persian rug.

De Wolfe was extremely particular about the equipment of dressing rooms and boudoirs. Many drawers were needed to contain letter-writing equipment, among other things, to save having to go into another room to get them. A hollow table on casters was also thought to be an asset in a dressing room, as

were a heated towel rack, a wall cabinet, lots of shelves and hooks, and a shallow bottle closet. The wall had to be lined with closets, painted with bright colors inside, and "fitted with perfumed pads."[17] Even the clothes hangers had to be covered with chintz. With its practical mirrors, multitude of storage, and comfortable chairs in various sizes for attending to her makeup, having her hair done, or putting on her shoes, Anne Morgan's sunny, sparkling dressing room represented a feminine ideal that de Wolfe wanted all women to be able to achieve in their own homes.

Anne Morgan's dressing room. (Collection of The New-York Historical Society)

1911–12

Amanda and Jay P. Graves Residence
Waikiki
Spokane, Washington

*A*s the upwardly mobile wife of the mining, railroad, and real-estate tycoon Jay P. Graves and a frequent traveler to New York City, Amanda Graves (née Cox) undoubtedly recognized the enormous prestige that came with hiring Elsie de Wolfe, America's most famous decorator. Indeed, in the creation of their house, she and her husband demonstrated a high level of aesthetic discrimination. Kirtland Kelsey Cutter (1860–1939), of Cutter & Malmgren, was chosen as the architect of Waikiki, a Native American word meaning "many waters" that was taken from the name of a road forming a boundary of the estate. Cutter and his partner, Karl Gunnar Malmgren (1862–1921), had a reputation for creating striking buildings executed in Tudor revival, English Arts and Crafts, Craftsman, and Georgian revival styles. They were for many years the architects of choice for Spokane's engineering and mining elite. For the landscaping, the Graveses selected a nationally eminent firm, Olmsted Brothers of Brookline, Massachusetts, whose portfolio included Central Park in New York City and the winding, park-like Spokane neighborhood of Rockwood, which Graves had helped develop.

The thousand-acre estate of Waikiki, located on the north side of Spokane, was purchased by Graves in 1904. He had come, with his wife and son, from the farming town of Plymouth, Illinois, to Spokane Falls, as it was then called, in 1887 and very quickly established

Opposite: Front facade. (Northwest Museum of Arts and Culture, East Washington State Historical Society, Spokane, Washington)

Portrait of Jay P. Graves (Northwest Museum of Arts and Culture, Eastern Washington State Historical Society, Spokane, Washington)

a foothold in the area's expanding business world, concentrating on copper mining, the development of a local railroad system, and the rapid growth of Spokane as a residential center. Through his leadership of the Spokane Washington Improvement Company, for example, he developed Rockwood and had it planned by John Charles Olmsted and Frederick Law Olmsted Jr., who had come to that part of the country to design the Alaska-Yukon-Pacific Exhibition of 1909 in Seattle. Graves' ownership of the Spokane & Montrose Motor Railroad Company also made access to this new residential area possible.[1]

Despite his success in business, Graves maintained an abiding interest in farming, and over the next three decades he concentrated on developing a model farm estate, raising Jersey cattle, purebred sheep, and

poultry. By 1920 an article in a local newspaper reported, "Waikiki is now held by breeders of blooded cattle throughout the country as representative of the highest degree in this field of endeavor."[2] Graves, it noted, was to be found on the farm more frequently than he was in his office.

The picturesque Tudor revival house was designed by Cutter in 1909 and completed in 1912. An artificial lake was dug, and a number of outbuildings, including greenhouses and a garage for four cars, were created. The gardens immediately around the house consisted of terraces, rustic nooks, and a covered walk, and Cutter created a dramatic entrance a half-mile from the house. With its timbered stucco exterior, gables and dormers, high shingled roofs, and four tall chimneys—only one of which was functional—the house was an elegant monument to a newly minted fortune.

A covered front porch led to a large vestibule and through to a cross-shaped grand hall, which served as a combination living room–reception hall. At the rear of this impressive space was a large bay window, facing north and overlooking the Little Spokane River. In keeping with the English style of Waikiki, oak paneling and leaded glass were widely used throughout the building. In the grand hall, the large stone fireplace was topped by a carved oak panel featuring a "dolphin on the crest of a wave, splashing water into a basin."[3] An enormous terrace ran along the back of the house; terraced gardens filled the land below.

Other downstairs rooms included, on the west side of the house, a Georgian-style paneled library and a loggia that led to a 250-foot-long, brick-wall-enclosed, formal sunken garden. The library had built-in bookcases, a large fireplace of Siena marble, and rich plaster cornices. It also had a handsome coffered ceiling painted a typical de Wolfe color, "old ivory."[4]

As for the dining room, also accessed from the grand hall, the oak-paneled, Queen Anne–style room with molded beams, was described as being "softer and warmer" than the other rooms, with wall-mounted lights and a large alabaster ceiling fixture. French windows opened to the terrace.

Little documentation of the furnishing details exists, although the sum of $14,000 was dedicated to the interior decoration of the house (compared with $20,000 for the construction costs), which included "elegant furniture and specially designed silverware." The latter was kept in a walk-in vault off the butler's pantry.[5] Mention also was made of "three large Austrian carpets," designed to reflect the patterning on the coffered ceiling. Smaller Oriental rugs were also used. What little description of the interior exists suggests that it was entirely consistent with the styles de Wolfe was creating for other homes around that time.

The upstairs interiors were equally typical of de Wolfe's approach, expressing her decorating preferences for the private spaces in a domestic dwelling. "The second floor of the entire structure is provided with eight chambers with baths," reported the *Spokesman-Review*. "These rooms are finished in ivory and white enamel with oak floors, a sewing room, numerous clothes and linen closets, vacuum cleaning room and a hallway."[6]

Writer John Fahey suggested that Amanda Graves played a considerable role in the creation of Waikiki: "She approved Cutter's plans, and in her private quarters she called for flowered wall fabric, full-length mirrored closets along one entire wall, and tiered hat racks in a closet along another wall." These practical details undoubtedly would have been suggested by de Wolfe, who always was attentive to the disposition of dressing rooms and boudoirs.[7]

Elsie de Wolfe, photographed by Baron de Meyer, c. 1911–12. (Collection of the Elsie de Wolfe Foundation)

In fact, de Wolfe might have been describing Graves' dressing room in *The House in Good Taste*. "Another scheme, when . . . the dressing-room was too large for comfort, was to line three walls of it with closets, the fourth wall being filled with windows," the decorator explained. "These closets were narrow, each having a mirrored panel in its door. This is the ideal arrangement, for there is ample room for all one's gowns, shoes, hats, veils, gloves, etc., each article

Main entrance. (Northwest Museum of Arts and Culture, East Washington State Historical Society, Spokane, Washington)

having its own specially planned shelf or receptacle. The closets are painted in gay colors inside, and the shelves are fitted with thin perfumed pads. They are often further decorated with bright lines of color, which is always amusing to the woman who opens a door. Hat stands and bags are covered with the same chintzes employed in the dressing room proper. Certain of the closets are fitted with the English tray shelves, and each tray has its sachet. The hangers for the gowns are covered in the chintz or brocade used on the hat stands."[8]

The one extant photograph of Amanda Graves' sitting room illustrates a number of familiar de Wolfe touches. Among these are plain paneled walls, patterned curtains, wall-mounted sconces, a glass-topped dressing table with neoclassical-style patterns painted on the surfaces of its drawers—probably by Everett

Shinn—and a mirror hanging behind it, a floor lamp with a pleated shade, well-positioned small table lamps, covered radiators, a screen, and a Georgian revival chaise longue with a striped cover and cushions.

The Graveses moved into Waikiki at the end of 1912 and commenced to make it a center of Spokane society, entertaining, among other guests, Belgian royalty. Amanda Graves suffered from a heart condition, however, and from 1916 to 1920, the year of her death, her social life was considerably limited, and she rarely ventured from the house. Jay Graves remarried, but by 1934 the effects of the depression upon his finances were such that he could no longer afford to maintain Waikiki. In 1936 he sold it to Charles E. Mar and built a smaller house in Rockwood. Waikiki is now owned by Gonzaga University and is used as a retreat.

Rear view. (Northwest Museum of Arts and Culture, East Washington State Historical Society, Spokane, Washington)

Amanda Graves' sitting room. (Northwest Museum of Arts and Culture, East Washington State Historical Society, Spokane, Washington)

1905–14

Villa Trianon
57 Boulevard St. Antoine
Versailles, France

"The perfect house, which is neither immense nor vulgar . . ."[1]

Elsie de Wolfe's relationship with France began in 1889 when she and Bessy Marbury, whom she had befriended several years earlier, went on a cycling trip through Normandy. The following year, the two women, their friendship growing and their Francophilia deepening, visited the castles in Touraine, a trip that they undertook on a very small budget.[2] According to the design journalist Ruby Ross Goodnow (later the decorator Ruby Ross Wood), "They used no trains or buses, they patronized no hotels and they had a heavenly time."[3] De Wolfe wrote an article about the trip for *Cosmopolitan* for which she received $200.[4]

This trip was the beginning of the women's long-term love affair with France. For de Wolfe in particular, it involved a sudden immersion into the history of French architecture and decorative arts. A young woman rapidly rising through the ranks of society, de Wolfe surely was aware that travel in Europe also offered an opportunity for her to be able to reinvent herself. Other elements of that reconstruction had already been realized through acting out dramatic roles and wearing couture clothes. Soon it was to be completed through the activity of interior decoration.

De Wolfe's initial introduction to France occurred while she was still an amateur actress. In 1890 she took acting lessons in Paris, and later in the decade she became absorbed in learning about 18th-century French decorative arts with the assistance of a number of

Opposite: Library. (Vogue, March 1, 1914, courtesy Condé Nast)

French playwright Victorien Sardou. (My Crystal Ball, *1923*)

renowned collectors and aesthetes, including Count Robert de Montesquiou-Fezensac (1855–1921), Baron Jérôme-Frédéric Pichon (1812–1896), the owner of the exquisite 17th-century Hôtel de Lauzan on the Île St. Louis, and Pierre de Nolhac (1859–1936), an art historian who, in 1900, would become the curator of the Château de Versailles.

The decorative arts knowledge de Wolfe absorbed was fed into the designs for the sets and costumes she created for her theatrical performances. For example, she used a painting in the Louvre as a source of inspiration for the 18th-century costume of Fabienne, in Victorien Sardou's play *Thermidor,* a role she performed in 1891 and for which she went to some

effort tracking down picturesque old fabric to use in its construction.[5] For other roles she wore gowns, peignoirs, and wrappers designed by haute couturiers such as Charles Worth (1825–1895), Jacques Doucet (1853–1929), and Jeanne Paquin (Jeanne Becker Jacobs, 1869–1936), among others, thereby establishing a reputation as a billboard for the latest in fashion. By the end of the decade she was overseeing the sets and costumes for productions such as *A Marriage of Convenience,* in which she performed in 1897.

In Paris, de Wolfe also visited the Musée Carnavalet, which is devoted to Parisian life since its days as a Roman outpost, where she could examine fine 18th-century furniture and interiors firsthand. Most importantly, she was also beginning to participate in the antiques business, what her friend Clyde Fitch (1865–1909), the theatrical director, called "old-shopping."[6] In the early years of the 20th century, fine 18th-century French furniture could still be purchased at relatively affordable prices, and de Wolfe learned much from the Georgia-born Minna, Marchioness of Anglesey, an avid antiques collector with a passion for 18th-century French decorative arts.[7]

Although the neoclassicism of France during the reigns of Louis XV and Louis XVI was to inspire many of de Wolfe's decorating projects over the next two decades, it was not the only stylistic option available to her at that time. Many contemporary French architects and decorative artists were rejecting historicism and aligning themselves with the sinuous, nature-inspired forms of what came to be called Art Nouveau. Several of de Wolfe's fellow Americans responded to this "New Art," and in 1900 Lady Anglesey went so far as to purchase the salon of Art Nouveau furniture exhibited by the Bon Marché department store in the Grand Palais at the 1900 Paris Exposition Universelle. De Wolfe, however, was shocked by her friend's new fascination and denounced the style that had turned her compatriot's head as "the first warning of the avalanche of bad taste which burst upon us in 1900 and had its way until the beginning of the war." She also recalled her intense dislike of the movement's "awful chairs and tables supported by flowers contrived to look as if they were growing from the ground. And the mantelpieces of fleurs-de-lis and rushes, carved and painted in their natural colors of purple and yellow and green!"[8]

The actress' preference for a softer, more elegant style in architecture and the decorative arts was reflected in her choice of, and decorating decisions relating to, what was to become her home in France from 1905 onward, Villa Trianon. Back in 1897, Edith Wharton and Ogden Codman Jr. had advocated the French 18th-century styles as the most appropriate ones for an American interior decorating renaissance, noting, "In Paris, for instance, it is impossible to take even a short walk without finding inspiration in those admirable buildings, private and public, religious and secular, that bear the stamp of the most refined taste the world has known since the decline of the arts in Italy."[9] De Wolfe, herself in constant search of refinement, found much to admire in this view.

In 1903, de Wolfe and Marbury had first seen the villa, a large but architecturally undistinguished early-19th-century house situated on the edge of the gardens of the Château de Versailles on Boulevard St. Antoine, not far from Marie-Antoinette's *hameau.* From 1899, they had spent their annual French summer holidays in a small pavilion on the grounds of Lady Anglesey's Versailles estate, which had belonged to Madame de Pompadour's doctor, François Quesnay. Then in 1902 the couple moved to a house on Boulevard St. Antoine, a few doors from the house that would hold them rapt for decades. From their first

Rear facade. (Vogue, March 1, 1914, courtesy Condé Nast)

sighting, through the wrought-iron gates of the dilapidated Villa Trianon, the highly impressionable, upwardly mobile actress' romanticized vision of France's heroic and aristocratic past was reinforced. "There was an air of mystery about the crumbling walls with their ivied trellis," she recalled. "We loved the overgrown gardens and the glimpses we could get of the house with its shuttered windows. To us it was like a beautiful woman who had a tragic history and had grown worn and faded before her time. We felt that all it needed was a little encouragement to bring about a second blooming."[10]

Marbury claimed that the house had been built for the surgeon of Marie Antoinette, and later it became home to Louis d'Orléans, Duc de Nemours, a son of King Louis Philippe. It had two cottage-style outbuildings and came with two acres of land. The fact that the site had been part of the park of the Château

Entrance to Villa Trianon with guest house at right. (Vogue, March 1, 1914, courtesy Condé Nast)

Rear terrace. (The House in Good Taste, *1913*)

Treillage arch in the garden. (The House in Good Taste, *1913*)

Topiary in the garden. (After All, 1935)

Music pavilion. (My Crystal Ball, *1923*)

de Versailles, and that the deed still reserved a right-of-way for the king of France, clearly enhanced its appeal. The purchase, which took place with the help of the playwright Victorien Sardou, was a fairly drawn-out and complicated process, but eventually Marbury, who, unlike de Wolfe, had a reliable income, became the owner of the villa for about $12,000. The refurbishment was undertaken entirely by de Wolfe.

The restoration of Villa Trianon began in 1906, the summer before the opening of the Colony Club, and continued until the decorator's death in 1950. The first six years were intensive, and by 1912 the villa had been utterly transformed. Funding was made available

both by Marbury and by Anne Morgan, who had played a key role in Colony Club and who, from 1907 onward, became the third member of what came to be called the Versailles triumvirate. For nearly five decades de Wolfe continually worked on both the interior and the gardens, constantly refining them and testing interior decorating ideas that she would use subsequently in a professional capacity. Though she had residences on two continents and decorated them with equal passion, Villa Trianon arguably was her only real home.

The drive was to the side of the house, through wrought-iron gates and up a short drive that took visitors directly into the gravel forecourt. Concerned as

Pool in the garden. (My Crystal Ball, *1923*)

always with privacy, de Wolfe reoriented the primary face of the house from the forecourt to the large garden at its rear where she built a terrace that ran along the full length of the back of the structure. The terrace served to link the house with the garden, and it was the place where the household dined in good weather. This was the decorator's first opportunity to relate the interior and the exterior of a house, as neither 122 East 17th Street nor the Colony Club had had a garden. Although her little balcony at the former, and the trellis room and roof terrace at the latter, had attempted this linkage, they both had suffered from the constraints of an urban setting. At the villa, however, the garden became the most important room in the house.

One part of an article published in *Vogue* in 1914 concentrated on the garden of Villa Trianon, pointing out the way in which the *tapis vert* at the center of this symmetrical, formal design led across to a grand trelliswork arch, "overgrown with vines and set with old marbles," that was situated at the rear of the garden.[11] The theatrically overscaled arch recalled similar trellis-work garden structures at The Mount, Wharton's house in Lenox, Massachusetts, and at its center de Wolfe installed a fountain, flanked by classical statues.

Nolhac had discovered the design for the original Great Park of Versailles created by André Le Nôtre at the time of Louis XIV, and de Wolfe decided to work to a plan similar to that of the landscaping genius. Like her predecessor, she introduced a scheme of rectangular beds, both broad and narrow, planted with roses, larkspur, and daisies, and bedecked with statues, urns on plinths, and marble benches as well as specimen topiaries trained into whimsical shapes—segmented cones, or a neoclassical urn. Knitting it all together were tailored paths made of "little round pebbles of different shades of yellow and pink."[12] By the early 1920s, the pebble walks would be replaced by more substantial stone slabs. A statue by Claude Michel—an 18th-century sculptor better known as Clodion (1738–1814)—of a nymph embracing a fawn in her arms received special mention in *Vogue*, as did another by the Swiss sculptor James Pradier (1799–1852).

In 1908, Anne Morgan bought an extra piece of land for the garden, and an impressive neoclassical-style folly—a green-and-cream music pavilion—was constructed on it. Composed of a tall octagonal room with small projecting wings, this little "house in the garden" was designed by the landscape architect Achille Duchêne.[13] Its walls were covered, both inside and out, with green-painted trelliswork, as was the shallow dome of its glass roof; de Wolfe also sheathed the villa's two picturesque outbuildings, including one that she remodeled, into a guest house, with green trelliswork. Bas-relief plaster panels, which Pierre de Nolhac allowed the decorator to copy from originals

at the Château de Versailles, surmounted the pavilion's French windows, and carved garlands of fruit and ribbons were mounted on the trelliswork panels near the dome. The interior light fixtures, made of painted metal, were in the shape of flowers and butterflies. The furnishings consisted of cane-backed side chairs and Louis XV–style armchairs upholstered in a graphic butterfly petit point. There was also a piano and an 18th-century statue of Euturpe, the goddess of music, formerly owned by the Marquis de Gontaut-Biron, whose collections de Wolfe would vainly tempt Henry Clay Frick to buy.[14]

Flanked by large stone urns holding flowering plants, marble steps led from the pavilion to a rectangular reflecting pool with a single jet of water, created after the removal of the old vegetable garden. In 1909, a party was given to mark the opening of the music pavilion, and Count Boni de Castellane—an heiress-hunting aristocrat who had married the railroad scion Anna Gould—decorated the garden for the event, which included a dinner for 60 guests on the lawn. Soon after its construction, however, the pavilion became devoted to dance, with appearances by de Wolfe and Marbury's friends Irene and Vernon Castle, the Astaire and Rogers of the early 20th century.

The visual harmony and the sense of gentle, restrained luxury and tastefulness that characterized Villa Trianon's garden were extended to the interior of the 16-room house. The dominant colors were shades of gray and varied blues that recalled many of the flowers grown in the gardens, especially the delphiniums and Canterbury bells. A wide central hall bisected the first floor of the house. To the left of the hall were a salon, a writing room, a library, and a telephone room—a sweep of spaces that was connected by open arches instead of doors. To the right of the hall was situated a servants' hall, at the front of the house,

Large salon. (Collection of The New-York Historical Society)

overlooking the gravel forecourt, and a dining room at the rear, overlooking the music pavilion and reflecting pool. French doors at the back of the house allowed diners and guests in the salon to access the terrace. Upstairs, five bedrooms were linked to five bathrooms, four of which de Wolfe installed, shocking the French plumbers hired to do the work, as it seemed to them like an unnecessary extravagance.

De Wolfe described the decor of the house as being "of the period but . . . not at all elaborate."[15] The house may have belonged to a royal duke at one point in its history, but the decorator had no intention of introducing a regal aesthetic. As she had in 122 East 17th Street, she rejected lace curtains in Villa Trianon,

instead primarily using simple muslin panels. After consulting with Ogden Codman Jr., de Wolfe installed in the salon 18th-century blue-and-white wood paneling that had been given her by Minna Anglesey; it was a victim of the marchioness' sudden infatuation with Art Nouveau. The elegant carved boiserie provided a cool, aristocratic foil for a number of charming pieces of furniture, some antiques—a Louis XV table among them, upholstered in blue brocade—old tapestry, and chintzes. Others were modern, including "easy chairs with linen coverings which took their design from the textiles woven by Oberkampf during the eighteenth century."[16] As in many of her interior schemes, de Wolfe was happy to mix old and new as long as the

Painting of the large salon by Walter Gay. (Collection of the Elsie de Wolfe Foundation)

total visual effect, rather in the manner of a stage set, was achieved. In the large salon, a tapestry of a rural scene almost filled a panel on one wall. Mirrors and antique lighting fixtures also were used throughout the house to great effect, helping to provide an illusion of spaciousness and a soft ambience. De Wolfe explained how she wired fixtures that had been made for candles to retain the illusion of candlelight.[17] As in 122 East 17th Street, 18th-century paintings and prints covered the walls and created focal points for the eye.

In another reminder of the decorations of the house on East 17th Street, de Wolfe used in Villa Trianon's dining room a slightly ponderous Renaissance revival dining table lightened by a coat of pale gray paint. The polished wood chairs were sturdy and slightly provincial in appearance, with Adam-style splat backs and seats upholstered in lively stripes the colors of which complemented the rose-patterned Savonnerie carpet. Opposite the fireplace stood a marble console against a wall partially paved with a grid of tightly set sheets of mirror measuring more than a foot square, amplifying the light from the garden-facing windows. Behind the head of the table stood a white-and-gold wall fountain crowned by a swagged urn, its base banked with potted plants, rather like that in the entrance hall of de Wolfe and Marbury's house on East 55th Street. Though welcoming and cozy, Villa Trianon's dining room was not the most inspiring of the villa's rooms—the heavy white-silk curtains, another cast-off of Minna Anglesey's, were top-heavy

*Dining room. (*Vogue, March 1, 1914, *courtesy Condé Nast)*

with swags and seemed crowded by the architecture, indicating they probably had been made for taller, slightly wider windows. Yet it was comfortable, airy, and loosely historicist, with several elements of de Wolfe's emerging decorative vocabulary firmly in place: stripes, florals, mirrors, and pale paint.

Upstairs, the white-paneled bedrooms "were furnished with painted beds, inlaid tables, and chests of drawers, chaise longues or wall couches, and chairs upholstered in chintz or linen."[18] De Wolfe's formula for bedrooms, developed first in East 17th Street and reiterated at the Colony Club and elsewhere, was applied once again in her French home. Efficiency was achieved in the bedrooms by the inclusion of spacious wardrobes and dressing tables and hygienic white enamel finishes, while etchings, sketches, and watercolors on the walls added to the warm atmosphere of the rooms. The decorator described the bedroom furniture she used in the villa as "graceful and feminine . . . such as the ghosts of the fair ladies of the Park would adore."[19] De Wolfe's boudoir was decorated with a green-and-rose-striped wallpaper overlaid with a bold damask-like pattern of stylized flowers and vines, its visual complexity punctuated by clusters of gilt-framed

Console in the dining room. (The House in Good Taste, *1913*)

art ranging from well-mannered landscapes to an antique design for curtains hanging above a chinoiserie lacquered cabinet. Over the Louis XV–style daybed, plump with cut-velvet cushions and a fur lap robe, hung what appeared to be a large copy of one of Goya's portraits of the Duchess of Alba; on the parquet floor was spread a highly patterned Aubusson carpet rich with roses and leafy swags.

In 1912 Marbury, de Wolfe, and Morgan decided to add an extra wing to the villa, at about the same time the vegetable garden was erased in favor of the reflecting pool. The banking heiress funded the so-called Morgan Wing, which housed her private quarters on the second floor and a spacious windowed promenade that came to be known as the Long Gallery on the first floor. The addition wasn't built until 1914,

however, and because of the war, it remained undecorated for another five years after that.

Villa Trianon inspired the gracious vision de Wolfe shared with others, both friends and clients, many of whom had never even been to France. To them the decorator offered a fanciful ideal of an aristocratic past, an elegant and evocative philosophy of design that was readily adopted by clients who wished to be modern without relinquishing the hard-won status symbols of antiques, paintings, and sculpture. Even de Wolfe's French friends were astonished by the transformation of the house, observed Bessy Marbury: "They connected the trend of modernism with American enterprise, and could not imagine us capable of reverence and of reserve," she wrote in her memoirs in 1923. "Their surprise was very great therefore, when they found us restoring the past while recognizing the importance of hygiene, and the necessity of present day convenience."[20]

The villa provided a means through which de Wolfe could construct and reinforce her own sense of self more completely than by simply adorning her body with couture clothing. No longer able to live out her fantasies on the stage, she created in the town of Versailles a comfortable, romantic backdrop for herself and her circle against which she could realize her dreams. Here she would create the beauty she felt she had been deprived of as a child growing up in a New York brownstone. Gérald Van Der Kemp, a later chief curator of Versailles who knew de Wolfe well, recalled that the decorator's immersion in Villa Trianon and its history, real and imagined, was complete: "She was absolutely convinced that she had been a lady of the court of Louis XV."[21] Above all, in Versailles de Wolfe was nearer than anywhere else to the aesthetic achievements of 18th-century France that she revered, lessons that had played such an important part in encouraging her to aspire to something more than ugliness and mediocrity.

Elsie de Wolfe's boudoir. (Vogue, March 1, 1914, courtesy Condé Nast)

1913

Grace and Ormond G. Smith Residence
Shoremonde
Oyster Bay, New York

One of the most complete and luxurious sets of interiors that Elsie de Wolfe created on Long Island was Shoremonde, a country house for the Ormond G. Smiths, a well-traveled couple who shared de Wolfe's passion for France and French culture.

Schooled in France and the United States and later made a Commander of the Legion d'Honneur, Ormond Gerald Smith (1860–1933) was a partner in Street & Smith, publishers of popular magazines like *People's* and *Picture-Play Weekly*—it would also publish *Mademoiselle* and *Charm* under the stewardship of Smith's son, Gerald—as well as hundreds of inexpensive novels known as penny dreadfuls. Smith also was famed for having discovered or nurtured the careers of numerous prominent American writers, including O. Henry and Dorothy Parker.[1] (Another of his achievements was the creation of fictional detective Nick Carter, whose mystery tales were a mainstay of Smith's magazine empire.) The success of Street & Smith, which had been founded by Ormond Smith's father in 1855, gave him the financial security with which to create a grand country residence.

To design the house, the Smiths chose the New York–based architectural firm of Hoppin & Koen, established in 1894 by Francis L. V. Hoppin (1867–1941) and Terrence Koen (1858–1923), both former McKim, Mead & White associates. Hoppin already had a number of Classical revival successes to his name, including the novelist Edith Wharton's

Opposite: Entrance portico. (Architectural Record, Aug. 1916, courtesy of the Art Institute of Chicago)

South portico. (Architectural Record, Aug. 1916, courtesy of the Art Institute of Chicago)

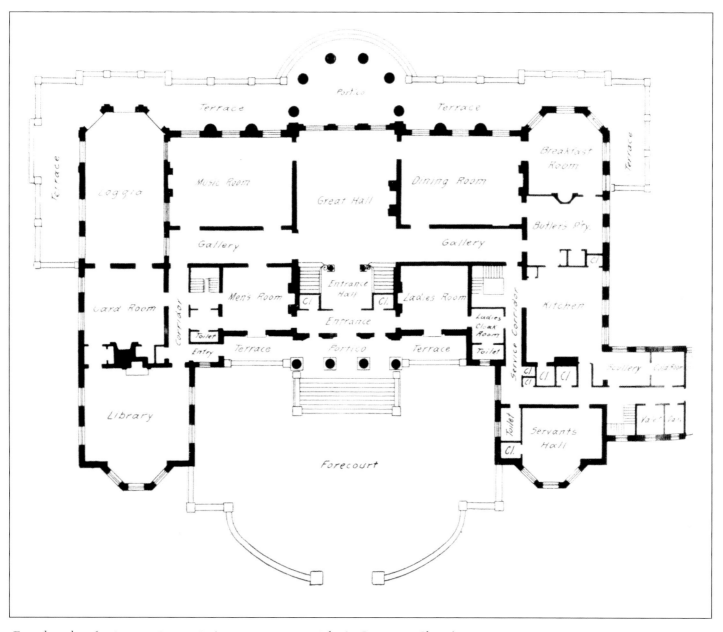

*First-floor plan. (*Architectural Record, *Aug. 1916, courtesy of the Art Institute of Chicago)*

country house, The Mount, and this may have influenced the literary Smith's choice of architects. Commissioning de Wolfe for the interiors of the house, however, was likely a more personal choice: de Wolfe's close friends Sarah and Eleanor Hewitt were cousins of Smith's wife, the former Grace Hewitt Pellett (1871–1924). The choice of the Long Island village of Oyster Bay, barely 25 miles from New York

City, as the location for the house was natural; the Smiths had been renting houses for the summer season in the area for some years.

Located on a 250-acre parcel of land overlooking Long Island Sound with a mile of waterfront, a private yacht harbor, and its own lighthouse, Shoremonde was a particularly majestic example of the Federal revival style, its massive three-story central

Men's room. (Architectural Record, Aug. 1916, courtesy of the Art Institute of Chicago)

Ladies' room. (Architectural Record, Aug. 1916, courtesy of the Art Institute of Chicago)

block flanked by two-story bay-fronted wings set at right angles.[2] In addition to a formal sunken Italianate garden, a cutting garden, a small lake, and an enclosed vegetable garden laid out in elegant parterres, the house was accompanied by a multitude of outbuildings, which included a garage, an overseer's house, and workmen's cottages. The exterior of the 180-foot-long, $1 million house was clad in red brick copied from 18th-century English examples, trimmed with granite, and anchored by a formidable portico with Corinthian columns set atop a flight of white marble steps.[3] Another portico, this one semicircular, was found at the rear of the house, flanked by terraces that wrapped half the house.[4]

The interior schemes that de Wolfe developed for Shoremonde, which was completed in 1913, were

Dining room. (Architectural Record, Aug. 1916, courtesy of the Art Institute of Chicago)

*Trellis room. (*The House in Good Taste, *1913)*

Fountain in the trellis room. (The House in Good Taste, *1913*)

among the most sumptuous she had created to date. They also were the most varied she had produced within in a single dwelling. It was undoubtedly highly successful and a very rich scheme, as evidenced by the words of a writer in the August 1916 issue of *Architectural Record,* praising the decorator's work: "In decorating the interior the services of Miss Elsie de Wolfe were wisely invoked and she has assuredly given distinction and grace to this Georgian mansion."[5]

To either side of the entrance hall was a suite for the use of guests, each comprised of a sitting room and an adjoining lavatory. The ladies' room was dominated by what was described as "an unusual shade of mauve"

(one of de Wolfe's favorite colors at this time, as evidenced in the East 71st Street show house). The men's room was distinguished by delicately painted, low-relief decorations in the manner of James and Robert Adam; with a color scheme that was largely red and blue with touches of silver. In the center of the men's room, on a black wool rug with a diamond-patterned border, stood a spade-footed wood desk with an Adam-style armchair. Modern upholstered armchairs finished with brocade woven with 18th-century motifs of griffins and oval medallions were set close to the fireplace, itself nestled in a shallow, full-length arch and surmounted by an elaborate gilt-wood mirror that was adapted from a 1774 Robert Adam design for Derby House in London.[6] As for the 40-foot-long by 30-foot-deep great hall at the heart of Shoremonde, the two-story space was sparsely furnished with "just enough pieces to avoid the uncomfortable feeling of bareness," the marble balustrade of its gallery overhead draped with Middle Eastern rugs and tapestries.[7]

The music room and dining room were situated to the left and right of the great hall. In the music room, de Wolfe used a rich color scheme that combined mulberry-purple hangings with blue draperies, while the dining room, its oak paneling offset by pale marble pilasters, held a majestic Chinese Chippendale table and an equally large Kermanshah rug. Directly off the dining room was the breakfast room, its bay window looking out over the rear terrace and sunken garden. It was described as a typically English room "paneled and painted in cream color, the chintz curtains displaying a bold pattern design in old rose and pale green, over a gray-green rug."[8]

The breakfast room was balanced on the other side of the house by an even larger enclosed loggia lined with trelliswork and furnished with four button-tufted chesterfield sofas, painted furniture, and enamel-flowered sconces. The space was a de Wolfe pièce de resistance and was illustrated in *The House in Good Taste*. She also included a photograph of the room's baroque white-marble fountain, with its base of three entwined dolphins.[9] The *Architectural Record* evocatively described the room as containing "pale green lattice work against a terra cotta wall" and added, "The draperies are of striped taffeta silk in pale pink and green, the couch and chairs are covered with cream and green striped [leaf-pattern cut] velvet, the floor is of marble mosaic, the rug terra cotta with black border."[10] Among the furniture was a zinc-lined plant-holding table similar to those in the winter garden at the Lake Forest home of the J. Ogden Armours and Canton wicker chairs identical to those used in the rooftop winter garden of the Colony Club. De Wolfe proudly described Shoremonde's trellis loggia as "classic in its fine balance and its architectural formality, and modern in its luxurious comfort and its refreshing color. Surely there could be no pleasanter room for whiling away a summer day."[11]

The loggia led to a card room that opened into the library, which was described as having "blue and silver hangings against lime wood in the manner of Christopher Wren" and "painted ceilings in bas-relief."[12]

Typical of de Wolfe's approach to the private quarters in a domestic dwelling. Of the 26 bedrooms in the house—a dozen for family and guests and 14 for servants—seven were here, all with linked bathrooms and closets, one with a dressing room and one with a morning room, or "boudoir." The servants' quarters were situated on the right wing of the house on this floor. De Wolfe's commitment to stylistic variety in this house was visible in the guest rooms, one of which she treated in the "Chinese manner"

with "black and gold lacquer," while another was in the Directoire style with red-and-blue chintz hangings.[13] The design for the fabric of the latter room was, apparently, "suggested by an ancient document," although no details were provided.[14] As usual when presented with a feminine space, de Wolfe devoted thorough attention to the design of Grace Smith's boudoir. Using deep-green-painted, Louis XVI–style panelings as a calming background for a multitude of patterns, de Wolfe decorated the room with a faded Aubusson rug of rose, green, cream, and blue; double-armed sconces with porcelain flowers; and curvaceous reproduction French furniture covered with brocaded silk and needlework upholstery. Grace Smith's boudoir ranks as one of de Wolfe's most fresh and charming private spaces, lively with complementary patterns but restrained in the amount of furniture and art and its deployment—one large framed picture was casually propped against the wall on top of a chest of drawers—reinforcing the decorator's easygoing, modern approach to traditional interiors.

The interior of Shoremonde was judged a great success by the *Architectural Record,* which noted that both the architect and the interior decorator had ably confronted the challenge of conforming to period design without being too literal or too lavish. They had "steered through the Scylla and Charybdis of interior decoration, in carefully avoiding the ostentatious and the commonplace."[15]

After only six years' residence, Shoremonde was sold in 1919 to the automaker John North Willys for a reported $800,000.[16] A year later, for $500,000, the Smiths bought Stepping Stones, de Wolfe client Anne Vanderbilt's country house in nearby Jericho.[17] Grace Smith died in 1923, at age 52, leaving behind a 10-year-old son and her husband, who survived for another decade.[18]

1913–15

Projects for Friends

*A*n important part of Elsie de Wolfe's life revolved around the activities, both charitable and entrepreneurial, of her friends. In 1909, for example, she decorated the garden of the Lenox Library—site of the future Frick mansion—for a benefit, and in the following year she supported Bessy Marbury in a venture with the New Theatre by creating sets and costumes for an opening performance. Between 1913 and 1915, at the height of her success as an interior decorator, de Wolfe continued to create settings for projects initiated by members of her close group of female friends, Marbury and Anne Morgan in particular.

One early project came into de Wolfe's hands thanks to Morgan, who was a member of the woman's department of the National Civic Federation. The Federation's Vacation Savings Fund, later known as the Vacation Association, was organized by a number of prominent women across the country, including Morgan, Eleanor Robson Belmont, Gertrude Robinson Smith, and Daisy Harriman, and its aim was to ensure that thousands of working women could afford to take a holiday at a respectable country boarding house. In 1912 the philanthropists launched a vacation-funding scheme financed by the purchase of savings stamps.

One of the association's aims was to combat the loneliness of the often unmarried female city worker and to provide her with a social life and a cultural education. To these ends, the association decided to open a headquarters building with lodgings. Back-to-back

Opposite: Front facade of the Vacation Association building, c. 1920. (Barnard College Archives)

Elsie de Wolfe, 1915.
(Collection of the Elsie de Wolfe Foundation)

buildings were rented at 38 West 39th Street and at 35–37 West 38th Street, the former for the headquarters and the latter for lodgings. They were opened, fully furnished and equipped, on January 1 and April 1, 1914, respectively.[1]

De Wolfe oversaw the renovation and decor of the interiors of both buildings. The first floor of the headquarters contained administration offices, a restaurant, and lounges for the so-called taxpayers (it was decided the word *members* was not inclusive enough); the second floor was dedicated to a reception room where men were welcomed; and the third floor comprised a lounge, a writing room, and a dressing room with baths.[2] This floor was the "Colony [Club] in miniature," and the dressing room was equipped with "dressing tables, cubicles for changing clothes and private bathrooms in which the girls could soak in warm, relaxing tubs."[3] The residential building, which was to be "run on the plan of a good English lodging house," consisted of single and double bedrooms, which cost $5.00 and $5.50 to rent.[4] (These rates were waived for women who earned salaries lower than $15.00 per month.[5]) By the time she came to design these interiors, de Wolfe had considerable experience in creating communal living and leisure spaces for women, albeit at different social levels, for the Colony Club and Barnard College.

A considerable budget was dedicated to the refurbishment of the Vacation Association's headquarters. In 1913 the annual report showed that just $1,152.98 was spent on fixtures and fittings, though this figure rose to $13,303.33 in the following year. In her biography of de Wolfe, Jane S. Smith described the association's decor as similar to de Wolfe's work at Barnard College, explaining that "sturdy oak replaced the more delicate mahogany of [the Colony Club] . . . and plain carpets were used instead of Oriental rugs, but the similar arrangement of the rooms and their familiar atmosphere of well-upholstered convenience proved Elsie's contention that her principles of simplicity, suitability and proportion could be used for any setting on any budget."[6] One observer noted that the rooms were "much more attractive than the average boarding house."

One of the weekly activities provided at West 39th Street was arranged in collaboration with Bessy Marbury. Dancing lessons were given by a teacher who came from Castle House, the tea-dance café that was one of Marbury and de Wolfe's joint business projects. Other activities included weekly dances, a drama club, singing classes, costume balls, museum tours, and illustrated lectures.

Vacation Association meeting at the 39th Street clubhouse, c. 1920. (Barnard College Archives)

At the same time they were involved with improving the lot of working women, Marbury and de Wolfe also were moving into enterprising new ventures. Castle House, for instance, was a collaboration with the celebrated dancers Irene and Vernon Castle. The couple had married in 1911 and worked in France at the Café de Paris, where they came to the attention of de Wolfe and Marbury.[7] With the support of several society leaders, including Mamie Fish and Almira Rockefeller, Marbury and de Wolfe persuaded the dancers to be the stars of a teatime dancing venue that would be open from 4:00 to 6:30 each afternoon. A writer in *Vogue* explained, "The charming walls of Castle House became a setting within which one might take tea and twirl or be taught to dance at its courtliest and smartest artistic best."[8]

Castle House was located at 26 East 46th Street, opposite the Ritz-Carlton Hotel, in what had been the fashionable dressmaking establishment of Josefa Osborn. The dance hall was opened on December 13, 1913, and it quickly became popular. Music was provided by the Society Orchestra, an influential African-American jazz band led by James Reese Europe (1880–1919).

Marbury's deep-rooted entrepreneurialism went hand in hand with a desire for social reform, and the absence of alcohol at Castle House was used to offset widespread anxiety about the immoral climate many believed was engendered by the new dance movements. A genteel environment was crucial, and de Wolfe gave Castle House "a highly tasteful interior appropriate to its ambitions."[9] Irene Castle recalled its elegance: "When Elsie de Wolfe decorated it, few changes were

Irene and Vernon Castle dancing in Castle House, c. 1914. (Museum of the City of New York)

made in the panels and crystal chandeliers [of Osborn's shop]. You entered it by going two steps down to the door and into a foyer. In the background was a fountain surrounded by ferns and small palms. . . . The smaller room had plain walls and cloth-covered lights with mirrors going around the room. Both were furnished with benches and chairs covered by tie-on mats or cushions."[10]

Castle House survived for only two seasons, but it was quickly followed by two new venues at which the dancers appeared. The first, Castles in the Air, was a roof garden on West 44th Street, on top of the Schubert Theater. In July 1914, the oceanside Castles by the Sea opened on Long Island.[11] Marbury had also managed dancing classes the Castles held on the cruise ship *Viktoria Luise.*

At the end of 1914, Marbury and de Wolfe collaborated on the Strand Theater Roof Garden. Like Castle House, this establishment, which opened its doors in January 1915, was an alcohol-free entertainment venue and offered its clientele the opportunity to dance to a jazz band, eat "corn beef hash and apple pie," and be waited on by the same group of society women who had supported Castle House. Anne Vanderbilt, the second wife of William K. Vanderbilt, joined the existing triumvirate as a fourth member,[12] and while she and Marbury managed the Roof Garden, Morgan had charge of the cafeteria and de Wolfe decorated it.

"That the surroundings are beautiful, no-one can deny," a contemporary article explained. "Blue and gold is the color scheme employed. As one enters the roof garden the first thing to greet the eye is a real Hindoo in magnificent dress. . . . For those who do not care for tea there is an idealized soda fountain, designed by Miss de Wolfe. The dancing floor is oval in shape and around it are chairs and tiny tables. . . . Blue velvet curtains bound in gold braid and inverted lights which are hidden by the wall's wainscoting are artful features not overlooked by those who love beauty in their surroundings."[13] Describing the same setting slightly differently, in her 1989 thesis on Marbury, Rebecca W. Strum wrote that "the ambience of the Strand Roof Garden was garden-like; the many windows let in all available sunlight. De Wolfe decorated the room in pale

Set at the Princess Theatre for the production of Nobody Home, *1915. (The New York Public Library)*

green and white, with silver-gray tables and chairs, and green wicker lounges upholstered in a gaily colored chintz. There was a green latticed soda fountain and a separate smoking corner . . . with large wicker chairs and files of newspapers."[14]

Lunch at the Roof Garden could be taken between 11:30 a.m. and 2:00 p.m., and tea and dancing took place from 4:30 to 6:30 p.m. General dancing took place after 8:00 p.m. For a couple of years, the Roof Garden was a success, but ultimately it couldn't compete with nightclubs that provided alcohol. Marbury sold it in early 1917.

During the first year of the Roof Garden's existence, Marbury and de Wolfe took on an even more ambitious project. For some time Marbury had wanted to open her own theater. In April 1916 she discussed the possibility of managing the 39th Street Theatre for Lee Schubert, but the plan didn't materialize.[15] She also developed another, again unrealized, idea—very likely to have been instigated by de Wolfe—that involved running the theater as a cabaret, with "seats covered in chintz slip covers . . . The alleyways on both sides were to be decorated with trellises and plants to imitate gardens where the audience could cool off during intermissions."[16] Back in 1915, however, Marbury had decided to become a producer and to engage de Wolfe as her set designer, primarily as a ploy to prevent her companion from returning to war-torn France.

In the summer of 1914, Marbury had found a partner, F. Ray Comstock, who wanted to work with her to create productions for the small Princess Theater at 104 West 39th Street, built by Lee Schubert and his collaborators a couple of years earlier. Their aim was to find a new theatrical formula that would put this little space on the map. The Princess was elegantly outfitted with a fireplace in the lobby, applied

Cover of the sheet music for a song written by Jerome Kern for Nobody Home, *c. 1915. (Museum of the City of New York)*

wall moldings, chandeliers in the main hall, and decorative metalwork on the stairs.[17] Together Marbury and Comstock developed the concept of the intimate musical comedy, six of which were produced between April 1915 and November 1918. Only two of them involved Marbury, however. *Nobody Home* opened in April 1915, and *Very Good Eddie* opened in December 1915 and ran through the following year. Both shows had two sets, a small cast, and a small chorus, each member of which was dressed differently. De Wolfe created the sets and coordinated the costumes.

Guy Bolton and Paul Rubens wrote the script for *Nobody Home*, Jerome Kern composed the music, and P. G. Wodehouse wrote the lyrics. Although Hickson of

The sheet music for a song written by Jerome Kern for Very Good Eddie, *c. 1915. (The Museum of the City of New York)*

Fifth Avenue was credited with the design of the costumes, de Wolfe, according to Strum, "chose the colors of the costumes to complement the colors of the sets. In Act I she used pale green and white, with red accents, repeated in the details of her representation of the Ritz Carlton lobby." For the set in Act II, an apartment on Central Park West, de Wolfe "broke the walls into angles and included five doors. The walls were ivory white and the moldings and trim were black. She added two orange trees growing out of tubs, painted on opposite walls. A bird in a black, orange, and white cage hung near a black and orange striped sofa. Matching chairs were placed around the room."[18] It was a strikingly modern set, appropriate for the new theatrical form that was being presented. As a press preview from the time explained, "The scenery and stage accessories have been designed and planned by Elsie de Wolfe, the world famous decorator of homes of the smart set and will present many novelties in the way of stage decoration."[19]

Designing the sets for this musical represented an important turning point for the decorator. She began to move away from a reliance upon historical styles and to embrace the new and contemporary. As she explained in an interview in *Strand* magazine, she felt that America needed to find a style of its own, one that was not so dependent on European antecedents: "Now we are beginning to realise that beautiful as an Italian villa is on the shores of the Adriatic, it may not be suited to the shore of a New York or New Jersey lake."[20]

Nobody Home also gave de Wolfe an opportunity to develop her ideas about color. "I carefully plan style or period," she said, "but colors never. I just feel them. . . . I felt orange to be right for that particular room."[21]

She also worked on Marbury's other production with Comstock, Bolton, and Kern at the Princess Theater, *Very Good Eddie.* This time Act I took place on the deck of a Hudson River cruise boat, while Act II was enacted at the Rip Van Winkle Inn. The costumes of the chorus members again were designed by Hickson, and de Wolfe had responsibility for the second-act set. Once again she included five doors, each one surrounded by columns, but this time the set had two levels. A central staircase led to a landing and a window, and de Wolfe once more relied on black, white, and orange.

In 1916 de Wolfe returned to France and became increasingly engaged with the war work that would result in her receiving the Legion d'Honneur. For personal reasons, her intense friendships with Marbury and Morgan began to subside, as did de Wolfe's interest in participating in her friends' charitable and commercial endeavors.

Set at the Princess Theater for the production of Nobody Home, *1915. (The Museum of the City of New York)*

The finale of Nobody Home, *1915. (The Museum of the City of New York)*

1906-37

Elsie de Wolfe's Showrooms
New York City

etween 1905 and 1919, the scale and number of Elsie de Wolfe's decorating projects expanded considerably. From the moment she decided to create her own letterhead, engraved with a little wolf logo, and go in search of professional interior decorating commissions as a means of earning a living, to the years immediately following World War I, when she began to withdraw from the multimillion-dollar business she had created and spend more time in France, her decorating operation went through several transformations. To accommodate these changes, she eventually was obliged to occupy three different business premises. Few business records survive, so little is known about the details of the way in which de Wolfe managed her office, but from the material that does remain, it is clear that she worked with a substantial—and constantly changing—team that included numerous assistants, a secretary, and people looking after her accounts. "Where she formerly worked alone or, at the most, with one assistant," a newspaper article of 1910 explained, "she now keeps fourteen busy all the time and she has so many demands on her time that she finds it absolutely impossible to accept more than half the contracts that are offered to her."[1] By 1914 the quantity of work coming into her office was said to be so substantial that she was earning $175,000 net a year—more, it was claimed, than any of the lawyers in New York.[2]

Opposite: Elsie de Wolfe, with one of her Pekingeses, c. 1915.

Some of the archives that contain information relating to de Wolfe's oeuvre reveal details of the contributions made by some of her assistants. During the work undertaken on her East 55th Street house, for example, Paul Chalfin—later the creator of the interiors of Vizcaya, James Deering's home in Miami, Florida— was employed as an assistant, while the abilities of an assistant known only as Miss Butler were praised by Henry Clay Frick during the decoration of his New York house. Among the staff decorators was Winifred de Wolfe, wife of the decorator's brother Edgar.[3]

Elena Bachman, who married the architect Mott B. Schmidt in 1925, and H. Joan Hofford acted as assistants on the projects de Wolfe undertook for Nell Pruyn Cunningham in the 1920s. When she went on her summer spending sprees in Europe, the decorator needed someone trustworthy back in New York to undertake the day-to-day work. It is also known that she worked with a multitude of subcontractors. The artist Everett Shinn, for example, collaborated with de Wolfe on several projects, most notably painting furniture for the Colony Club.[4] She also subcontracted work

Showroom in the Elsie de Wolfe Studio at 2 West 47 Street, c. 1915. (Collection of the Elsie de Wolfe Foundation)

to metalworkers, cabinetmakers, and muralists, as well as numerous other artists and craftsmen.

Back in 1905, de Wolfe had begun her decorating career from her home at 122 East 17th Street. Such were the space demands of storing items to be used in her early projects, the Colony Club in particular, that she was soon forced to establish a commercial office elsewhere. Letters from de Wolfe to Stanford White and Everett Shinn from March 1906 onward bore the address of 4 West 40th Street, her first office, and described the basis of her business as relating to

the supply of both "Interiors" and "Objets d'Art." The address of the property purchased by Bessy Marbury in France—57 Boulevard St. Antoine, in Versailles—was also included in de Wolfe's letterhead as her "Paris Branch" at that time, and the designer's cable address was given as ELSIEMISS.[5] Although no images of the interiors of 4 West 40th Street have been identified, de Wolfe worked from there for nine years, the busiest period of her career. Located in a remodeled mansion that also contained private apartments as well as other design-related businesses, it must have been able to

Corner of the showroom in the Elsie de Wolfe Studio at 2 West 47th Street, c. 1915. (Collection of the Elsie de Wolfe Foundation)

accommodate a sizable operation.[6] Eight years later, when de Wolfe was working for Frick, the 4 West 40th Street address was still on the letterhead, although that of her Paris branch had changed to 39 Rue Caumartin.[7] For example, an April 24, 1915, letter to Frick from Josephine Kneissel, one of de Wolfe's finance managers, was sent from the West 40th Street address.[8] A couple of months later, however, de Wolfe wrote to Frick from 2 West 47th Street, evidence that she finally had to move her office to a new location in a commercial building that also contained the offices of the society architect Bertram Grosvenor Goodhue.[9] A subsequent move to the Cammeyer Building at 677 Fifth Avenue eventually took place "on or about the first of November 1921."[10]

In line with the significant amount of press coverage that the decorator was attracting at that time, her new West 47th Street "studio," as it was called, which she moved into in 1915 and introduced with a reception co-hosted by Bessy Marbury, Anne Morgan, and society actress Julia Hoyt, not surprisingly caught the attention of *Vogue*.[11] A double-spread article described it as "one of the most attractive studios in New York."[12] It consisted of two floors—one contained a mixture of salons, offices, and studios, which were carefully decorated for visits from both existing and potential clients, while the other housed workshops where interior items were created for the decorator's many projects. With its checkerboard floor made from squares of black and white marble, antique wall fountain, and 18th-century French console table, the entrance hall, which visitors encountered as they left the elevator, recalled those of the houses on East 71st and East 55th Streets. The large showroom, entered through glass doors, featured mirrored columns and a wide array of furnishings shown against walls painted a deep, soft gray. It also contained a recessed,

mirrored display case filled with Venetian glass. Painted French chairs, solid carved English tables, armchairs with the familiar striped upholstery fabric, Chinese porcelain jars transformed into lamps with gently shirred silk shades, hanging baskets of glass flowers (reminiscent of those used at Planting Fields, the Coe house, in the 1920s), and other glass and porcelain ornaments were all displayed for potential purchase. De Wolfe's openly espoused eclecticism was on view for all to see, illustrating her strong belief that "against a proper background, furniture of all periods may be assembled."[13]

The little anteroom, entered from the West 47th Street showroom, however, exhibited a more consistent example of a specimen de Wolfe interior. Here, paintings of bonsai trees inspired by images on Chinese porcelain jars were applied to dull-green walls to form a background for a small sofa slipcovered in green silk with yellow piping, two French side chairs, and sconces with blue beaded fringes. De Wolfe's private office was decorated in the Georgian style, featuring blue wood-paneled walls with gilt detailing, a black-and-white marble fireplace, and a niche filled with Chinese porcelain. On the window wall, a gap between thin cream silk curtains, sprigged with rose and green flowers, and the window sashes was occupied by a "deep shelf where goldfish bowls and Chinese bird-cages are placed."[14] (Goldfish had followed de Wolfe through many projects, from the little conservatory in East 17th Street to the hallway of East 55th Street.) Her desk was of black and gold lacquered wood.

The Elsie de Wolfe Studio displayed the sophisticated, sumptuous style that had become her hallmark. An increased eclecticism and a greater use of materials connoting luxury—gilt, cut crystal, marble, mirrored glass, and lacquered wood among them—had begun to characterize her decorating style, showing a subtle

Anteroom in the Elsie de Wolfe Studio at 2 West 47th Street, c. 1915. (Collection of the Elsie de Wolfe Foundation)

change from the restrained but comfortable neoclassicism she had undertaken between 1905 and 1914.

In June 1916, a year after she had moved offices, de Wolfe returned to France. She dedicated most of the next 18 months to war work, playing a part, alongside Mathilde de Rothschild, in the application of the hot ambrine wax treatment to soldiers who had sustained burns. On her return to New York in autumn 1919, de Wolfe found that her decorating business had thrived in her absence. A move to even larger premises was again necessary. "This time," she explained in her autobiography, "I took a whole floor on upper Fifth Avenue."[15] Providing an insight into the nature of the new space she had taken on in a new six-story building

erected on the site of Brigadier General Cornelius Vanderbilt's mansion, she explained, "As it has always been arranged more like a private house than like a shop and it has a spacious front showroom, I thought it would be a perfect setting for a large party, so I gave a dinner for eighty of my friends."[16]

Now the business promoted itself as "Elsie de Wolfe—interior decorations, antique furniture, objets d'art," an indication of the firm's range. Before the war, period furniture had been considered the only appropriate furniture for high-class interiors; now new furniture in modern styles was becoming more acceptable to elite clients in France and, to a limited extent, in the United States. For the time being, where the American

Elsie de Wolfe's private office at 2 West 47th Street, c. 1915. (Collection of the Elsie de Wolfe Foundation)

market was concerned, de Wolfe mostly stayed with historical styles, using both antiques and reproductions. Photographs of her 677 Fifth Avenue showroom depicted, among other objects, 18th-century furniture—sofas, side tables, chairs, gilt mirrors, screens, footstools, chandeliers, and table lamps—arranged against paneled walls reminiscent of a large drawing room, which suggested to her clients the level of elegance they could achieve in their own interiors.

The Fifth Avenue showroom remained the heart of de Wolfe's American decorating business up until the first public sign of the firm's demise on May 1, 1937, when it filed for bankruptcy. With de Wolfe now married to the British press attaché Sir Charles Mendl,

spending most of her time in France, and the level of competition that existed by that time, the firm was unable to remain financially viable. For 15 years Elsie de Wolfe Inc. operated out of 677 Fifth Avenue, its staff depending heavily upon de Wolfe's well-established language of interior decoration.

De Wolfe's associates did not always achieve the same level of success as the firm's founder, however. An interior created for the Daniel Jacklings' apartment in San Francisco in 1919, for example, which Winifred de Wolfe designed in the English-manor style with a molded ceiling, paneled walls, tables, and high-backed armchairs, had a formulaic feel that lacked her sister-in-law's flair. Later, in the 1930s, the firm created a

Showroom at 677 Fifth Avenue, 1922. (New York Public Library)

number of interiors in a modified Venetian Baroque style, which began to seem rather old-fashioned in the context of the more modern-looking interiors that were becoming popular among wealthy Americans.

De Wolfe had made a few more attempts to reanimate the showroom and to enhance the firm's profile. In 1932, for example, she conceived the idea of hosting a permanent exhibition of American-made furniture in an attempt to help the country's manufacturing industry during the depression. She even managed to persuade Eleanor Roosevelt, who exhibited furniture made by her Val-Kill firm at de Wolfe's showroom in 1933, to endorse the project. In 1932, Elsie de Wolfe Inc. also exhibited the extravagantly mirrored furniture

and objets d'art created by French designer Serge Roche, examples of which would appear in numerous de Wolfe interiors, including Gary Cooper's California home and Hope Hampton's Manhattan town house. It was a little too late to save the firm, however, and the showroom closed in 1937.[17]

Furniture from the firm was auctioned at the Plaza Art Auction Galleries in New York a year later. A newspaper report explained, "Elsie de Wolfe is selling her stock and in the future will specialize as a consulting decorator."[18] Upon the firm's closure, de Wolfe's business records were apparently destroyed. The details of how America's most famous decorator had run her firm for more than three decades were forever lost.

1914–15

Adelaide and Henry Clay Frick Residence

1 East 70th Street

New York City

"In good taste, comfortable and livable."[1]

Elsie de Wolfe's work for Henry Clay Frick (1849–1919) made her a rich woman. She was paid a commission of 10 percent of the cost of the antiques she bought for the steel magnate, in addition to a fee for all furnishings she had made in her own workrooms. So ambitious was the project, and so generous the budget, the commissions and fees brought her a substantial income, probably in excess of a million dollars.

The Frick mansion is one of the best documented works of de Wolfe's career, as much correspondence between decorator and client survives. The material provides an unequaled insight into her working practices and into the relationship she developed with one of the most important male clients of her long career. Frick was a married man, but his houses in Pittsburgh, New York City, and Prides Crossing, Massachusetts, seem to have been planned and furnished without significant input from his wife. The combination of Frick's ambition, wealth, and connoisseurship and de Wolfe's characteristic determination and commitment resulted in a set of interiors that was among the closest to her decorating ideal.

The house at 1 East 70th Street was not Frick's first attempt to create a grand residence, nor was it his first encounter with interior decorators of note. Following his move to Pittsburgh from the Mennonite farming community of West Overton, Pennsylvania, he built his wealth in the coke (coal residue) and steel industries and his partnership with Andrew Carnegie. After his

Opposite: Second-floor corridor with cove lighting, c. 1914. (The Frick Collection, New York)

Henry Clay Frick. (The Frick Collection, New York)

marriage to Adelaide Howard Childs (1859–1931, of a Pittsburgh boot-making family), Frick bought a house called Homewood in 1882. Renamed Clayton, it was to undergo a number of enlargements and refurbishments.[2] In 1890, A. Kimbel & Sons of New York created an Eastlake-style, high Victorian interior for Clayton, but in 1903 Frick commissioned Cottier and Company, a decorating firm with offices in London and New York, to update it in the Edith Wharton and Ogden Codman idiom at a cost of a $100,000.[3]

In 1889, Frick decided to build a summer house, and he hired the Boston architects Arthur Little and Herbert W. C. Browne, friends of Ogden Codman, to design Eagle Rock, an extravagant Georgian-style seaside mansion in Prides Crossing, north of Boston. Cottier and Company was employed once again to direct the interior decoration, while the powerful

English art dealer Joseph Duveen was hired to acquire antiques and artworks.[4] A relationship was established at this time between de Wolfe and Duveen, who acted as an agent for the decorator, an association that was to continue at East 70th Street. De Wolfe eventually contributed furniture to Eagle Rock as well, such as a Chippendale table with 18 matching chairs, which she discovered at Partridge's in London.[5]

In 1905, Frick and his family were renting William H. Vanderbilt's mansion on 640 Fifth Avenue, a year before Eagle Rock was ready to inhabit. At this time Frick decided to build a house in New York that would act after his death as a museum for his collection of fine and decorative arts. In 1906, the industrialist bought a large lot on Fifth Avenue between East 70th and East 71st streets, then the site of a private library that was about to be moved to the New York Public Library, being designed at the time by the architects Carrère & Hastings. In 1911 Frick chose one half of that architectural team, Thomas Hastings, to create a palatial Beaux Arts house. The designs were completed by the following summer, and construction began a few months later.[6]

In his determination to make 1 East 70th Street a symbol of his social standing, in August 1913 Frick brought into the project, through the agency of Joseph Duveen, one of the most high-profile decorators of the day, Sir Charles Allom of White, Allom, & Company. The distinguished knight had overseen the redecoration of Buckingham Palace seven years earlier.[7]

By this time, however, Frick already had some preliminary dealings with de Wolfe. Early in 1913, she had brought to Frick's attention the collections of the late Sir John Murray Scott; this extraordinary cache of ancien-régime antiques, stored at that time in Scott's apartment at 2 rue Lafitte in Paris, had not yet been made accessible to the public.[8] On January 27, 1914, de Wolfe contacted Frick again, suggesting that she take charge of the feminine aspects of the New York house, for which she considered herself better suited than Allom. "Please don't forget *me!*" she wrote. "I am specially good at detail and the fitting up and the *comfort* of women's rooms, the intimate little tricks that no mere man, no matter how clever he may be, can ever know."[9] Frick responded positively to the suggestion and by the middle of March established his financial agreement with de Wolfe: "I am to pay you 10% above

cost for anything you may from time to time purchase for my house, you at all times making the closest bargain possible."[10]

Though de Wolfe was by then a celebrity and nominal author of a bestselling book, *The House in Good Taste,* it is not clear how she and Frick were introduced. He may have heard of her from Arthur Little, who had worked with de Wolfe on Suffolk House for the James W. Lanes a couple of years earlier,[11] or it is possible that he learned of her work through Thomas

Adelaide Frick's bedroom, c. 1914. (The Frick Collection, New York)

Adelaide Frick's boudoir, c. 1914. (The Frick Collection, New York)

Hastings, whose wife was on the board of governors of the Colony Club and was a close friend of de Wolfe. Given de Wolfe's fame, he undoubtedly was aware of her reputation for creating the kind of "tasteful, livable" decoration he desired for his New York house and of the high level of professional competency of her West 40th Street operation.

Between March and September 1914, an enduring, respectful relationship developed between de Wolfe and the millionaire. Frick traveled with her to France to shop for furniture, praised her good

taste, and gave her large amounts of money to spend on his behalf. He chided the decorator for her lack of bargaining skills, sorted out the problems that occurred between Hastings and de Wolfe's assistant, Miss Butler. When de Wolfe felt her advice was insufficiently heeded, Frick quickly reassured her of his complete trust.

De Wolfe and Frick, and to a lesser extent, his wife, Adelaide, and their daughter Helen, worked closely on the furnishing and decoration of most of the second- and third-floor rooms in the New York

Adelaide Frick's bathroom, c. 1914. (The Frick Collection, New York)

mansion. The second-floor spaces included Adelaide's bedroom, boudoir, and bathroom; Helen's bedroom, bathroom, and private library; and five other bedrooms and four bathrooms. On the third floor, de Wolfe was to decorate four more bedrooms (including the house-keeper's) and four additional bathrooms. Despite this multitude of responsibilities, she also wanted charge of the decoration of the ladies' reception room on the ground floor, as well as the breakfast room and Frick's second-floor sitting room. These rooms had been given to Allom, but de Wolfe believed they would be better handled by her. "I feel," she explained, "that all my schemes as planned should go together, and that it will be the greatest mistake if these rooms are not carried out by one person. To take two of the principal rooms right out breaks the harmony."[12] Frick did not give way at first, but by September of the following year de Wolfe was in London looking for items for the sitting room with the aim of creating "a much more human interior, livable and comfortable."[13]

Between May and September 1914, de Wolfe acquired many furnishings for Frick in Europe and

*Furnishings bought for Henry Frick by Elsie de Wolfe in 1914
through Jacques Seligmann. (After All, 1935)*

implemented decorative schemes for most of the above-mentioned rooms. Typically, she was in search of French and English items with which to create soft, alluring rooms with subtle color schemes and an extensive use of ornamental textiles and trimmings. Adelaide Frick certainly played some role in the decision making, although usually only in the form of a veto. Her husband made it clear whose taste had the upper hand when he told de Wolfe to have his wife's bedroom

"completed in blue, as per your samples. If Mrs. Frick does not like it after it is finished we will change it."

The arrangement that de Wolfe developed with suppliers of antiques and artworks involved taking the goods on a "sale or return" basis, thus allowing Frick and his wife to decide whether or not they could live with her selections. Many pieces entered the house on approval but were later rejected, sometimes, de Wolfe felt, too rashly. On a recurrent basis, de Wolfe urged

Console table bought for Henry Frick by Elsie de Wolfe in 1914. (The Frick Collection, New York)

Writing desk by Jean-Henri Riesener bought by Elsie de Wolfe in 1914 for Mrs. Frick's boudoir. (The Frick Collection, New York)

clients to wait until rooms were complete before they passed judgment and not to reject schemes on the basis of drawings or samples, which did not necessarily reflect the true impact of the realized interiors.

In May 1914 de Wolfe was in London, staying at the Ritz Hotel. She had dealings with a number of local suppliers of antiques and artworks, among them Sir Sidney Greville, S. J. Phillips, Basil Dighton, Lenygon and Morant, Frank Partridge, Charles of London, and S. E. Letts. As usual, she was shopping for several projects at once, but Frick had the most money to spend and had most of her attention. Her London purchases ranged from a Chippendale breakfast table to a silver mustard pot to Chinese pictures reverse-painted on glass (which ended up in her bathroom at Villa Trianon and inspired the mirror decorations of her bathroom at 10 avenue d'Iéna). Nearly everything had an 18th-century origin.

At the end of the month de Wolfe met Frick in Paris. They were welcomed with open arms by dealers and shopped widely at Stettiner, Eduoard Jonas, Arnold Seligman, Doucet, Lepeltier, Mathelin, and Jansen, among others. Stettiner supplied a bureau for Helen Frick's room at a price of 4,500 francs, and Jansen had a matching table that cost 8,000 francs. Jansen also had a mantel for Helen's room, which de Wolfe called "simply perfect! It is in old white marble, which has become a beautiful color with age, and has two blue Sèvres plaques."[14] However, as a letter from de Wolfe to Frick later recounted, Jansen sold the mantel to someone else, and it had to be replaced by one purchased from Seligman.

Doucet was the source for a bust of Claudine Houdon, created by the sitter's father, the neoclassical French sculptor Jean-Antoine Houdon (1741–1828), which de Wolfe decided to carry back to New York herself. "I could not bear to have anything happen to

173

Corner cupboard, attributed to Martin Carlin, bought for Henry Frick by Elsie de Wolfe in 1914. (The Frick Collection, New York)

[it]," she exclaimed to Frick. It ended up in his private sitting room on the second floor. Jonas supplied a "very fine table," which de Wolfe recommended for the drawing room. For the bathrooms, she bought desk sets and lamps and shades in colors that would "harmonize with the décor of the adjoining bedrooms."[15] De Wolfe habitually bought from established antiques dealers and decorating firms, as well as from private sales, and during the summer of 1914 several unique opportunities arose from which Frick was able to benefit. Most important was the availability of part of the

fabled Wallace Collection—largely French antiques and Old Master paintings assembled by the 4th Marquess of Hertford and his illegitimate son, Sir Richard Jackson—which Frick had seen a year earlier at the apartment of the late Sir John Murray Scott. Seligman had secretly given de Wolfe and Frick access to Scott's musty rue Lafitte home, whose rare contents were awaiting a venue for their sale. In June 1914, the collection finally went on public display in the Hôtel de Sagan, a palace at the end of the Faubourg Saint-Germain that was Seligman's home. De Wolfe had already recommended several pieces to Frick as "fine genuine things of the class you want in your house," among them a Reisener table with bronze mounts, a secretaire–bonheur du jour, and a black table, presumably of lacquer.[16] On May 28, 1914, de Wolfe reminded Frick of the last item: "Do not lose sight of the black table in the J.M.S. house. It is a marvel, and as soon as this collection is shown to the public, will surely sell."[17] Baron Edmond de Rothschild eventually bought the table, and although the secretaire–bonheur du jour was shipped to New York, Frick finally rejected it as being too expensive.[18] In a June 4 letter to Frick, de Wolfe informed him that Scott's collection was now on public view, though minus the black table: "Our friend is now out in the open and the purchase is known. I am glad you had the first chance anyway."[19]

Frick was less interested in another sale with aristocratic provenance, that of the Gontaut-Biron Collection, with which de Wolfe had tried to tempt him in an effort to enhance her commission. This perhaps explains why Frick complained so frequently of his decorator's inability to drive a hard bargain when it came to costly antiques; de Wolfe doubtless wished to maximize her percentage so her negotiations were not overly rigorous.

Among the furnishings found in Paris that summer were a table and two stools for Adelaide Frick's boudoir;

a Louis XVI armchair covered with green velvet for the library; a Sèvres inkstand; a tapestry covered stool for the dressing table in Helen Frick's room; a crystal writing set with a diamond monogram for Frick's wife (it was so expensive that de Wolfe suggested Frick think of it as a Christmas present); Ming vases that were subsequently made into lamps for his daughter's private library and two pink Chinese lamps for her bedroom; an old marble lamp for his wife's boudoir; and, for her bedroom mantel, two small candlesticks that the decorator described as "very fine, and I think well bought; 3,500 francs."[20] Curtains were also ordered.

Meanwhile, everything was not going so smoothly in New York, as Hastings was interfering with de Wolfe's plans for the interior. The decorator's assistant, Miss Butler, cabled her boss to let her know what was going on. "I saw the gilt mirrors for three of the guest rooms on the second floor recent and they are perfect horrors. . . . I cannot imagine anything more suggestive of a hotel reception room."[21] Frick took de Wolfe's side and brought Hastings into line with a curt missive: "It is to Miss de Wolfe I am looking that the furnishings she is doing for me will be in every respect in good taste, simple and livable."[22]

De Wolfe promised that everything would be complete by the summer of 1914. She had not anticipated the outbreak of World War I, however, and the difficulty she would have in leaving France and returning to the United States. In early August she traveled from Baden-Baden, Germany, to Biarritz, France, and on to Spain, where she was trapped for some time until she could finally get to Le Havre, from where she finally sailed for New York on September 26. Remarkably, her late return did not significantly delay the Frick project. Although de Wolfe was still working at 1 East 70th Street the following year, the job was substantially complete by autumn 1914, when the Fricks moved in.

De Wolfe's rooms for Frick were complete creations with consistent color schemes, filled with museum-quality furniture by leading cabinetmakers, with custom-made finishing touches. As her husband had decreed, Adelaide Frick's elegant bedroom was predominantly blue. Along one wall stood a neoclassical Italian parcel-gilt single bed, upholstered and draped with a graphic blue-and-cream silk, woven with sunflowers; reputedly dating from the 1700s, the fabric also was used for window curtains. To deflect drafts and provide privacy, an upholstered screen of blue-and-cream petit point stood between the headboard and the door to the hall. The eclectic shapes and periods of the seating de Wolfe had assembled—antique child's armchair to modern button-tufted chaise longue to practical club chair on casters—were offset by a variety of

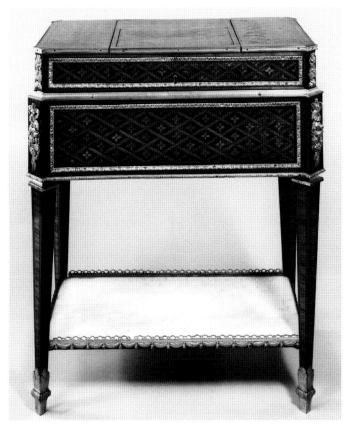

Work table by Martin Carlin bought by Elsie de Wolfe in 1914 for Mrs. Frick's boudoir. (The Frick Collection, New York)

Guest bedroom, c. 1914. (The Frick Collection, New York)

sumptuous materials in shades of smoky blue: damask, cut velvet, and flowered silk. To balance the densely patterned Chinese carpet, de Wolfe had the ceiling lined with canvas panels exuberantly painted with medallions depicting putti engaged in pastoral pursuits. This was possibly the creation of Everett Shinn, who painted murals for other de Wolfe clients. Though Adelaide's walls were hung with engraved reproductions of 18th-century portraits of aristocratic English ladies by Gainsborough and other Georgian artists, the room was accented with treasures like a Louis XVI secretaire and a side table, reportedly by Riesener; the

table's storage compartment was camouflaged by a door disguised as a shelf of leather-bound books.[23]

Adelaide's boudoir next door was lined with blue-painted 18th-century boiserie set with contemporary paintings by François Boucher. Near the center of the room stood a little Riesener desk from the Scott collection. Glass-front wall cabinets were filled with Sèvres and Vincennes porcelain, and a pale blue modern carpet, probably a Superba Wilton broadloom like the one de Wolfe used in her dining room on East 17th Street, softened the parquet floor.

Guest bedroom, c. 1914. (The Frick Collection, New York)

Curiously situated between her parents' suites and connected to both by doors, Helen Frick's bedroom and bathroom were simple and relatively modest. Not unlike the stylish but practical bedrooms in de Wolfe's own homes, the decorations were suitable for a rather serious woman in her mid-20s, though executed in confectionary shades of pink and green. Next to the single bed stood a three-drawer Louis XV table made of tulipwood and kingwood, which de Wolfe had bought from Lewis and Simmons.

The guest bedrooms decorated by de Wolfe exhibited individual color schemes and differing, though largely formal, period formats. One was finished in green and had a chinoiserie theme with accents of Regency faux bamboo; another was predominantly Georgian. Each had a fireplace, a chaise longue, a dressing table, a mirror, good lighting, and a bedside table, following the familiar de Wolfe formula for bedrooms. The decoration of the connecting bathrooms was color-coordinated to the rooms they served.

Henry Clay Frick was not to bask in the glory of his house for long; he died in 1919, five years after taking up residence. Following his wife's death in 1931, 1 East 70th Street was transformed into a private museum, as Frick had planned. The second and third floors were turned into offices, and much of de Wolfe's work was undone, the furnishings dispersed to other Frick family houses.

$\mathcal{1915}$

Magnolia and George Sealy Residence

Open Gates

Galveston, Texas

$\mathcal{I}$n 1915, before she left for France and war work, Elsie de Wolfe undertook a partial redecoration of Open Gates, a house purportedly designed by Stanford White for George Sealy (1835–1901) and his wife, the former Magnolia Willis (1854–1933).

It has been claimed that the architect was chosen by Magnolia, whose husband told her to find "the finest architect in the country."[1] Evidence supporting this attribution is contained in a specifications manuscript relating to the interior of the house in the McKim, Mead & White office archive. The manuscript detailed the "work to be done and material furnished for the completion of a part of a dwelling house for George Sealy, Esq., Galveston, Texas, in accordance with the drawings and specifications prepared by and under the general superintendence of McKim, Mead & White."[2] Specifications were provided for the paneling, doors, staircase, floors, cabinetwork, fireplaces, and decoration. The document does not mention White by name, but it does outline a number of extravagant details typical of White's work, including the use of bronze in the hallway, gold paintwork in the drawing room and music room, and "walls covered with yellow silk and ceiling painted in imitation of sky."[3]

Whether or not White designed Open Gates, local architect Nicholas Clayton certainly oversaw its construction. He also built an elaborate carriage house on the grounds in 1891. The result of White and Clayton's work was a remarkable mansion in the neo-Renaissance

Opposite: Exterior. (The Rosenberg Library, Galveston Texas)

Elsie de Wolfe, painted by Albert Sterner, 1915. (Collection of the Elsie de Wolfe Foundation)

Bedroom, partially refurbished by Elsie de Wolfe in 1915. (The Rosenberg Library, Galveston, Texas)

style that boasted a colonnaded front, a high-pitched, gabled roof made from tiles brought from Belgium, corner towers, and a tall chimney. An earlier house on the site had been removed after Sealy purchased the property in 1881; the building and landscaping of the new residence were completed in 1889, after a year and a half of construction.[4]

By the turn of the century, the Sealys had come to dominate Galveston society. Pennsylvania-born George Sealy, a son of Irish immigrants, had started off as a farmhand. He then joined his elder brother in Texas in 1857 and made his money through shipping, banking, and a stake in the Gulf, Colorado, and Santa Fe Railroad. He married Magnolia Willis, the daughter of a business associate, in 1875, and they had five daughters and three sons. Magnolia Willis had come from a mercantile background in southern Texas and was educated in a New York boarding school. She also traveled frequently to fashionable destinations of her social class, including the spas of Hot Springs,

Bedroom, partially refurbished by Elsie de Wolfe, 1915. (The Rosenberg Library, Galveston, Texas)

Virginia and, when in New York City, stayed at the Hotel Fifth Avenue. Like so many other wealthy women of her generation, Magnolia Sealy played a leading role in the church and in local philanthropic pursuits—she was instrumental in having Galveston Island planted with the pink and white oleanders that became the city's horticultural symbol—and she was a prominent member of the Women's Health Protective Association. In 1900, the year of a devastating hurricane in Galveston, Open Gates became the refuge for

more than 400 people. Margaret Burton, one of the Sealys' daughters, later recalled that "for weeks there was 15 ft. of sea water there which reached to the beautifully polished oak floors above."[5]

Open Gates was so called because its doors were constantly open to the community, and it was frequently a site of lavish entertainments. Magnolia seized numerous opportunities to display her taste to the social group she led and through which she defined herself. When George Sealy died in 1901, she pursued

Second bedroom, partially refurbished by Elsie de Wolfe in 1915. (The Rosenberg Library, Galveston, Texas)

an active life as a wealthy widow, traveling frequently to Europe and making many furniture purchases.

Magnolia Sealy's decision, at the age of 61, to employ de Wolfe to renew the interiors of Open Gates was a mark of her continued interest in fashion and taste and of her need to express herself, and impress others, through the choice of interior furnishings supplied by the most famous decorator of the day. Photographs of Open Gates taken around five years after de Wolfe completed the commission indicate that

she did not undertake a complete refurbishment but rather updated what had come to look like an out-of-date White interior.

The rooms that most clearly show de Wolfe's hand, not surprisingly, are the bedrooms, although it has been suggested that she also refurbished the library. The main emphasis seems to have been the addition of new draperies, rugs, and upholstery, although there are signs that she added some furniture as well. Magnolia Sealy's bedroom, for example, contained a hand-painted

Another view of refurbished bedroom. (The Rosenberg Library, Galveston, Texas)

furniture suite that was described by her daughter Margaret as "distinctly French, it being painted in festoons of pink roses, green leaves and garlands, also turquoise ribbons all on tan satin wood like the museum pieces painted years ago by a famous artist called Verni[s] Martin."[6] The room contained an old bed that de Wolfe most likely refreshed with the addition of a draped curtain, a tightly fitting bedcover, and a roll pillow of the type shown in several illustrations in *The House in Good Taste*. While the

heavily carved Italianate furniture of another bedroom was unlikely to have been de Wolfe's choice—it either dated from the original interior decoration or had been added later by the Sealys—the chintz curtains, covered with a floral pattern, were undoubtedly a de Wolfe contribution. She likely supplied the della Robbia–style bas reliefs suspended from the picture rail—similar casts were used in a trelliswork hall at the home of de Wolfe clients Henrietta and Benjamin Guinness as well as on the walls of the roof

Third bedroom partially refurbished by Elsie de Wolfe in 1915. (The Rosenberg Library, Galveston, Texas)

garden of the Colony Club—and almost certainly painted the walls a lighter color as a complement to the flowery fabrics.[7] The use of the same chintz for the curtains and for a high-level bed surround reinforces the likelihood that de Wolfe played a role in creating this highly feminine space.

In another bedroom, the suite of furniture—a bed, a desk, two side chairs, and a dressing table with a three-sided mirror—all had matching rococo swags painted on their light-colored surfaces, reminiscent of the work Shinn so frequently executed for the decorator's projects. The chintz curtains and matching window seat were additional de Wolfe hallmarks.

Although de Wolfe's input at Open Gates was only partial, and she had to work around the earlier, heavier decor, the project illustrated the decorator's skill at counteracting the oppressive eclecticism of the late Victorian era by introducing an airier attitude more in keeping with the modern domestic interior of the early 20th century.

1915 – early 1920s

Mai and William R. Coe Residence

Planting Fields

Oyster Bay, New York

*I*n 1913, William Robertson Coe and his fashionable second wife, Mai (1875–1924), purchased the Long Island estate Planting Fields. It seems very likely that Elsie de Wolfe collaborated with the painter and decorator Everett Shinn on a couple of interiors there. First they worked on a little tea house situated in the grounds of the main house, and later they collaborated on a bathroom–dressing room in the house itself. The tea house formed part of what was then referred to as the Blue Pool Garden, which had been designed in 1914 by Guy Lowell of the Boston firm of Lowell and Sargent.

The garden had been conceived as a formal element of the landscaping for a house built in 1906 and owned by New York lawyer James Byrne. In 1918, that house burned down and Coe commissioned a new house, Coe Hall, which was designed in the Tudor revival style by the New York architecture firm Walker and Gillette. Coe Hall was completed in 1921. In the same year in which building commenced, Guy Lowell's partner, Andrew Robeson Sargent, died, but the garden continued to be developed by Fred Dawson of Olmsted Brothers under the supervision of Mai Coe, whose bedroom in the new house looked directly out onto it.[1] Due to the complexity of the circumstances surrounding the creation of Coe Hall and its 409-acre estate, work was continually being undertaken from the time the Coes bought the property through the early 1920s.

Tea house, c. 1926. (Mattie Edwards Hewitt, courtesy Planting Fields Foundation Archive)

Mai Coe, c. 1916. (Planting Fields Foundation Archive)

In contrast to the Colony Club, where de Wolfe had been in charge and had hired Shinn to create murals for the strangers' dining room, the Planting Fields commission seems to have been Shinn's in the first instance. Mai Coe was known for her cultural interests and for her desire to use 20th-century American artists—among them Shinn and Robert Chanler, who were both close friends of Coe's—in the creation of her stylish home.

Born Mary Huddleston Rogers in New York City, the daughter of Henry Huddleston Rogers, one of the founders of the Standard Oil Company, Coe's wife had had a sophisticated education, wore couture clothing, and had traveled extensively in Europe. Her husband, the chairman of the board of an insurance company, in sharp contrast, had been born in England, the son of a cashier at an ironworks. The couple had met on a transatlantic crossing and had married in 1900. In 1911 they leased the Bryne mansion before purchasing it two years later.

The Blue Pool Garden, including the tea house, and the interior decoration of Coe Hall were Mai Coe's initiatives. The tea house was situated at the south end of the garden containing the reflecting pool, which was constructed on the site of the Byrnes' former tennis courts. Lowell had transformed a little garden house located to the west of the Blue Pool Garden, which had been there for some time. He had raised the building's height, added large textured bricks to its surface to match the Byrne house, put terra-cotta tiles on its roof, and added a fireplace, a chimney, and brick pergolas to either side of it. In one of the pergolas he had installed a period-style stone bench set with a lead relief sculpture.[2]

The interior of the building was put into Shinn's hands. In 1915 the painter created a pair of striking rococo-revival lunettes for it, one of which was positioned over Lowell's fireplace and the other on the facing wall over two small windows.[3] Executed in light-hearted evocation of Watteau and Fragonard, using pastel pinks, greens, and blues to reflect the colors of the Blue Pool, they were paintings of voluptuous lounging women, in 18th-century dress, surrounded by parrots and baskets of flowers. The colors used for the interior of the teahouse, including the light aqua of the latticework that covered its inner walls and the rose pink marble used for the fireplace, were led by those in the lunettes.

Records from Planting Fields report that the Tea House chairs were designed and hand-painted by Shinn. The gold-trimmed, blue velvet curtains were supplied by

View of the Blue Pool Garden from the Tea House, c. 1926. (Mattie Edwards Hewitt, courtesy Planting Fields Foundation Archive)

Interior of the Tea House, with a lunette and painted decoration by Everett Shinn, 1915. (Planting Fields Foundation Archive)

the New York architecture and decorating firm of Schleich and Smeraldi in November 1915 at a cost of $467. Led by John D. Smeraldi, a muralist and furniture designer, the firm designed the Marine Roof nightclub of the Hotel Bossert in Brooklyn, undertaken between 1909 and 1916, as well as interiors for the Ritz-Carlton Hotel in Atlantic City. The records also reveal that Shinn worked on the interior in April and May of 1915 (receiving payments of $500 and $300, most probably for the lunettes) and that he remodeled the Tea House in June, for a sum of $2,000.[4] The source of the statuary for the pool garden and some decorating in 1918 was the society hostess and decorator Mrs. Nathaniel Bowditch Potter (née Mary

Sargent, d. 1962), sister of the Coes' landscape architect Andrew Robeson Sargent.

Although de Wolfe was not mentioned by name, she was likely involved with Shinn in some capacity in the installation of the interior of the tea house and the purchase and fabrication of the items for it, as they had undertaken so many similar projects together over the years. It was de Wolfe, for example, who had engineered the future Ashcan school artist's early decorative work. In 1907, at de Wolfe's encouragement, he elaborately repainted the playwright Clyde Fitch's piano, a project for which Shinn became renowned, and she then commissioned him to work with her on the Colony Club, arranging for him to see painted French antiques in the Hewitt sisters' collection that might act as inspiration. She also had hired Shinn to decorate some furniture and contribute a panel for an unidentified house in Westbury, New York. De Wolfe could have overseen the installation of the tea house's latticework, which covered the walls of the interior right up into the roof area, as well as the positioning of the lunettes and of a mirror over the mantelpiece. Possibly she supervised the painting by Shinn of the cane-back chairs and the glass-topped hexagonal table that was introduced into

Everett Shinn lunette in the Tea House, c. 1915. (Planting Fields Foundation Archive)

Mai Coe's bathroom, with paintings by Everett Shinn, c. 1926. (Mattie Edwards Hewitt, courtesy Planting Fields Foundation Archive)

the interior in November. She also might have acquired the Oriental rug, or perhaps she oversaw the fabrication and installation of the lights, designed by Shinn to match the flower baskets in the paintings, which took the form of latticed metal baskets containing hand-painted metal flowers. The sterling Bronze Company was paid $1,008.10 for providing fixtures, most likely the metal baskets in question. The baskets of flowers painted on the chairs, sofa, and table harmonized with the paintings and the lights.

A few years later, Mai Coe also commissioned a number of exotic interiors within the main house. A breakfast room that had American-Western-inspired paintings featuring buffalos on its walls was created by Chanler in 1922—William Coe had a special interest in the West. Her own bedroom, in which Chanler painted more murals a year later, had a chinoiserie theme. A Louis XVI reception room was created by the decorating firm of Alavoine et cie, and there were a number of English-style rooms designed by Charles of London, including William Coe's bedroom, a great hall, a dining room, a family den, and two guest rooms.[5]

Shinn and de Wolfe may well have worked together on the creation of Mai Coe's bathroom–dressing room, which led from her Chanler-decorated bedroom. Its decor was intended to complement the interior of the tea house, which could be seen from the dressing room's windows. Here Shinn created seven painted panels, commissioned by Mai Coe in 1921; the best known of them later came to be called "Ladies on a Swing." Executed in a style similar to the lunettes in the tea house, these long, thin panels, which were framed and positioned around the room, were theatrical representations of woman dressed in 18th-century clothing and surrounded by drapery and flowers. De Wolfe's involvement in the project, however slight, can be authenticated by the existence of a May 21, 1920, letter to Coe from the architects, Walker and Gillette, confirming that they had paid de Wolfe $60.30 for "2 Venetian Hanging Baskets and 2 Glass Bowls" (similar to those sold in her showroom) that were used in the interior, the former as light fittings.[6]

With its dull-ivory walls and woodwork, the space had all the hallmarks of a de Wolfe private interior. It took its color cues, once again, from Shinn's paintings, pastel shades being combined with blue and gold, the latter used for the velvet curtains and for the canopies that Shinn painted onto the paneled cabinets situated on the west wall of the bathroom.[7] The violet marble sink had cabriole legs, and the shower boasted a violet marble base and gold-plated fixtures, tarnished for effect. The dressing table, which featured Shinn-painted floral swags on its drawers, had a protective glass cover, good lighting from a table lamp with a pleated shade, a three-part mirror at its rear, and a stool upholstered in needlepoint—typical of a de Wolfe dressing room. A final exotic touch was provided by the presence of six silver pedestals for a number of color-coordinated live cockatoos. As had so many other de Wolfe bathroom–dressing room interior schemes, Mai Coe's quarters combined modern equipment and conveniences—the shower in particular—with period furniture items and theatrical fantasy.

Mai Coe died in 1924 and therefore did not have long to enjoy the extravagant interior and garden that she had commissioned. The work that might have been undertaken by de Wolfe constituted only a fairly small component of this ambitious project. Nonetheless, the Planting Fields project exhibited a high level of continuity with de Wolfe's prewar work and demonstrates her continued relationship with Shinn in these years.

1921

Elisabeth Marbury Residence
13 Sutton Place
New York City

*A*fter her return to France in 1916 and increased involvement with war work, Elsie de Wolfe kept a distance from many projects that were passing through her New York office. She continued to be involved, however, with special commissions, particularly when they involved celebrities or friends.

The 10-year lease on the East 55th Street house de Wolfe created with Ogden Codman Jr. came to an end in 1920. Bessy Marbury had never really moved into the house that de Wolfe had created for both of them, and since the decorator had shifted her life abroad in recent years, the theatrical agent began looking for a home of her own. This belated declaration of independence happened around the same time that Anne Vanderbilt, following the death of her husband, William K. Vanderbilt, in July 1920, decided to sell her enormous Fifth Avenue mansion and move to a smaller, more manageable house. At this time Anne Morgan also left her quarters at her mother's home at 219 Madison Avenue. Marbury was the first to settle on Sutton Place as her new neighborhood, and by the end of 1921, all three women were ensconced in newly built or extensively remodeled houses there.

The growing commercialism of the fashionable areas of New York City was forcing middle- and upper-middle-class people living below 42nd Street to settle in relatively undiscovered areas. Marbury discovered one such neglected location in Sutton Place, a two-block

Opposite: Rear facade. (My Crystal Ball, 1923)

Elisabeth Marbury. (My Crystal Ball, *1923*)

stretch between 57th and 59th Streets on what was then Avenue A, in a largely industrial area on the banks of the East River. A developer had already bought a group of 18 houses in the area and was selling them. Marbury purchased 13 Sutton Place and hired Mott B. Schmidt, a young architect, to oversee an architectural modification that would cost a reported $20,000.[1] De Wolfe was asked to create the interiors.

Born in Middletown, New York, and raised in Brooklyn, Schmidt had trained at Pratt Institute of Technology between 1904 and 1906, and he embraced the fashionable Beaux Arts approach to architectural design. Following a two-year tour of Europe, he

returned to New York to learn his trade.[2] In 1912 he established an architectural practice and created, among other buildings, two town houses on Monroe Place in Brooklyn. It has been speculated that de Wolfe used the buildings as a decorator's show house, though no documentary evidence to confirm this has been found. It seems probable that de Wolfe first became aware of Schmidt's work in 1915 when he designed a shop for one of her competitors, the decorator Alice M. Swift, at 11 East 55th Street, just doors down from de Wolfe and Marbury's own house.[3] By 1921, when de Wolfe and Schmidt frequently began working together, the architect was not an unknown quantity. He had remodeled two houses for Colony Club member Pauline Emmet and her husband, Greville, and had seen his work published in *Architecture* and *Architectural Record*. Schmidt's fiancée, Elena Bachman, also worked in de Wolfe's office. However their paths crossed, decorator and architect ended up working together on Marbury's Sutton Place renovation and, subsequently, on the grander houses of Anne Morgan and Anne Vanderbilt.

The migration of these wealthy women to Sutton Place led equally adventuresome members of society to follow, and before long they had been joined by prominent ladies like Margaret Cammann and Margaret Olcott. *Gossip* magazine was quick to print insinuating comments about what it mistakenly saw as an all-female community, conveniently failing to note that among Sutton Place's new residents were professional men with families and that several of the Social Register ladies—among them, Cammann, wife of a banker, and Olcott, married to a popular tenor—arrived with equally prominent husbands in tow.[4] Schmidt was remodeling a house for himself just a block away on East 57th Street, so he was already familiar with the area and a participant in its up-and-coming status.[5]

Schmidt's first completed Sutton Place commission was Marbury's little three-story house, an old brownstone that she purchased in late 1920 and which he sensitively modified to "maximize the use of its limited space."[5] On the first floor, Schmidt placed the kitchen and butler's pantry at the front of the house, adjacent to the hall and curving staircase. The dining room occupied the full width of the back of the house, where it opened to a terrace overlooking the river and a common garden that would come to be shared by the neighboring homes. Occupying the full width of the house at the front on the second floor was a sitting room with charming bow windows, fitted with windowsill gardens of moss and potted plants. This served as de Wolfe's reception room when she was in New York. Marbury's library occupied the river side of the house.[6] The third floor was dedicated to two small bedrooms, de Wolfe's hung with antique Chinese paintings on glass, Marbury's furnished with the same white-enameled French furniture she had used at East 17th Street and East 55th Street. Servants' quarters were relegated to the attic.

The interior decors of the Marbury, Morgan, and Vanderbilt houses, created by de Wolfe to suit the personalities of their inhabitants, were highly individual. In designing interior schemes for three strong women who needed their homes to provide the hospitality and work spaces required by their positions, the decorator used her skills to paint livable evocations of her friends' characters.

For the 65-year-old Marbury, doyenne of the theater, literary, and political worlds, de Wolfe created a fairly conservative, relaxed, yet refined home. In the library, the room in which an increasingly ill and obese Marbury ended up spending most of her time in the last dozen years of her life, the decorator introduced a voluminous rolled-arm sofa covered in highly

glazed dark green chintz. The walls were lined with modest fitted bookshelves, and slipper chairs were upholstered in tone-on-tone flowered damask. The rest of the room combined equally familiar components: Chinese jar table lamps with pleated and lightly fringed silk shades, a large, plain mirror above the sofa to enlarge the space, a Chinese carpet, double-branched wall sconces sparkling with crystal lusters, and patterned chintz curtains and cushions. Marbury's bronze-mounted mahogany desk was a 19th-century reproduction of a Louis XVI antique, while her desk chair was either an American Colonial-style Windsor

Front entrance. (Collection of The New-York Historical Society)

Second-floor landing, with Marbury's library beyond. (Collection of The New-York Historical Society)

chair or a large Georgian armchair (contemporary photographs show both combinations). Through the addition of multitudes of framed photographs of friends and family hanging on the walls and hundreds of books—many antique, and others were signed first editions and presentation copies from the authors— the room quickly became a statement of the social connections and intellectual life of the woman who lived there.

In sharp contrast to the cluttered library and the dark and cozy dining room—a present from de Wolfe, it had Charles II period paneling and Jacobean crewel-work curtains—the sitting room that de Wolfe created for herself across the hall from the library was all Old World elegance. The recesses of the Georgian pine paneling were fitted with antique floral wallpaper. A Louis XVI side chair that had been used in the East 17th Street house found its way here, as well as a small

Elisabeth Marbury's library. (Collection of The New-York Historical Society)

wood-and-porcelain Chinese screen like one in Anne Vanderbilt's drawing room; several Chinese paintings on glass hung above and near the fireplace. Leopard-spot and real leopard upholstery provided a novel touch, used on a pair of Louis XV–style side chairs (leopard-spot velvet) and a modern round hassock (real leopard skin). Inspired by 18th-century French interiors, which often incorporated fabrics with animal-skin motifs, the decorator had acquired a taste for exotic hides, real and

simulated. A further example of de Wolfe's interest in whimsical fabrics was her selection of a cotton printed with greyhounds or whippets to upholster an 18th-century-style armchair. Dramatic marbleized finishes for doorframes and baseboards constituted another interesting element of the decoration of Marbury's house. Though not necessarily a de Wolfe hallmark, the technique is evidence that the decorator was conscious of contemporary trends, since similarly marbleized

Elsie de Wolfe's sitting room. (Collection of The New-York Historical Society)

woodwork, influenced by a contemporary interest in 18th-century Venetian interiors, was adopted in the early 1920s by decorators like Ruby Ross Goodnow, Paul Chalfin, and others.

Thirteen Sutton Place proved the ideal environment for the aging, largely housebound Marbury. It acted as a memory bank: all the personal items— her books, textiles, photographs, Catholic devotional items, Bokhara rugs and Hamadan runners, a modern painting of a vase of anemones—that she had amassed over the years were at her fingertips.[7] Its thoughtful clutter, traditional sense of comfort, and lack of pretension were an artful reflection of Bessy Marbury's generous personality. When she died in 1933, the house and its contents were inherited by de Wolfe. She promptly opened it for public viewing, sold the contents at a two-day auction, and set sail for France.[8]

Fireplace in Elsie de Wolfe's sitting room. (Collection of The New-York Historical Society)

1921

Anne Vanderbilt Residence

1 Sutton Place
New York City

Though they had known each other casually since the 1880s, Anne Vanderbilt, the second wife of the industrialist William K. Vanderbilt (her third and richest husband) became a member of the de Wolfe–Marbury–Morgan group in the years immediately prior to World War I, thanks to a shared interest in social welfare.[1] She had participated in the Strand Theater Roof Garden project and had become attached to the three other women, especially Anne Morgan, with whom Vanderbilt was to maintain a close relationship until her death.[2]

After William K. Vanderbilt died in the summer of 1920, his elegant widow (née Anna Harriman, 1859–1940) sold the chateau-size family mansion at 660 Fifth Avenue and joined Bessy Marbury in the unprepossessing setting of Sutton Place.[3] She purchased 1 Sutton Place, a large corner building, in early 1921, for $50,000.[4] Like Marbury, she hired Mott B. Schmidt and Elsie de Wolfe to transform it. It quickly emerged, however, that Schmidt's challenge was not a question of modifying the existing house, but rather of demolishing it and building anew.

The replacement that Schmidt designed was a restrained 17th-century English Renaissance–style house that would cost $150,000. The architect's hallmark was inspired simplicity and historicist inspiration, and the entrance to the four-story house, which faced

*Opposite: Entrance hall staircase with Allyn Cox mural. (*The Practical Book of Decorative Wall Treatments, *by Nancy McClelland, 1926)*

Anne Harriman Vanderbilt, far right. (Barnard College Archives)

57th Street, was, according to Schmidt, inspired by "one of the beautiful doorways in King's Bench Walk, London, designed by Sir Christopher Wren."[5] Through his use of artfully stained cement and worn bricks recycled from the earlier 19th-century, three-bay-wide town house on the site, the architect cleverly managed to make the new structure look satisfyingly old, and critics admiringly commented on its evocation of historic houses in the Chelsea area of London.[6]

In the basement, Schmidt located the servants' hall, a storage area, and the services, which included vacuum cleaning machinery. The first floor was divided into a large dining room at the rear that opened to a small

terrace, a reception room at the front, a pantry, a coat-room, and a dressing room and bath. On the second floor, a long drawing room with three windows faced the river, and three windows of a bedroom and attached bath faced 57th Street. The third floor consisted of a maid's room at the front of the house, and at the back of the house, a large private suite for Vanderbilt, with a boudoir, a bathroom, five closets, and lingerie storage, plus a bedroom-bathroom suite for her maid. Vanderbilt's bedroom was on the fourth floor, at the end of a private spiral staircase, with a roof terrace overlooking the East River.

Given the thrice-widowed Vanderbilt's personal sophistication and comfortable fortune—her last

East 57th Street facade. (Architectural Forum, August 1924, courtesy Kingston University)

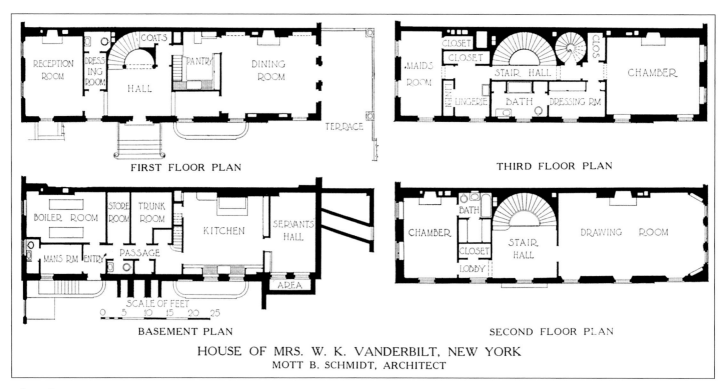

FIRST FLOOR PLAN

THIRD FLOOR PLAN

BASEMENT PLAN

SECOND FLOOR PLAN

HOUSE OF MRS. W. K. VANDERBILT, NEW YORK
MOTT B. SCHMIDT, ARCHITECT

Plan. (Architectural Forum, *August 1924, courtesy Kingston University)*

husband left her a trust fund of $8.25 million, to which she added $3 million from the sale of the family mansion—it is not surprising that her interiors were considerably more refined than Marbury's around the corner or even Anne Morgan's, which would be built next door. Befitting Vanderbilt's glamour, a dramatic chinoiserie theme ran through her rooms, reflecting de Wolfe's commitment to 18th-century decoration as well as her client's long interest in Chinese furniture and art objects.[7] In her country home on Long Island, Stepping Stones, Vanderbilt, perhaps at de Wolfe's instigation, installed an exquisite 18th-century octagonal room of paneling painted with rococo-style chinoiserie scenes of cranes, mandarins, and dragons.

Large, moody Dutch nautical-theme paintings filled the walls of the dining room, whose windows faced the busy East River. In the center of the Persian carpet on the room's black-and-white marble floor was a severe Chinese dining table banked with curvaceous antique Queen Anne chairs, their seats upholstered in old tapestry. Elsewhere in the room stood various pieces of 17th- and 18th-century English furniture, including a glass-front cabinet with knobby turned legs. The "little Georgian parlor" at the front of the house (it was labeled as a reception room on Schmidt's architectural plans) was walled with antique deal paneling that had been shipped from England, against which de Wolfe placed cheerful floral-pattern chintz curtains, a lacquered chinoiserie secretary, and three large ceramic chickens atop a bookcase the lower doors of which were painted with trompe l'oeil images of shelves and books. The result was homely yet elegant, a waiting room where guests could freshen up in a connecting dressing room and bath before being taken up to see the mistress of the house.

In the large drawing room—with paneling painted the brilliant blue of Vanderbilt's eyes—were a plump sofa and matching armchair covered in a Jacobean-style floral-print fabric, fitted corner cupboards for books, Queen Anne tripod side tables with lamps made from Chinese jars, and a French ceramic column. Wall sconces in the fanciful form of pagodas with small ceramic figurines picked up on the Oriental theme that ebbed and flowed throughout the house, as did Chinese statues, small Chinese folding screens of wood set with porcelain plaques, and a highly polished Chinese lacquer armoire. Noteworthy was de Wolfe's inspired treatment of the door between the blue drawing room and the yellow stair hall: on either side, two Italian paintings of storm-tossed landscapes—probably dating from the 18th century—were mounted like panels, one above the other. As an approving visitor recalled, the effect was "a joy to behold."[8] The yellow-hall side of the door was flanked by two paintings by Walter Gay, a talented expatriate American artist who specialized in depicting interiors and who was collected by several members of the de Wolfe–Marbury circle. One painting depicted a detail of what appears to be the drawing room at de Wolfe's house on East 17th Street, the other the octagonal chinoiserie room at Vanderbilt's former country house.

The most dramatic chinoiserie feature of Vanderbilt's house was the entrance hall, where de Wolfe had commissioned the artist Allyn Cox to create a fantastical mural for the plainly carpeted stairwell. Doubtless inspired by the presence of two Vanderbilt treasures—a pair of six-foot-tall wood-and-ceramic pagodas that were once part of the furnishings of the Royal Pavilion in Brighton—the artist painted the architecturally featureless stairwell with a dramatic trompe l'oeil image of a Chinese statue positioned in a bamboo-trimmed niche and surrounded by

Drawing of the entrance by Mott B. Schmidt. (Architectural Forum, *August 1924, courtesy Kingston University*)

flowering cherry trees and stands of feathery bamboo.[9] He also may have been responsible for the painting the raised paneling of the hall and an adjacent anteroom, which were decorated with romantic chinoiserie scenes of fishermen, scholars, ladies, and butterflies. The American decorator Nancy McClelland praised Cox's use of paint to create architectural and sculptural illusion. "Breaking into a wall is sometimes attended with considerable difficulties," she wrote of the Vanderbilt stairwell, "and it is pleasant to know that the surface may be left unbroken, while at the same time the desired effect may be obtained by simili-architecture, done with paint."[10]

*Dining room, looking toward the garden terrace. (*Architectural Forum, *August 1924, courtesy Kingston University)*

*Dining room leading to entrance hall. (*Architectural Forum, *August 1924, courtesy Kingston University)*

Chinoiserie corridor leading from entrance hall to dining room.
(Architectural Forum, *August 1924, courtesy Kingston University*)

"Little Georgian parlor." (Architectural Forum, August 1924, courtesy Kingston University)

Though Vanderbilt had numerous homes—including an estate in suburban Westchester County, a country house on Long Island, a town house in Paris, a horse farm in Normandy, and a villa in Cannes—I Sutton Place was the fulcrum of her life.[11] From there, she participated in philanthropic projects, among them her work with Anne Morgan on the development of the American Women's Association Clubhouse at 353 West 57th Street, a residential hotel for working women. It was an enormous undertaking, resulting in the fifth-largest hotel in the city, its 1,250 rooms housed in 27 stories of red brick.[12] Plagued by a heart condition, Vanderbilt died in 1940, of a stroke.

Upstairs in the private rooms, the theme of Far Eastern exotica continued, though reduced to mere accents. Vanderbilt's boudoir on the third floor, for example, was lighted by more pagoda sconces, and though the guest room on the second floor was the repository of gloomy Pilgrim-era antiques, on its mantel was gathered a flock of colorful Chinese ceramic birds. No photographs seem to exist of Vanderbilt's fourth-floor bedroom, whose riverfront terrace was next to Anne Morgan's own. Overall, the upstairs rooms combined the qualities of convenience and comfort with visual delight, the familiar vocabulary of de Wolfe's schemes for areas destined for sleeping and dressing.

Corner of the "little Georgian parlor." (Architectural Forum, August 1924, courtesy Kingston University)

*Drawing room. (*Architectural Forum, *August 1924, courtesy Kingston University)*

Antique door leading from the hall to dining room. (Architectural Forum, *August 1924, courtesy Kingston University*)

*Fireplace in Anne Vanderbilt's boudoir. (*Architectural Forum, *August 1924, courtesy Kingston University)*

*Second-floor guest room. (*Architectural Forum, *August 1924, courtesy Kingston University)*

Anne Morgan Residence

3 Sutton Place

New York City

As her closest friends began moving to Sutton Place, Anne Morgan decided to leave her mother's house on Madison Avenue and join the uptown migration. Initially she considered remodelling an existing Sutton Place property but instead acquired adjoining town houses—No. 3, next to Anne Vanderbilt's new house, and No. 5, owned by Emeline and Stephen Olin, Vanderbilt's sister and brother-in-law—and had them razed and replaced by a single new building designed by Mott B. Schmidt. The restrained Colonial revival red-brick facade borrowed features from two Philadelphia landmarks, the 1765 Samuel Powel house and the Benjamin Wister Morris house.[1]

As in the Marbury and Vanderbilt projects, Schmidt used the full width of Morgan's second floor to great spatial effect, placing a 38-foot-long drawing room across the front and a T-shaped library and reception room at the rear, with an elliptical stair threading through the center of the house. So Morgan and her guests could enjoy the communal garden and view of the bustling East River, Schmidt placed the dining room at the back of the first floor to access a terrace—as he did in Marbury and Vanderbilt's houses—and the kitchen at the street front. Bedroom suites and servants' quarters were on the third and fourth floors, and a small garden could be found on the flattened peak of the slate roof, enclosed by Chinese Chippendale-style railings; the basement contained elevator machinery, a refrigerating plant,

Opposite: Reception room. (Architectural Forum, *August 1924, courtesy Kingston University*)

Anne Morgan. (Collection of the Elsie de Wolfe Foundation)

an incinerator, and vacuum cleaner machinery. The entire project, including the purchase prices of the original houses, reportedly cost $300,000.[2]

Just as Schmidt revisited his successful maximizing of space in the Marbury and Vanderbilt houses here, so de Wolfe found inspiration in the chinoiserie theme that she had introduced into those houses. The focal point of Morgan's riverfront reception room on the second floor, for example, was an extravagant Chinese Chippendale gilt-wood mirror positioned above a Louis XV–style fireplace surround of white

marble inlaid with shaped panels of dark figured stone; the walls were lined with Chinese Export wallpaper hand-painted with exotic birds and butterflies flittering through groves of bamboo. As in the drawing room of de Wolfe's house on East 55th Street, sconces in the form of sprays of enameled flowers flanked the fireplace. Nearby stood a fine lacquered 18th-century secretary with misty mirrored doors and a Louis XVI lyre-back side chair. A Georgian chandelier, whose tiers of crystals arched up and down like a fountain, was suspended from the ceiling. In the fireplace itself was placed a pair of fanciful pagoda-shape andirons. Even Morgan's bathroom conformed to the theme, with an old chinoiserie cabinet adapted to create the washbasin. The banking heiress' dressing room was hung with antique Chinese processional wallpaper, which was supplied by Charles R. Gracie and Sons.[3]

The remainder of the house, however, had a rich but restrained Colonial simplicity in keeping with its American Georgian facade. A set of 18th-century English Chippendale furniture was in the dining room, which was paved with a diamond-patterned black, yellow, and white marble floor and anchored by a fireplace in the neoclassical style. Wall sconces and an early-19th-century family portrait over the mantel broadcast an atmosphere of austere ancestral elegance.

The library, adjoining the chinoiserie reception room, also had a strong 18th-century ambience. Its walls were sheathed with waxed pine paneling from an English Georgian room and were hung with reverse-painted Chinese glass paintings like those de Wolfe had at Villa Trianon and her apartment on Avenue d'Iéna. It was a contemplative but inviting space with bookcases recessed into the walls, dramatic fluted Ionic pilasters, and sumptuous fabrics: a Fortuny-like printed linen on the daybed, a chinoiserie brocade, and leafy tapestries on the comfortable

Front facade. (Architectural Forum, *August 1924, courtesy Kingston University*)

Rear facade. (Architectural Forum, *August 1924, courtesy Kingston University*)

Drawing of the garden entrance. (Architectural Forum, August 1924, courtesy Kingston University)

Garden entrance. (Architectural Forum, *August 1924, courtesy Kingston University*)

armchairs. At the foot of the daybed was a light fur blanket, probably chinchilla, recalling the "glorified and diminutive coverlet . . . lined with the soft long-haired white fur known as mountain tibet" that de Wolfe advocated as an elegant foot-warmer in *The House in Good Taste.*[4] Brass grilles were set into the doors of the bookcases, and double-arm sconces backed with large gilt-and-crystal stars were fixed to the paneling. Morgan's office upstairs was darkly paneled, too, though it was enlivened with emblems of the heiress' personality: framed photographs, a silver loving-cup trophy, and potted geraniums in the windows.

Facing Sutton Place on the third floor, the so-called west boudoir (likely Morgan's own) was a semi-recreation of the sitting room the heiress left behind at her former home on Madison Avenue. Identical double-arm wall sconces, probably brought from her previous residence, illuminated its plainly painted walls. Recessed glass-front cupboards like those at 219 Madison Avenue were painted with chinoiserie scenes inside and housed a few antique covered porcelain bowls. A wing chair was covered with the same dramatic black-and-white cut velvet that had been used in Morgan's former sitting room. It was a comfortable, unpretentious space that represented de Wolfe's art at its most subtle, and as

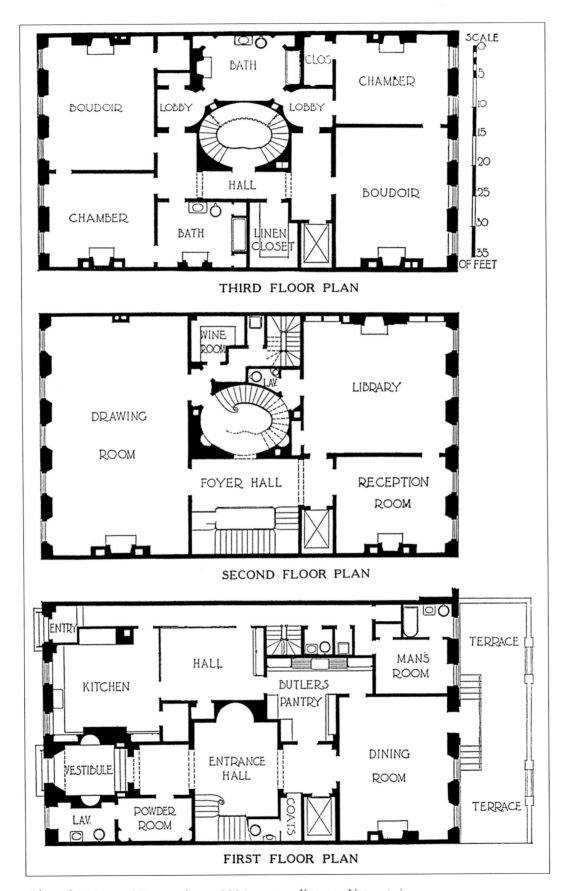

SCALE

5
10
15
20
25
30
35
OF FEET

THIRD FLOOR PLAN

BATH CLOS CHAMBER
BOUDOIR LOBBY LOBBY
CHAMBER HALL BOUDOIR
BATH LINEN CLOSET

SECOND FLOOR PLAN

WINE ROOM
LAV.
LIBRARY
DRAWING ROOM
FOYER HALL RECEPTION ROOM

FIRST FLOOR PLAN

ENTRY
HALL MAN'S ROOM TERRACE
KITCHEN BUTLERS PANTRY
VESTIBULE ENTRANCE HALL DINING ROOM
LAV. POWDER ROOM COATS TERRACE

Plans. (Architectural Forum, *August 1924, courtesy Kingston University*)

Dining room. (Architectural Forum, *August 1924, courtesy Kingston University*)

a character study it accurately reflected Morgan's modesty, unflappable calm, and good taste.

Another de Wolfe touch could be seen in the faux-marble-painted entrance hall of the house, with prim wood stools and chairs upholstered in racy leopard-spot velvet. The same print, this time executed in chintz, was used for curtains in the lavatory on the ground floor.

In the years following World War I, Anne Morgan continued to pursue social causes on both sides of the Atlantic, including the rehabilitation of northeastern France and the spearheading of the American Women's

Association's clubhouse project with Anne Vanderbilt.[5] The quietude of Sutton Place provided a convenient refuge when she found herself in town.[6]

Like the Vanderbilt and Marbury residences, 3 Sutton Place was not designed for a young woman, hence its relative aesthetic gravity and lack of stylistic novelty. In fact, excepting a few vibrant elements— including Allyn Cox's extravagant chinoiserie murals for Anne Vanderbilt and splashes of leopard-spot patterns in Marbury and Morgan's houses—numbers 1, 3, and 13 Sutton Place bore the stamp of conservative, upper-crust ease.

Library. (Architectural Forum, *August 1924, courtesy Kingston University*)

Corner in the library. (Architectural Forum, *August 1924, courtesy Kingston University*)

Anne Morgan's office. (Architectural Forum, *August 1924, courtesy Kingston University*)

*West boudoir. (*Architectural Forum, *August 1924, courtesy Kingston University)*

Condé Nast Apartment
1040 Park Avenue
New York City

Throughout her long career, Elsie de Wolfe decorated only a handful of interiors for which the dominant client was a man. Whether a bachelor like James Deering, a widower like Henry Adams, a divorcé like Condé Nast, or married men like Paul-Louis Weiller, Henry Clay Frick, and J. Pierpont Morgan—men whose finely honed tastes and domineering personalities effectively thrust their wives, who traditionally would have been de Wolfe's primary contacts, to the decorative sidelines—they had one characteristic in common: refinement.

Condé Nast (1874–1942) was probably the most refined and tasteful of all of de Wolfe's male clients. He has been described as "urbane, socially irreproachable, devoted to party-giving and informed on art, the theatre, decoration, sports and finance."[1]

De Wolfe's relationship with Nast was already longstanding by the time she came to create the interiors for his apartment. They first came into contact with each other around the time Nast bought *Vogue* in 1909, when de Wolfe was already well established in her decorating career. She was heavily dependent on the taste-conscious media for her professional advancement, and her presence in magazines served to enhance her reputation as a star decorator offering her services to the rich and famous. It was a dependency that lasted throughout her life.

Before Condé Nast bought *Vogue*, it had been owned by Arthur Turnure, who ran it as a New York–based magazine showing out-of-town women what was available in the best dress

Opposite: Mirrored window wall of the drawing room, c. 1925. (Pierre Brissaud, the Elsie de Wolfe Foundation)

Elsie de Wolfe in the early 1920s.
(Collection of the Elsie de Wolfe Foundation)

Company, a firm that produced home dressmaking patterns.[2] There, according to Edna Woolman Chase, one of *Vogue's* editors-in-chief in the first half of the 20th century, he discovered that "it is the women of this country who do the buying."[3] When Nast bought *Vogue* in 1909, he took to it a new philosophy that did not involve looking for large circulation numbers but that aimed, rather, to develop a publication "authoritative in matters of taste, or dress, or whatever it dealt with." He wanted it to appeal to people who had money but "whose criterion was taste rather than mass popularity."[4]

De Wolfe first appeared in *Vogue* in 1911, outfitted for a fancy dress party as an 18th-century shepherdess. She had already appeared in the popular press many times before, thanks to Elisabeth Marbury's highly effective agency, depicted as a fashionably dressed actress complete with her dogs and photographed against the backdrop of her stylish home on East 17th Street. Her early appearances in publications such as *Broadway Magazine* and *New York Journal* were aimed at a narrow audience. Nast's ambitions for *Vogue* coincided perfectly with de Wolfe's aspirations—and Marbury's for her. For his part, publicizing the famous decorator to the stars of American high society provided Nast with a model of taste lived out to the limits, and he was to exploit that example many times in the future.

De Wolfe appeared frequently in *Vogue* in the years after 1911. In 1914, for example, the magazine ran a feature on her house in Versailles, and in 1915, when she was celebrating her 50th birthday, Nast published a stylish portrait of her. Photographed in profile, she was wearing a felt hat, white gloves, and a choker necklace. "For travelling and sport wear," the caption read, "there seems to be nothing so smart this season as the hat of French felt—light or dark to suit

shops. When Turnure died in 1906, the magazine managed to survive for the next three years without a publisher, but Nast's subsequent ownership took it into a new era. Born in Missouri, Nast had studied law at Washington University in St. Louis but had decided not to go into legal practice. Instead he began his working life in a small printing plant, and quickly he moved upward to a job as advertising manager at *Collier's* in New York. Highly successful there, he went on to a senior position at the Home Pattern

Drawing room, c. 1924–25. (Collection of The New-York Historical Society)

the occasion," indicating that de Wolfe was still seen as a trendsetter as she moved into her middle age.[5] Indeed, pictures of de Wolfe in fashionable clothing continued to appear in *Vogue* through the 1920s and 1930s; her ability to be at the forefront of couture did not diminish as she grew older.

When Nast bought a magazine called *Dress and Vanity Fair* (which quickly became simply *Vanity Fair* in

1913), de Wolfe began appearing in its pages as well.[6] His purchase of *House and Garden* followed a couple of years later, promoting de Wolfe and her work many times during the subsequent decades.

Nast's magazines also connected de Wolfe with other people who were to play important roles in her life in the interwar years, among them John McMullin, a *Vogue* journalist who became a close companion to the decorator, and Main Bocher, a magazine editor who moved to Paris and established himself as Mainbocher, one of the 20th century's top fashion designers.

The spare Francophile reception room of a New York apartment occupied by Nast soon after his purchase of *House and Garden* and illustrated in the November 1915 issue of *The Decorative Furnisher* might have been decorated by de Wolfe. The space displayed a number of de Wolfe hallmarks of the period, among them white, painted Louis XV bergères dressed in pale damask and lightweight cane-seated side chairs. The publisher lived in that apartment with his first wife, Clarisse Coudert, and their young children, Natica and Charles. In the early 1920s, following the couple's divorce, Nast moved into an apartment at 1040 Park Avenue in New York. This time he hired de Wolfe to create some of the most stunning interiors of his life and her career.

In August 1928, Nast devoted several pages of *Vogue* to de Wolfe's designs for his Park Avenue duplex penthouse. *Vogue* had gone from strength to strength in the years following World War I, and Nast had become a very wealthy man. In 1921, he had bought a new printing establishment in Greenwich, Connecticut, and had commissioned Guy Lowell—the designer of the tea house at Planting Fields, the estate of de Wolfe's client Mai Coe—to lay out the gardens. Commenting on the large amount of money he had been willing to invest in what was little more than a factory, Edna Woolman Chase pointed out, "His taste was impeccable and he was willing to pay to gratify it."[7]

In spite of his extravagance, Nast did not own much private property. He rented a number of residences in the United States and the United Kingdom but only ever bought two—a house at Sands Point, Long Island, and his 5,100-square-foot Park Avenue apartment. The latter served as a home but also, more importantly, as a setting for his many parties and therefore as an advertisement for the man and his magazines. It was a 20-room duplex (the first of its kind to be popularized) in a building designed by Delano & Aldrich, the society architects whose work included the second home of the Colony Club, also on Park Avenue. Nast lived and entertained in the Park Avenue residence for 18 years. His first party, held on January 18, 1925, celebrated the inauguration of the apartment and de Wolfe's decorations; another fabled party was held for Charles Lindbergh after his historic flight, and yet another was organized for George Gershwin after the opening of his famous musical *Porgy and Bess*. The Gershwin fête involved up to ten days' work on the part of Nast's long-term secretaries.[8] Chase described Nast's organization of his parties as very fastidious.

Although the fashions depicted in *Vogue* were always up-to-the-minute, Nast chose more conventional, historically inspired styles for his own interiors. As was always the case in de Wolfe's projects, however, there were several modern twists.

The 14th-floor section of the apartment at 1040 Park Avenue was devoted to Nast's private quarters. The drawing room was decorated in the familiar French style typical of much of de Wolfe's work. It featured a mantelpiece of dark marble topped by a mirror set into wood paneling, graced by a neoclassical bust of a female figure and flanked by wall sconces. Louis XV side chairs, upholstered in pale green floral-patterned damask, and a sofa were arranged in conversation groups around tall, elegant 18th-century French side tables. The floral curtains were made of green damask panels hung over undercurtains of blue taffeta. A black lacquered eightfold chinoiserie screen, formerly owned by a Duke of Beaufort, and an elaborate glass chandelier completed the sense of opulence and refinement that defined the space, which was made to look even

Ballroom, c. 1924–25. (Courtesy Condé Nast)

bigger through the inclusion of full-length mirrors inserted between the windows.[9] Recalling the drawing room in de Wolfe's East 55th Street house to some extent, Nast's version was grander, fancier, and more formal. The colors, however, were familiar elements in de Wolfe's oeuvre: blue-green walls and some gold highlights, either painted or actually gilt, on the cornice. A large Savonnerie rug of gray, rose, and green covered the parquet floor.

The dining room was equally formal and was finished in gray, echoing de Wolfe's earlier scheme for her own dining rooms at East 17th Street and East 55th Street. The cool, pearly color was not the only example of de Wolfe revisiting her popular past. According to Ruby Ross Wood—the ghostwriter of *The House in Good Taste* and later a top Manhattan decorator in her own right—who attended a party held in the apartment in 1928, de Wolfe's beloved Monnoyer grisailles were mounted there.[10] Nancy McClelland found the decoration of the dining room to be particularly effective, praising its "general coolness and restraint" and pointing out with approval that the applied panel moldings of the room were actually executed in trompe l'oeil.[11]

Even grander and more dramatic than these two living spaces, however, was the large ballroom, or salon,

Chinese Chippendale mirror in the ballroom, c. 1924.
(Pierre Brissaud, the Elsie de Wolfe Foundation)

which opened out onto a roof terrace that had been glassed over with a 75-foot-long conservatory designed by Delano & Aldrich. The walls of the ballroom, which was extended in 1926, were covered with a theatrical 18th-century Chien Lung wallpaper that depicted flowers and birds in brilliant shades of pink and blue. The wallpaper had been found in the attic at Welbeck Abbey, the seat of the dukes of Portland in Nottinghamshire, and was later used in the ballroom at Beau Desert, the Welsh estate of de Wolfe's old mentor Minna, Marchioness of Anglesey. Nast and de Wolfe clearly relished its noble provenance.

De Wolfe amplified the chinoiserie splendor of the wallpaper in the ballroom's furnishings. A Chinese Chippendale mirror was suspended over the mantelpiece situated at one end of this vast room, and the draped curtains had Chinese-style pagoda pelmets, completing the oriental splendor of the space. Ruby Ross Wood called it a "fine room" but criticized the window dressing as "pink sill curtains under too grandiose valance boards of bad gilt," clearly finding the overall effect excessively ostentatious and the gilding too bright and new.[12] During parties, the ballroom's curtains were dramatically parted to reveal bouquets of flowers placed on the tables of the roof terrace and the festive twinkle of strands of electric Christmas-tree lights with crystal drops. Wood was equally disparaging about the library, a room located at the end of the salon. She didn't like the imitation walnut paneling, nor, worst of all in her eyes, the "horrible leopard-skin chintz" used for the undercurtains. For her, these features represented "Elsie de Wolfe in her dotage." She coveted, nonetheless, a small, walnut-framed, 18th-century needlework sofa with zigzag motifs, which was in the same room.[13]

De Wolfe's former protégée was not alone in finding some aspects of the interior decor of 1040

Park Avenue unacceptable. Nast's daughter Natica, a young woman by that time, who also lived in the apartment, objected to an 18th-century dressing table that de Wolfe had bought for her room. Edna Woolman Chase claimed that de Wolfe's intentions for the room included "mirrored cornices, eggshell taffeta curtains," and "fruit-wood bergeres in petit point or toile de Jouy."[14] Natica Nast had simpler taste and wanted a practical dressing table with "lots of drawers and a triple mirror."[15] De Wolfe is claimed to have protested, "That dressing table came out of Versailles and it cost ten thousand dollars. If it was good enough for Marie Antoinette, it's good enough for you."[16] A clear generational shift in taste was being played out, de Wolfe's pre-1914 decorating language having a limited appeal for a younger generation.

There were enough admiring clients left, however. A comment by Chase made in her 1954 book about her life at *Vogue* showed that there was still an enormous amount of respect for de Wolfe's work at the time of her decoration of the Park Avenue apartment, even though the decorator's life was becoming increasingly focused on social pursuits. "When you were in a room de Wolfe has decorated," the editor-in-chief of *Vogue* explained, "you were at ease. The lights were well placed for reading and the chairs were comfortable. In her guest-rooms the beds were first-rate, there was a place where you could conveniently remove your shoes and stockings, there was always a full-length mirror, and the lights of the dressing table were intelligently arranged . . . She might sometimes be fancy. She was never foolish."[17]

The Nast interiors were, without doubt, among the fanciest and most flamboyant that de Wolfe was to create in her entire career. As in all her work, however, she also created a series of rooms that performed a specific, if rarefied, function. The glamour of the decor was linked, undoubtedly, to its purpose—to cement

Terrace leading to the ballroom, c. 1924–25.
(Collection of The New-York Historical Society)

Nast's position as the taste-conscious publisher of the world's most stylish magazines and, by extension, as an arbiter of international chic. Although 1040 Park Avenue was a home, its private rooms were hidden, and its fame was based on its role as a background for elegant parties attended by famous people. As such, following de Wolfe's own decorating philosophy, it may not have been simple, but it was eminently suitable.

Cash-strapped by the 1930s, Nast frequently rented out the apartment furnished, before dying in 1942. His funeral was held in the drawing room. Its contents were sold at auction, and the apartment later was sold and cut up into smaller units.

The library in the Condé Nast apartment, c. 1924–25. (Courtesy Condé Nast)

A private sitting room, c. 1924–25. (Collection of The New-York Historical Society)

circa *1920–28*

Nell Pruyn Cunningham Residence

103 Warren Street

Glens Falls, New York

Throughout the 1920s, a regular customer at Elsie de Wolfe Inc. was Nell Pruyn Cunningham, who was furnishing her home in Glens Falls, a prosperous lumber town on the Hudson River near Albany. Although de Wolfe probably was not directly involved in the Glens Falls project nor in the decoration of Cunningham's summer cottage on Lake George in the Adirondacks, the extensive correspondence between Cunningham and the studio provides an insight into the way de Wolfe's firm operated and how its staff perpetuated the hallmarks of de Wolfe's prewar traditionalism.

Independently wealthy, Nellie Knickerbacker Pruyn (1875–1962) was the youngest daughter of Samuel Pruyn, a co-owner of Finch–Pruyn, a paper mill he founded with lumber merchant Jeremiah W. Finch. Her eldest sister, Charlotte (1867–1963), married a Boston lawyer, Louis Fiske Hyde, in 1901 and six years later returned with him to Glens Falls. Soon after, Charlotte, the then-unmarried Nellie (known as Nell), and their sister Mary Eliza Hoopes (1870–1951) decided to erect adjoining houses on the Hudson, alongside the mill that was the source of their fortunes. Henry Forbes Bigelow of the Boston architecture firm Bigelow and Wadsworth designed the houses, which were completed by 1912.

The Hydes' home was the most splendid of the stucco-clad trio, a Florentine Renaissance palazzo that was filled with an impressive collection of art and antiques.[1] The

Opposite: The living room–library, 1952. (The Hyde Collection Archives, Glens Falls, NY)

Nell Pruyn Cunningham.
(The Hyde Collection Archives, Glens Falls, NY)

home of Mary Eliza Hoopes and her engineer husband, Maurice, was Colonial revival, while Nell's was unclassifiably picturesque, with a Spanish-style central courtyard at its heart and a shaped Flemish-style gable dominating the roofline in the manner of Cape Dutch houses in South Africa. Pruyn's correspondence with the de Wolfe studio began shortly after architect Charles Adam Platt added a service wing to the house in 1918–19.

The Hydes also had dealings with Elsie de Wolfe Inc. Two small tapestry-covered 18th-century French armchairs, signed Jacob, were purchased by the Hydes for $1,000 in December 1920.[2] Of the sisters, however, Nell was the firm's primary client, both before and after her 1924 marriage to Dr. Thomas Cunningham, a physician.

Between 1920 and 1928, Nell frequently shopped at Elsie de Wolfe Inc. and was in close contact with the studio's employees, judging by the amount of letters sent between Glens Falls and the de Wolfe studio, located at first at 2 West 47th Street and, from 1921 onward, at 677 Fifth Avenue. None of the letters actually was signed by de Wolfe. Some were written on her behalf by Josephine Kneissel, who had a financial role in the office. One 1924 letter was signed by Blanche Judge, who described herself as manager of the de Wolfe studio.[3] The majority of the correspondence was conducted by Elena Bachman or H. Joan Hofford, both of whom had decorating responsibilities within the firm.[4]

Bachman (d. 1955) was an especially active participant in the Glens Falls project. "I had a very nice time the other day with you and hope to see you again

Courtyard. (The Hyde Collection Archives, Glens Falls, NY)

Cunningham house with Charles Platt addition of 1918 at left. (The Hyde Collection Archives, Glens Falls, NY)

very soon," she wrote Nell Pruyn in 1921, indicating that she already had or anticipated a major role in the client-studio relationship.[5] She continued to correspond with Pruyn, describing the sale of a pink sofa, a rug, and two chairs, all of which had been sent to Glens Falls earlier for approval but which had been rejected. She also asked about fabric requirements for the Lake George cottage.[6] By October 1923, however, Hofford had become the main signatory of letters to Nell, a circumstance that continued until at least 1928.

A later communication from Bachman—now known as Elena B. Schmidt; she had married the architect Mott B. Schmidt in June 1922—bore the address of the latter's newly formed decorating business. Presumably she continued to participate in Pruyn's interiors although she was no longer associated with de Wolfe.[7] A 1928 letter by Hofford showed that Nell Cunningham maintained a link with the de Wolfe studio, while another written the following year indicated that Schmidt also was working with the Hydes.[8]

The living room-cum-library of Cunningham's house was the destination for many items supplied by de Wolfe's staff. These included a 19th-century portrait of a young girl, a white marble mantel, a 19th-century Italian hand-painted majolica bowl, a Louis XV ormolu cartel clock, a Louis XV stool with cabriole legs, and a French Directoire side table. The footstool and the clock had been purchased the previous December, while the side table appeared on a bill dated February 15, 1921. The February bill also cited the purchase of "a pair of chintz curtains and valances bound with blue taffeta and trimmed with blue tassels, lined with satin (living room)" and a "Pair of blue green glazed chintz curtains for door (dining room) trimmed with old rose glazed chintz."[9]

Though de Wolfe probably had no direct input on Cunningham's décors, the decorator's hallmarks were fully present. The same ram's head wall sconces de Wolfe had employed in her East 55th Street bedroom, among other places, were installed here. Many purchases were sumptuous textiles intended for upholstery, cur-

Georges Jacob chairs purchased from the Elsie de Wolfe studio by Charlotte Pruyn Hyde in 1920. (The Hyde Collection Archives, Glens Falls, NY)

Ram's head wall sconce. (The Hyde Collection Archives, Glens Falls, NY)

tains, and cushions: herringbone linen, Persian chintz, antique tassels, blue-and-gold Italian damask, henna velvet, and silk gauze. The small windows that looked down into the courtyard were hung with curtains selected by Elena Schmidt in 1925 and lined with bluish silver-gray taffeta.[10] At the center of the courtyard was a fountain topped with another studio find, a gilded bronze figure by the American sculptor Janet Scudder.[11]

Cunningham clearly depended on the de Wolfe studio to create a sophisticated home for a mature woman of means whose provincial address belied her worldly heritage—her paternal grandmother, a Christian missionary, spent years in Shanghai and Yokohama.[12] In Glens Falls, Elsie de Wolfe Inc. perpetuated the aesthetic preferences that had been established by its founder in the prewar years and that likely had influenced Nell Cunningham's taste as a young woman. De Wolfe's early appreciation for French antiques, English chintz, and antique Continental textiles still determined the interiors her staff decorators offered and which many of her clients sought.

Courtyard showing the Janet Scudder sculpture on the fountain. (The Hyde Collection Archives, Glens Falls, NY)

Frances and Zalmon G. Simmons Jr. Residence

RAMBLESIDE

Greenwich, Connecticut

In the late 1920s, Elsie de Wolfe, now Lady Mendl, oversaw an impressive domestic setting for Frances Simmons (née Grant, 1882–1964) and her husband, Zalmon G. Simmons Jr. (1871–1934), the president of the Simmons Mattress Company. The family firm had been founded in Kenosha, Wisconsin, by Simmons Sr. (1828–1910) in 1870. Like so many of the clients de Wolfe had worked with earlier in the century, the younger Simmonses were second-generation *nouveaux riches* who had set up housekeeping in Greenwich, a choice East Coast enclave known for long-established family money and Anglo-American refinement. They likely were particularly concerned about presenting themselves and their fortune in the most socially effective light, which meant building a traditional family house outfitted with impeccable interiors. Hiring de Wolfe, however, was not a case of simply approaching a star decorator and basking in reflected glory. The well-traveled Simmonses, as de Wolfe's biographer, Jane S. Smith, explained, were frequent visitors to Villa Trianon in Versailles, hence were relatively good friends of the decorator and familiar with her work on a firsthand basis.[1]

Zalmon Simmons Jr. began his ascent in the business world as a manager in the family factory, which manufactured brass and steel beds, wire mattresses, spring beds, folding chairs, and sofas. On the death of his father, he became president of the company, a position he held

Living room. (After All, 1935)

Elsie de Wolfe in the mid-1920s.
(Collection of the Elsie de Wolfe Foundation)

for 22 years. So successful was he at steering the firm's finances and cementing its reputation as the industry leader through innovative products and advertising that in 1923 he was able to relocate its offices to New York. Three years later, he launched the product most associated with the Simmons name: Beautyrest, a coil-spring mattress that revolutionized the bedding industry.

Considering Simmons' commitment to forward-thinking design, Elsie de Wolfe might seem a curious choice to oversee the interiors of his house. The mattress king, for example, employed the well-known industrial designer Norman Bel Geddes to modernize

his range of beds in the late 1920s. *Horizons,* the book Bel Geddes published in 1932 to promote his futuristic approach to design, contained an illustration of the undecorated all-steel beds he had created for Simmons, a curious reminder of the plain metal bed that de Wolfe designed, patented, and used at the Colony Club. Produced in 1928 and 1929, these brave new creations marked the manufacturer's increasing commitment to the aesthetics of modernity.[2] By handing over their home to de Wolfe, however, Frances and Zalmon Simmons made it clear that they preferred to live and entertain within the boundaries of conventional plutocratic good taste. The dislocation between Simmons' choice of style for his mass-market products and for his private world emphasized the fact that although consumers on every economic level would accept modern design in machine-made products, in domestic interiors they preferred safety and stylistic continuity. As far as Simmons and other new-money households were concerned, antique European furniture and historicist architecture were foolproof statements of real or imagined high social status. Still, the Simmonses—or more likely Frances, who was only in her mid-40s when de Wolfe began working on Rambleside—were not immune to the latest trends. Through the efforts of de Wolfe, the couple agreed to a few of the self-consciously glamorous touches that had crept into the decorator's oeuvre over the past decade.

In 1923 Simmons moved his offices from Kenosha to New York City and bought a 68-acre estate in nearby Greenwich from ship merchant Gustav Schwab, Jr.[3] He continued to purchase additional parcels until 1929, by which time he had acquired 116 acres in total. The recently built Colonial-style mansion on the property was drastically remodeled by architect Eric Kebbon in the style of a vernacular English country house.[4] Called Rambleside, it became a 25-room structure with a white-painted brick exterior, rustic stone window surrounds, a picturesque, multi-gabled roofline, and a Regency-style entrance porch supported by lacy black wrought iron and flanked by stone statues of 18th-century French rustics. Simmons gave two sections of the sprawling property to his sons, and on the land he kept for himself, two society landscape architects—Ferruccio Vitale, the award-winning dean of American gardening, and Isabella Pembleton, an alumna of the Lowthorpe School of Landscape Architecture for Women in Groton, Massachusetts—planted wild and formal areas and reinforced its landed-gentry air by digging an ornamental eight-acre lake.[5] Five acres of Rambleside were devoted solely to the cultivation of Frances Simmons' prize irises.

De Wolfe's interiors for the Simmonses skillfully addressed the couple's dual activities of everyday living and gala entertaining: dances, ladies' luncheons, garden parties, and weddings. The family lived at Rambleside year-round and required an all-purpose environment that was not only gracious but up-to-date. For the entrance hall, for instance, de Wolfe designed a floor of shining black marble inlaid with glittering strips of copper, surely a surprise after the fanlighted front door opened. Tall Oriental folding screens contributed to the modish drama of this introductory space.

To the left of the hall was the study, or so-called wood room, paneled with pine removed from an old house in the Bloomsbury area of London.[6] Leaving the hall from the right led the visitor through the stair hall and the music room into the library. A massive walnut-paneled space divided into two sections by square fluted columns, it had a teak floor and a black marble fireplace surround. Above the fireplace a painting of an 18th-century English gentleman in a giltwood frame gazed over an Aubusson-style carpet. Pilgrim-style

gateleg tables were set with brass bowls filled with flowers—one held an Art Deco figurine of an slender nymph—and modern Knole sofas were upholstered in flowered damask.

The entrance hall also led to the drawing room and the dining room beyond. Again paneled with wood and appointed with flowered chintz that brought Vitale and Pendleton's gardens indoors, the drawing room recalled that of any venerable English country house, which was surely one of de Wolfe's ploys to give the Simmons fortune, barely 50 years old, dynastic gloss. The walls of the dining room were covered with a fantastically overscaled Chinese wallpaper, perhaps a reproduction, a de Wolfe hallmark of the period as evidenced by similar papers used in the homes of Anne Morgan and Condé Nast. Chippendale-style chairs pulled up to a double-pedestal table—then as now a prerequisite of any interior inspired by traditional English decoration—completed the aristocratic effect. Flanking the curtained doorway to the glassed-in breakfast porch were mirrored niches the shelves of which were clustered with small artificial trees, likely Chinese or Japanese and made of semiprecious stones.

The remainder of the ground floor was dedicated to servants' quarters—an interesting location, considering that country-house convention relegated servants to cramped rooms in the eaves or distant wings—while one room was reserved for flower arranging. The second floor consisted of bedroom suites and bedrooms for family, guests, and staff. The master suite was made up of a bedroom, a sitting room, and two separate dressing rooms with baths; an adjacent glass-enclosed sleeping porch was used on warm evenings. More bedrooms were located on the third floor, which also contained a billiard room and a sunny playroom, presumably for the children of the Simmonses' sons, Zalmon III and Grant, who lived nearby.[7]

Front entrance, c. 1929. (Avery Architectural and Fine Arts Library, Columbia University)

Rear facade, with glassed-in breakfast porch. (Avery Architectural and Fine Arts Library, Columbia University)

Regency-style front porch, c. 1929. (Avery Architectural and Fine Arts Library, Columbia University)

Dining room. (After All, 1935)

The warm, monied atmosphere that de Wolfe brought to Rambleside—offset by more modern touches, such as the chic entrance hall—was aimed to reflect the gracious living to which the Simmons family aspired. Like Henry Clay Frick before him, however, Zalmon Simmons Jr. died only a few years after his house was completed. Four years later, in 1938, Frances Simmons sold the main house, the guest cottage, and 10½ acres of land to industrialist George Skakel, the father of Ethel Kennedy.

1929–30

Elsie de Wolfe Residence
10 Avenue d'Iéna
Paris

lsie de Wolfe's private life was dramatically transformed in the 1920s when she became Lady Mendl.

Though her union with Sir Charles Mendl, a press attaché to the British Embassy in Paris, was a *mariage blanc* between two friendly individuals with no romantic or physical attachments, this entrance into the lowest rung of the English aristocracy reinforced de Wolfe's distance from her New York brownstone origins. Marriage to a member of the diplomatic corps meant that she needed to enhance her role as a hostess, and she required a more appropriate base in Paris than her rue Leroux residence. Soon she settled on a spacious apartment in a mansion constructed in 1894 for Prince Roland Bonaparte by the architect Ernest Janty.[1]

Located on the top floor of this grandiose *hôtel particulier* near the Trocadero, the apartment also was intended to be a home for de Wolfe's *Vogue* journalist friend John McMullin and for the decorator's husband—although he retained his bachelor apartment. And she set about decorating her home with a sense of freedom and heightened appreciation of her new status. "Of the several homes in which I have lived," she wrote in her autobiography published three years later, "none has been so faithful a record of the person I am today as my apartment in the Avenue d'Iéna in Paris, where Charles and I live when in town."[2] Inevitably, the person

Opposite: Elsie de Wolfe seated in the large salon, 1938. (Cecil Beaton, courtesy The New York Public Library)

Elsie de Wolfe's bedroom, early 1930s.
(Collection of the Elsie de Wolfe Foundation)

de Wolfe was now representing differed from the one she had been trying to express in East 17th Street, at Villa Trianon, and in East 55th Street. More significantly, however, the Paris apartment was the only dwelling that she had created up until that moment in which she planned to be the sole female inhabitant.

De Wolfe still stood by the uncompromising words she had written in *The House in Good Taste* back in 1913: "It is the personality of the mistress that the home expresses. Men are forever guests in our homes, no matter how much happiness they may find there."[3] The woman de Wolfe set out to express through the

interior decoration of 10 Avenue d'Iéna was, as always, committed to the past and to the present. Rooms outfitted with antique furniture and 18th-century works of art were spiced with exotic materials, fanciful objets d'art of recent vintage, and an unsentimental approach to the practical aspects of life. "There I have blended the old that is good with the new that is pleasant to the eyes and touch," she explained.[4]

While the backward- and forward-looking aspects of de Wolfe's decorating approach had always coexisted, the growing influence of the Art Moderne interior, which was becoming increasingly visible in 1920s Paris and New York, had begun to affect her decorating strategies. Changes included the focused inclusion of dramatic animal skins—ocelot, leopard, zebra, chinchilla—as upholstery, along with large sheets of mirror, employed even more extensively than earlier in her career, and murals—neo-historicist under Everett Shinn, now whimsical by Marcel Vertès and Etienne Drian. These features had already been implemented in the postwar alterations to Villa Trianon, but the Avenue d'Iéna apartment was conceived as a gracious urban interior, far removed from the bucolic charm of Versailles.

Visitors to de Wolfe's apartment stepped out of a winding staircase into a vestibule at once soothing and strangely theatrical. A broad carpet of velvety brown wool edged with bands of black led like a runway to a massive black marble urn brimming with white flowers. Behind it hung a giltwood mirror mounted against a floor-to-ceiling curtain of brown velvet. Flanking the double doors to the apartment's entrance hall were Directoire tabourets of painted wood, upholstered with zebra hide. Neoclassical pomp against minimalist luxury, a touch of the veldt with Bonaparte chic: it was the new de Wolfe, coolly contemporary but still comfortingly recognizable. As a

Dining room. (After All, 1935)

Small salon. (After All, 1935)

magazine article about the interiors declared, "Throughout, old things have been used in the modern manner—a paradox that is extremely effective."[5]

Behind the doors, a perfectly round entrance hall was paneled with creamy boiserie punctuated with full-length niches—two mirrored and set with marble consoles and potted flowers, two arched and sheltering Louis XVI benches in pale blue satin. The traditional atmosphere was broken, however, by a discreet modernist intervention: a bowl-shaped metal and glass ceiling light with a stylized motif of leaping horses and riders.

The interiors of Avenue d'Iéna differed significantly from the "light, bright" spaces of de Wolfe's prewar years. The rooms had an unexpected sultriness, for example, in part thanks to de Wolfe's adoption of a

largely muted palette: subtly waxed woods in autumnal browns, cream-colored marble, and beige, with accents of ormolu, crystal, inky lacquer, and pale, smoky blue. In the Avenue d'Iéna apartment she seemed to be establishing an after-dinner atmosphere that lasted into the daytime. The result was a shadowy backdrop that highlighted the youthful appearance that de Wolfe maintained by surgical means.

Though not expressly modernist, the sepia palette of de Wolfe's apartment—the only truly bright space was her ivory bedroom and black, white, and mirrored bathroom—had a relationship to the beige color popularized by Paris' most celebrated designer of the time, Jean-Michel Frank. On the other hand, de Wolfe's careful use of faded gilt and

Elsie de Wolfe's bedroom. (Collection of the Elsie de Wolfe Foundation)

rock crystal mirrored the exuberant use of those mate-rials by José Maria Sert and Coco Chanel. But the dec-orator, who was aware of contemporary fashions, adopted the aesthetic of the moment and made it hers.

Instead of the personable clutter of Villa Trianon, de Wolfe edited the Iéna rooms down to spare arrange-ments of antique French furniture and select items of modern upholstery, set against warm wood—the 17th-century paneling and extraordinary *parquet de Versailles* in the main salon were taken from a château near Sarthe—or black-and-beige Oriental carpets.[6] Even the art de Wolfe chose to hang—largely red-chalk drawings, pastels, and sketches by Boucher, Watteau, Fragonard, Carmontelle, and other 18th-century favorites brought from Villa Trianon—displayed restrained colors.

Throughout this period, the decorator became identified with conspicuous connoisseurship through the adoption of extravagant bibelots, particularly crystal obelisks and miniature jade and crystal animals. Her embrace of these, rather than Giacometti sculptures and Neo-Romantic paintings, further served to distance her from the interiors du jour of her contemporaries.

These treasures—including a small 18th-century gold-and-diamond coach and a magnificent crystal ship in full sail—were frequently used as centerpieces on her dining table.[7] Ceiling-height Coromandel folding screens were another notable element of de Wolfe's newly rich decorating vocabulary. She stood one five-panel screen in each corner of her square dining room, effectively breaking up the room's boxy

*Elsie de Wolfe exercising in her bathroom, early 1930s.
(Collection of the Elsie de Wolfe Foundation)*

proportions while providing a darker, more dramatic counterpoint to the brightly painted Chinese Export wallpaper to which she had previously been devoted.

The most influential room at the Iéna apartment, however, was de Wolfe's bathroom. Launching a major trend in treating bathrooms as living spaces, the decorator combined sitting room, dressing room, boudoir, and bathroom into a single interior in which she spent hours exercising, putting on makeup, dressing, having her coiffure attended to by her fashionable Parisian hairdresser, Antoine, and drinking cocktails with friends. "It is to my boudoir-bathroom, dear to my heart, that I come home always with joy," she wrote.[8] It was, she added, "the last word in modern luxury."[9] The British Fascist leader Oswald

Mosley agreed, declaring it "one of the most voluptuous settings it was possible to encounter."[10]

A large room curtained with silver lamé, walled with white marble, and wrapped with a wide cornice of mirror etched with sea creatures, de Wolfe's bathroom was furnished as fully as any sitting room. There was an 18th-century stone chimneypiece, a white fitted carpet, and in one corner, an L-shape banquette covered for some years in zebra skin.[11] The room's opposite end contained a white marble bath set into an angular mirrored alcove fitted with shelves laden with dozens of scent bottles. To step in and out of the tub, de Wolfe used a round ottoman upholstered in zebra skin while a brown-and-cream Moroccan rug served as a bath mat.

Briefly, the center of the room held a square Chinese black lacquer table piled with books, but in 1929, de Wolfe commissioned a new table from the designer Pierre Legrain, who supplied a large mirrored globe topped with a mirrored plateau, all reverse-gilded with signs of the zodiac and mounted on a polished ebony base.[12] To one side of the fireplace de Wolfe placed a similarly treated mirrored secretary lined with pale sycamore, made to order by Max Ingrand.[13] With swan's-head taps and oyster-shell light fixtures added to the mix, the decoration spanned several evocative effects: fantasy, opulence, sumptuousness, voluptuousness, vibrancy, and, above all, relaxation.

Ten Avenue d'Iéna represented de Wolfe's successful blending of the prewar historic interior—and all the resonances of class and refinement that accompanied it—with a more up-to-date concept of decoration that responded to a society familiar with technological advancements, from motion pictures to transatlantic flights. Even though de Wolfe was in her mid-60s, she easily revitalized her stylistic vocabulary and, once again, created an interior aesthetic that the world was keen to emulate.

Early version of Elsie de Wolfe's bathroom, c. 1925. (After All, 1935)

Later version of Elsie de Wolfe's bathroom, c. 1940. (Collection of the Elsie de Wolfe Foundation)

Hope Hampton and Jules Brulatour Residence
1145 Park Avenue
New York City

The connections that Elsie de Wolfe made during her career as one of America's best-known actresses resulted in some of the decorator's first celebrity clients. She decorated homes for her onetime understudy Ethel Barrymore and the stage beauty Cora Brown-Potter. The actress Clara Bloodgood ordered a dressing table in 1907.[1] One of the decorator's earliest jobs involved painting the playwright Clyde Fitch's piano with neoclassical decorations. With the rise of the Hollywood film industry in the 1920s and the decorator's theatrical heritage, allied to her indisputable position as an international arbiter of good taste, de Wolfe was a doubly attractive mentor to screen stars anxious to live up to their newfound celebrity.

When de Wolfe broke her links with Bessy Marbury, Anne Morgan, and her other upper-class American friends in favor of the transatlantic social scene, she largely sacrificed her connection to the Old Guard and literary crowd that had attended the Sunday gatherings at East 17th and East 55th streets. People from the world of motion pictures filled the void. As Jane S. Smith, de Wolfe's biographer, observed, "In the twenties, Charlie Chaplin, Mary Pickford, Douglas Fairbanks, Constance Bennett, Norma Talmadge, and Anita Loos had all made their way to the Villa Trianon; in the thirties, they continued to arrive, along with new recruits like Gary Cooper, Marlene Dietrich and Irving Berlin."[3] Cooper had his Brentwood Heights house and Paris apartment decorated by de Wolfe, and the best-dressed comedienne

Opposite: Dining room, 1935. (Collection of The New-York Historical Society)

Elsie de Wolfe in 1934.
(Collection of the Elsie de Wolfe Foundation)

Ina Claire called on de Wolfe's services for her small apartment at the Hotel Pierre.

On the fringes of this parade of A-list stars was the silent-film actress Hope Hampton, who hired the de Wolfe studio to decorate the Park Avenue town house she shared with her husband, Jules Brulatour, in the upper reaches of New York's Upper East Side. Here the lavish use of crisp mirrored surfaces with mellow French furniture demonstrated de Wolfe's increasing desire to mix ancien-régime elegance with modern novelties.

The blonde and beautiful Hampton (née Mae Elizabeth Hampton, 1897–1982) played lead roles in second-tier silents, including *Love's Bait* (1921), *The Light in the Dark* (1922), *Hollywood* (1923), and *The Price of a Party* (1924). Like de Wolfe's own achievements as an actress, her talents were largely decorative, and she left Hollywood to sing light opera. Eventually, Hampton settled down into the role of a colorful Manhattan socialite.[4]

Brulatour, whom Hampton married in 1923, came to New York from New Orleans in 1898 and worked as a sales representative for a supplier of photographic equipment. Later he was named first president of the Universal Film Company. He also worked as a film distributor, investor, and agent, though he tended to describe himself as a "motion picture magnate."[5]

It is not clear how Hampton came into contact with de Wolfe, although thanks to the intersecting communities of fashion, film, and café society, there were myriad opportunities for the two women to have met. It can only be conjectured when de Wolfe became involved with 1145 Park Avenue, a ten-room, three-story house the actress purchased in 1921. She certainly was working there prior to April 1935, since that was the first time Hampton's house was photographed by Mattie Edwards Hewitt, whose files identified it as a de Wolfe project.[6]

With the probable collaboration of its founder—B-movie actress or no, Hampton was a celebrity and therefore worthy of de Wolfe's personal attention—the de Wolfe firm produced rooms with an appropriately cinematic sense of drama. The decor also recalled de Wolfe's apartment on the Avenue d'Iéna, the mirrors and animal skins of which were eagerly adopted by fashionable women of the interwar years who were trying to negotiate their entrance into modernity. Exterior improvements were made here as well. The Brulatours' L-shaped house was hemmed in by

Second-floor drawing room, 1935. (Mattie Edwards Hewitt, collection of The New-York Historical Society)

surrounding buildings, so de Wolfe lined its rear elevations with green-painted trelliswork similar to that used at Villa Trianon, giving ancien-régime distinction to what was little more than an airshaft.

De Wolfe learned from decorating her own homes how important it was to express the personalities of its inhabitants—especially females—as well as meeting their psychological needs and social positions or pretensions. She conjured a fantasy environment for Hampton in which the humbly-born Texan could be the glamorous personage she had become. As an article about the house in *Arts and Decoration* noted, Hampton,

Bathroom, 1935. (Collection of The New-York Historical Society)

assisted by the world's most celebrated interior decorator, "had the wisdom to make just the interiors she would like to live in, where she would feel most happy and at ease . . . the decoration and the owner are in perfect harmony."[7]

A wrought-iron staircase "dashingly carpeted in zebra-skin" wound through the center of the house, which the Brulatours would soon replace with a slightly more livable leopard-spotted carpeting.[8] Most of the furniture was Louis XV, antiques as well as reproductions, among them a pair of needlepoint-covered walnut chairs in the drawing room, but modern touches were included throughout to offset what might otherwise have been overwhelming historicism. The marble-floored entrance hall, for example, had mirrors set into its walls and doors and two mirrored consoles designed by de Wolfe's latest Paris discovery, Serge Roche. There was also a mirrored stool with plastered lion's-paw feet by the same designer, identical to one de Wolfe later used in Gary Cooper's apartment in Paris.

The theme of reflective surfaces continued to the second-floor drawing room, where a life-size portrait of Hampton was flanked by floor-to-ceiling trompe l'oeil pilasters cut from mirrored glass, echoing similar pilasters at Villa Trianon. Sumptuous fabrics were in abundance. Café au lait–colored curtains were trimmed with antique silver galloon and crowned by a baroque shaped pelmet. Eighteenth-century French furniture was upholstered in pale silks or fine needlepoint, and underneath it all was a fitted carpet of "suave oyster-white."[9] At one end of the room, a wall of mirrored folding panels parted to reveal the ivory-and-gold dining room, which an observer said "puts you in mind of courtly French banquet halls, done in miniature."[10] The mirror-topped, neoclassical-style dining table stood on a inlaid starburst at the center of the gray, white, and yellow marble floor. In one corner was a modern three-panel folding screen—reminiscent of the work of Etienne Drian, who painted whimsical murals at Villa Trianon—depicting streamlined urns brimming with flowers.

Hampton's private sitting room, "the heart of this sparkling little house," was located on the third floor.[11] This de Wolfe decorated in beige and chocolate brown, hallmark colors of her work in the 1930s, with slipper chairs, leopard-print cushions, and a broad modern sofa thick with fringe. White porcelain figurines were displayed in the built-in bookcases flanking the fireplace.

Next to the sitting room was the actress' beige-and-pistachio green bedroom. The quilted satin bedspread and mirrored walls were additional examples of the modern opulence that pervaded the house. At the same time, with its comfortable chaise longue piled with ruffled cushions and exquisite marble mantelpiece set with Chinese jade objets d'art, Hampton's bedroom was similar to countless other intimate retreats de Wolfe had created for women for decades.[12]

The bathroom and dressing room, on the other hand, was a miniature Galerie des Glaces. Fully-mirrored walls reflected crystal bibelots: a pair of obelisks and a horse figurine. The toilet was concealed beneath a Louis XVI–style *chaise percée* of the kind de Wolfe had been using since the early years of the century, and sconces dripping with clear-glass lusters and beads lighted the space. On the floor was a rug of skunk fur. Tall French doors framed by silk taffeta curtains opened to a private terrace enriched with elaborate green trelliswork panels and iron furniture.

The Park Avenue house remained Hampton's primary residence until her death. Given her position in the entertainment world, its interiors were more Hollywood than Trianon. Though continuing to incorporate the European antiques that signified elegance

and social cachet, de Wolfe's work in the 1930s also used modish elements—mirrored walls, mirrored furniture, plush carpeting in pale colors, graphic animal hides—that tapped into the era's cinema culture. The resulting interiors signaled a significant evolution in de Wolfe's aesthetic. Domestic interiors no longer needed to be gracious backgrounds for genteel pursuits; thanks to the influence of Hollywood, they could be film sets for the actress in every woman. As she had done with 18th-century French clarity early in her career, de Wolfe successfully marketed this latest step in her personal style to a new generation of admirers.

Bedroom, 1935. (Collection of The New-York Historical Society)

1935-38

The Duke and Duchess of Windsor
London, Paris, Cap d'Antibes, and Nassau

Elsie de Wolfe spent much time and energy socializing with and occasionally working for prominent Americans who wanted to become part of European society in the 1930s, advising on their decors, introducing them to haute couturiers, putting them in touch with the best jewellers, and entertaining them in her homes. The most important of these expatriate associations was her relationship with Wallis Simpson, later the Duchess of Windsor, which lasted for more than half a decade and gave rise to several significant decorating opportunities. The chemistry between these two American women abroad, who had many things in common—determination, a belief in self-improvement, an appreciation for high fashion and fine antiques—was considerable, and de Wolfe acted as Simpson's most influential mentor in matters of taste and decorum.

They met in London through John McMullin, a *Vogue* editor, sometime in the early 1930s.[1] At that time the former Wallis Warfield (1896–1986) was married to her second husband, Ernest A. Simpson, and had been living since 1929 in a flat at 5 Bryanston Court, a modern building in George Street near Marble Arch. Intensely interested in decor but untrained, Wallis Simpson initially sought the help of the popular English decorator Syrie Maugham to decorate the flat. Her closeness to de Wolfe, however, grew after spending a summer in the south of France in 1935 with the Mendls and others. A contemporary

Opposite: Salon in 24 Boulevard Suchet, Paris, 1938. (Collection of the Elsie de Wolfe Foundation)

Elsie de Wolfe, late 1930s.
(Cecil Beaton, collection of the Elsie de Wolfe Foundation)

in this area: "The exotic Elsie de Wolfe, wife of Sir Charles Mendl, virtually transformed Wallis during this period. . . . She taught her how to host a large dinner party, how to select a guest list which ensured a successful and interesting evening, and how to plan menus and ease conversation along."[4]

De Wolfe also introduced Simpson to her favourite couturiers—Mainbocher, Edward Molyneux, and Elsa Schiaparelli. Mainbocher, a former editor of *Vogue*, whose fashion career de Wolfe had help establish through her patronage, proved to be the most significant of the three couturiers for the duchess. He eventually designed her wedding dress.

De Wolfe also assisted her American friend in creating the interiors of a number of her homes and was given the remarkable opportunity to advise the king on the decoration of Fort Belvedere, his home in Surrey. In 1936 she was flown from Paris to Sunningdale, near Windsor, in his private plane to look at the house, though, given the timing of the abdication a few months later, it is likely that de Wolfe's suggestions were never acted on. Rumors also circulated that de Wolfe had been asked to decorate Buckingham Palace, and a contemporary newspaper reported that the plan was that she would "sweep stuffy Victorianism, plush out stately Buck Palace and redecorate its interior in Swank Modern Style."[5] With the king's abdication later that year, however, it was another potential commission that never materialized.

In October 1936, when Simpson, having filed for divorce from her husband, moved to 16 Cumberland Terrace, a four-story, John Nash–designed terrace house in Regent's Park, de Wolfe followed. "The cat has been let out of the bag," noted society columnist Cholly Knickerbocker.[6] "Elsie's latest coup," Knickerbocker continued, "is the commission to do over Mrs. Simpson's London house."[7] De Wolfe undoubtedly

newspaper reported that the decorator worked on the Bryanston Court flat around this time, probably giving it a face-lift with a new color scheme and furniture arrangement.[2]

The following two years, 1935–37, marked the development of Simpson's relationship with the Prince of Wales, later Edward VIII of England, and the scandal that developed around their courtship. During this difficult time, de Wolfe was on hand offering advice about social behavior and self-presentation. In 1935, de Wolfe published her book *Elsie de Wolfe's Recipes for Successful Dining*, thereby confirming her authority as more than a decorator but also as a hostess of renown and an expert in matters relating to modern social etiquette.[3] In his 1999 biography of the Duchess of Windsor, Greg King acknowledged de Wolfe's influence on Wallis Simpson

Modern Regency house in River Ridge, Connecticut, 1937. (The New York Public Library)

wanted this cat to escape, as the commission represented a huge success story, even though Simpson was only renting the seven-room, two-bath house for seven months.[8] The commission occurred at the moment when de Wolfe was finally relinquishing her interest in the work of her American office and leaving its operation in the hands of socialite Eileen Allen, a former actress and longtime friend.[9] On November 20, 1936, the artist and photographer Cecil Beaton visited the Regent's Park house and described a drawing room the decorator of which sounds very much under the influence of de Wolfe's beige period: "a charming feminine setting, with walls, carpets, curtains, and upholstery the colour of bleached olives. The flowers and exotic leaves are a bleached olive colour. The only colours in the room are the mauve orchids and crimson roses on an occasional table, and the pink in Mrs. Simpson's cheeks."[10]

In April 1937, Elsie de Wolfe reemerged in New York to mount an exhibition on the subject of Modern Regency style, said to be influenced by the furnishings the decorator had used in Simpson's home in Cumberland Terrace. The exhibition featured a set of interiors in this streamlined historicist style in muted, romantic colors such as blue, gray, rosewood, cedar, cinnamon, and citron. Among other items, a mirrored glass dining table with a leather top was on exhibit: the table, the article was claimed, "suggested the one Mrs. Simpson used in her London home."[11]

A number of British architects and decorators had espoused the idiom of Modern Regency, also known as Vogue Regency, some years earlier, as had American architects such as Paul Revere Williams in Los Angeles and John L. Volk in Palm Beach. It was the style used by Elsie de Wolfe Inc. in a house it had decorated

Elsie de Wolfe and the Duchess of Windsor in the drawing room of 24 Boulevard Suchet, Paris, 1938.
(Collection of the Elsie de Wolfe Foundation)

earlier in 1936.[12] In her commentary on this new decorating aesthetic, de Wolfe said that by referring to the past, rejecting the fussiness of the "modernistic," and adding color to the formal austerity of the "modern," she sought to "satisfy the needs of present day living."[13] It was de Wolfe's attempt to update her philosophy of interior decoration and to demonstrate what she had always believed: that looking at the past could inspire modern ideas. "Modern Regency," she proclaimed, "is in answer to a great need in this country—a need for a creative spirit, something that will, in times to come, be expressive of the days in which we live."[14]

In November 1936, Wallis Simpson's relationship with the king finally had the effect of destabilizing the monarchy, and she fled to France to avoid the publicity. There was some speculation that she might find refuge in Villa Trianon.[15] This does not seem to have been the case, however, although the decorator undoubtedly played a part in securing the former king his sanctuary in Baron Eugene von Rothschild's Schloss Enzesfeld near Vienna while he awaited the finalization of the Simpsons' divorce. Also, while Wallis Simpson waited in Château de Candé near Tours in the months before the marriage, de Wolfe was a visitor. Following the wedding, she played a part in the decoration of two Windsor homes, Château de La Croë on Cap d'Antibes, near Cannes, which the couple rented from 1938 to 1949, and a

Paris house, 24 Boulevard Suchet, rented from 1938 until the late 1940s.[16]

Like a set of a Noel Coward play, La Croë was a glamorous white villa set on 12 acres of land, with eight guest rooms and 250-foot swimming pool lined with blue tiles.[17] It was owned by Sir Pomeroy Burton, who modernized it in 1928 to the designs of Armand Albert Rateau and rented it to the Windsors for $16,000 a year.[18] They signed the two-year lease on April 22, 1938, and moved in just over a month later. Given the size of the house, it is likely that de Wolfe's work there was not entirely completed until later in the year.[19] Her task was to quickly advise on colors and arrange the furniture. It is unclear how many of La Croë's stylish contents were the Burtons'—they let the house partially furnished—nor is it clear what was brought there by the Windsors, de Wolfe, or the French decorator Stephane Boudin, head of Jansen, but the house was a compendium of de Wolfe's signature features.[20] There were a multitude of mirrors and a white-and-gold color scheme touched with blue and yellow. A flattering pink-and-apricot color scheme was used for the brunette duchess' bedroom, where de Wolfe introduced notes of modern whimsy. Especially noteworthy was a "dressing table and matching chest, painted with trompe l'oeil symbols of her relationship with the duke: duplications of his letters to her; an invitation bearing the royal crest; a fan; a pair of long white evening gloves; a lipstick; a jeweled handbag; and a pair of [the duke's] golf socks."[21] Probably painted in workrooms of the Paris decorating firm Jansen at de Wolfe's direction, the house conformed utterly to the decorator's belief in the importance, for women, of their most private domestic spaces being the rooms where they could most be themselves. The centrepiece of the duchess' bathroom was a 22-karat gold swan-shaped tub, which Sir Pomeroy had installed for his wife, Barbara, during his reported $2 million refurbishment of the house.[22]

Each guest room had a theme: the Rose Room, the Venetian Room, the Wedgwood Room, the Toile de Jouy Room, the Blue Room, and the Directoire Room. This individualization recalled the decorator's work decades earlier in the Colony Club and the Frick mansion. The Windsors spent Christmas 1938 at La Croë and were joined, among other guests, by de Wolfe and her husband, Sir Charles Mendl. McMullin assisted in the creation of the white-and-silver Christmas decorations, which were undoubtedly masterminded by de Wolfe, as was the appearance of the double-height seaside terrace, its grand colonnade hung with full-length curtains of boldly striped green-and-white cotton and streamlined wicker furniture with green cotton cushions piped and buttoned in white. "Dear Wallis, this snap will show you what Elsie has done to the terrace," McMullin wrote on a picture postcard to the duchess. "It is paved, has a big green awning, and deep stone seats with comfortable white cushions—as well as Regency effect or valance (by me) &c."[23]

Soon after acquiring Château de La Croë, the Windsors leased a four-story town house at 24 Boulevard Suchet in Paris. Stephane Boudin, who had designed the pavilion built on the grounds of Villa Trianon for de Wolfe's 1938 Circus Ball, is credited with the interior decoration.[24] De Wolfe, however, undoubtedly had an influence there, advising on the deployment of the duke's furniture from Fort Belvedere and York House, as well as Simpson's Cumberland Terrace furniture, all of which had been shipped from England to furnish La Croë.[25]

Owned by an Italian countess, the Louis XVI–style mansion had been built in 1932.[26] It consisted of three stories, with seven rooms for the Windsors on the first two floors and servants' quarters on the third. The first-floor salon was decorated in an updated Louis XIV style, with

Dining table in 24 Boulevard Suchet, Paris, 1938.
(Collection of the Elsie de Wolfe Foundation)

elaborately swagged dull-gold curtains and a scattering of small black lacquer tables. One of its most exotic features was a baroque-style sofa, covered with scarlet velvet that had been used previously, it was claimed, in a cardinal's robes; another was a modern Louis XV–style ormolu-mounted bureau plat entirely covered in etched and gilded mirror.[27] Though Boudin played the leading role in the Suchet interiors, another piece of evidence indicating de Wolfe's advice in the decoration of the house was suggested by the presence, in the so-called banquette room, of two luxurious low green velvet sofas. Shaped like a U and an L, each was deeply button-tufted and strewn with large

square cushions—recalling a banquette de Wolfe placed in her bathroom in Avenue d'Iéna and anticipating another that she would introduce a little later into her California home. The banquette room's windows were hung with satin curtains quilted in an oversize diamond or trellis pattern, a clear reference to de Wolfe's oeuvre; the lacy Chinese bamboo chairs and low black-lacquer tables subtly referenced the duchess' youthful travels in the Far East.

The dining room in Boulevard Suchet was painted cream with red details and gilding, and the large arched windows were draped with tassled crimson curtains chosen to match the 15 cream-and-red Louis XV–style chairs. Sheet mirror inset into the boiserie and arched doorways maximized the light, as did the black-mirror top of the William and Mary–style gilt mahogany table.[28] The duchess was allocated her own suite of rooms on the next floor, a division of space fully in line with de Wolfe's philosophy of the interior, which placed an emphasis on the privacy of its female inhabitants. The decor of the duchess' bedroom would not have been out of place on a Hollywood sound stage. The bed, designed by Boudin, featured a exaggerated scrolling headboard, covered in the same blue satin fabric that was used to completely curtain the walls. A painted Venetian rococo-style commode painted cream with pale blue scenes of the Italian countryside stood between the windows, and in the center of the room was a giant ermine fur rug in the shape of a flattened dahlia. The dressing table in the dressing room was "draped with alternating skirts of white and sapphire blue lace," while the cupboard doors were covered with mirrors.[29] The duke's spare, military-theme bedroom was furnished with a theatrical suite of Empire-style furniture painted scarlet and black, a club chair slipcovered in ivory-white satin, and an antique giltwood mirror topped with the Prince of Wales' feathers, part of the Fort Belvedere shipment.

Banquette room in 24 Boulevard Suchet, Paris, 1938. (Collection of the Elsie de Wolfe Foundation)

The duchess and de Wolfe remained close until the decorator's death in 1950. The Windsors were guests at the 1938 Circus Ball, and when in 1939 the Duke of Windsor was granted the role of governor general of the Bahamas, a newspaper reported, "Lady Mendl has been asked to brighten up the interior of Government House and is expected to leave for the Bahamas as soon as she has terminated her work in California. . . . One of her secretaries is in Nassau doing her best to add a temporary de Wolfe touch to the home for the arrival of the royal pair."[30]

In 1939 de Wolfe and the duchess set up a charity, Le Colis de Trianon-Versailles, the aim of which was to raise funds to send supplies to the soldiers on the front line. The following year they helped organize an exhibition, held at the John Wanamaker Auditorium in New York City, of clothes worn by members of their social set, themselves included. The proceeds went to French war charity.

For a period of around five years, the paths of these two American women had been closely intertwined, and there can be little doubt that the reputation for stylishness and sophistication that the duchess acquired was largely a result of her close relationship with Elsie de Wolfe.

1934–44

New York Hotels
New York City

*A*fter the death of Bessy Marbury in 1933 and the sale of the theatrical agent's town house at 13 Sutton Place, where the roving de Wolfe maintained a New York base, the decorator abandoned the idea of having a permanent residence in the United States. Instead, she began to spend a considerable amount of time not only living in fashionable hotels but adding these public buildings to her firm's repertoire.

In 1934, de Wolfe's firm decorated the Café Lounge and Bar of the Savoy-Plaza Hotel on Fifth Avenue, a McKim, Mead & White building. Romantic murals by the artist Hugh Troy depicting sleek greyhounds, handsomely gowned women on horseback, neoclassical temples, and lounging picnickers were featured in the decor as well as the hotel's advertisements.

A couple of years later, the firm decorated an apartment at the Hotel Pierre for actress Ina Claire, for whom it had also created stage sets. The apartment's living room displayed many familiar de Wolfe hallmarks, including a six-panel mirrored screen like those popularized by the English decorator Syrie Maugham, a Louis XV table, two modern chairs upholstered in leopard-print velvet, another covered with a feather-patterned chintz, mirrored flowerpots, and a mirrored coffee table.[1] Soon after, the firm worked on an apartment in Essex House, a prestigious new hotel located opposite Central Park.

Opposite: Painting by Dubjinsky of Elsie de Wolfe's suite at the Plaza Hotel, mid-1940s.
(Collection of the Elsie de Wolfe Foundation)

275

Elsie de Wolfe in 1941 with her cut-out glove.
(Collection of the Elsie de Wolfe Foundation)

and other publications. Another benefit was that her name-brand suite could be profitably leased when she was out of town.[3]

Similar recognition of the publicity value inherent in de Wolfe's patronage led important art and furniture dealers to lend the decorator furnishings for her hotel rooms with the promise that she eventually would sell them at good prices. This agreement provided her with rare items that she could not otherwise have afforded; more importantly, it brought her a substantial financial gain on all sales made—she typically charged double the dealer's asking price. If a guest admired a console or a chair, de Wolfe would arrange to sell it and later replace it with something else.

Particularly gratifying, personally as well as professionally, was a 1934 arrangement between de Wolfe and the St. Regis Hotel that provided her with a New York base for the next decade. Mindful of the considerable free publicity that would be generated with de Wolfe as a semi-permanent guest, Serge Obolensky, who called himself the hotel's "general consultant, promotion man, and trouble-shooter," was delighted to provide a suite at the St. Regis.[2] De Wolfe paid a minor discounted fee, while the St. Regis, owned by Obolensky's former brother-in-law, Vincent Astor, would reap valuable product placement. The decorator would entertain important guests at the hotel, which would be reported in women's magazines and major syndicated gossip columns, and her smartly decorated rooms would be published in *Vogue, House and Garden,*

Elsie de Wolfe in her suite at the Plaza Hotel, 1944.
(Collection of the Elsie de Wolfe Foundation)

Living room in the St. Regis Hotel, New York, 1941. (Collection of the Elsie de Wolfe Foundation)

When de Wolfe and her entourage hurriedly left Europe in 1940 as the Germans entered Paris, she found refuge on the 18th floor of the St. Regis. Soon afterward, de Wolfe began redecorating. On completion, her rooms' originality stunned reviewers, and the vibrant green, white, and terra-cotta color scheme was a decorating sensation.

De Wolfe's St. Regis living room appeared on the cover of the May 1941 edition of *House and Garden*.[4] It showed an elegant space with magnolia-green walls and snow-white upholstery. The white of the damask covering the sofa was repeated in the Aubusson rug on the floor, in the flowers arranged against light eucalyptus leaves in a vase in the corner of the room, and in a flower painting by socialite-artist Mary Benjamin Rogers suspended behind the sofa. On the sofa, blue, green, and terra cotta-colored cushions were scattered.[5] To upholster a small armchair and curtains at the window behind it, de Wolfe used a fresh white chintz printed with fern fronds in varied shades

Portrait of Elsie de Wolfe by Marcel Vertès, executed in the mid-1940s. (Collection of the Elsie de Wolfe Foundation)

of green. It was a design that became associated with the decorator, and she would use it extensively at her Beverly Hills house. For sparkle, de Wolfe brought in little gilded side chairs, a gilded coffee table with a mirrored top, and a number of small table ornaments. Underscoring the name-branding of the suite was a portrait of the decorator by an Austrian-born society painter, Baron Kurt von Pantz. The remaining rooms of the St. Regis suite were decorated in a similar vein and color scheme. It was a remarkably vital design statement for a woman born at the end of the Civil War. And as Obolensky admiringly recalled in his memoirs, because of de Wolfe's work at the St. Regis, "The new trend of good taste in hotel decoration . . . gained momentum very fast."[6]

The decorator maintained the St. Regis pied à terre until 1944, when Obolensky moved several blocks north to manage the Plaza Hotel for an Astor competitor, Conrad Hilton. De Wolfe instantly transferred her allegiances and her address.

For suite 317–325 at the Plaza, she created an even more dramatic environment than she had at the St. Regis. Against murals of frolicking nymphs by the French artist Marcel Vertès stood a white secretary that a de Wolfe protégé Tony Duquette painted with a baroque pattern. She used the same white-and-green scheme at the Plaza, but this time she reversed the colors. Dark green was used for the curtains, carpet, and lampshades, and the upholstery fabric was that familiar fern-leaf pattern; the paneled walls, on the other hand, were largely white. Mirrors and crystal chandeliers reflected and refracted the light, and an ornate red antique clock graced the mantel.[7] It was a light, exotic interior, described by the society columnist Cholly Knickerbocker as "one of Elsie de Wolfe's follies."[8]

Living room in the St. Regis Hotel, 1941. (Collection of the Elsie de Wolfe Foundation)

Like the St. Regis before it, the Lady Mendl Suite served as a personal home, a professional advertisement, and a desirable piece of real estate. In 1948, Marlene Dietrich reserved it to rest between acting assignments. It also was a very convenient base for de Wolfe whenever she passed through New York on her way to California or France.

The décors de Wolfe created for her rooms at the Plaza and the St. Regis once again provided evidence of her uncanny ability to conjure innovative, influential interiors, even into her 80s, and the continued importance of marking every place she lived, even if only temporarily, with her taste and personality.

1942

Elsie de Wolfe Residence

After All

Beverly Hills, California

"The ugliest house in Beverly Hills."[1]

The last house that Elsie de Wolfe decorated for herself was in California. With the outbreak of war in Europe, she and her entourage left Paris and returned to the United States. Following a period in New York in 1941, she and her husband, Sir Charles Mendl, went to Los Angeles and rented a house at 1125 San Ysidro Drive.[2] Leaving Villa Trianon and her Paris flat had been emotionally wrenching for the decorator. On the positive side, relocation presented her with an opportunity to explore new ideas in a landscape seemingly devoid of the history that had always inspired her decorative work. In 1942, de Wolfe moved into a dark red, Hispano-Moorish-style stucco house in Beverly Hills. With its high ceilings, generously scaled rooms, and large garden, it had enough potential for the decorator to disregard its visual drawbacks and reinvent it as thoroughly as she had recast her old house on Irving Place. The dominant industry—motion pictures—of the house's location also gave de Wolfe an opportunity to reenter the world of stage-set fantasy from which she had originally emerged.

Since 1919, when she began adding theatrical leopard-spot upholstery to Villa Trianon, de Wolfe had been gradually moving away from her dependence on 18th-century France and absorbing decorating strategies from more progressive contemporaries. At the same time, she was becoming increasingly fascinated with, on the one hand, the illusionistic possibilities of interior decoration and, on the other, the importance of bibelots as personalized aesthetic

Opposite: Entrance hall, with balustrade decoration by Tony Duquette. (Collection of the Elsie de Wolfe Foundation)

Elsie de Wolfe in the garden, 1940s.
(Collection of the Elsie de Wolfe Foundation)

refugee, and though the home she created there compensated significantly for the temporary loss of Villa Trianon, After All never gave any indication that it was anything more than a stylish stopgap.

From the beginning of her decorating career, de Wolfe had understood that fabrics and draperies—the soft structures of the interior—could be as effective at creating evocative space as hard structures, such as walls and ceilings. Her box bed at 122 East 17th Street, with its enveloping curtains, for example, bore witness to her love of the transient, intimate spaces that draped fabrics could create. She had also long been conscious of the importance of small portable items—the objects on a desk, a dressing table, or a mantel, for instance—which had always played key roles in her interiors, though in a restrained fashion born out of her repudiation of Victorian ostentation and over-elaboration.

By the 1940s, however, when de Wolfe became much more nomadic than in her earlier life, the movable, flexible aspects of interiors had come to dominate the fixed, hard structures, which allowed for less adaptative use. Both of these decorating strategies offered a more intimate, internalized, and personalized definition of the interior, one that did not depend on the architectural shell. Above all, an emphasis on these features meant that the soul of an interior could be moved from place to place with ease. It was no coincidence that the idea of the tent, the most nomadic inhabited structure of all, featured strongly in de Wolfe's work in these years. As she moved from city to country, France to the United States, her persona moved, and with it, her ideal interior.

She approached the renovation of 1018 Benedict Canyon Drive with a small budget and without the dependence she had had in Villa Trianon on the inclusion of expensive pieces of furniture or luxurious fabrics, which in any case would have been difficult to

accents. Situated in the heart of "Dreamland," as Hollywood was frequently called, Beverly Hills was the perfect place in which to pursue this idea of fantasy and to indulge in what to others might have looked like decorative excess. The early 1940s proved to be a period of extreme self-confidence for the decorator, whose reputation allowed her to employ whatever effect she wished without any thought of criticism, inappropriateness, or, most importantly, permanent habitation. The house on Benedict Canyon Road, which she would call "After All" after the title of her autobiography, was a way station, a pied à terre.[3] It was not Villa Trianon, the center of her peripatetic life. On one of the cushions in the new house was embroidered the phrase "It Takes a Stout Heart to Live Without Roots."[4] De Wolfe had come to Beverly Hills as a

Main entrance. (Collection of the Elsie de Wolfe Foundation)

obtain due to the restrictions imposed by wartime rationing. She once semi-accurately described the interiors of the house as "all junk." After All was to be a party house, more in line with the temporary structures that she had created in the garden of the villa for social occasions or the pavilions that dotted the gardens of the Versailles estate of Minna Anglesey, one of which de Wolfe and Marbury rented for several years.

Indeed, from the outset, the decorator saw her time in Beverly Hills as a brief interlude before she could return to France, and the Benedict Canyon house was to be a stage for entertaining the the wealthy inhabitants of Hollywood, who could likely become clients. Before de Wolfe could get

to work on the interiors, however, some basic changes had to be made. These involved painting the exterior of the house white; filling in the large swimming pool; adding a parking area around a newly planted mature olive tree; and making the garden seem larger than it was through a clever distribution of outside mirrors—a technique that she had perfected over the years and counseled friends and clients to adopt.[5] And here, as at her suite at the St. Regis, the palette, indoors and out, was dark green, snow white, and jet black, accented with grace notes of coral red. Among these were a little table with a red-leather top, the red-lacquer clock reputedly given her by Henry Clay Frick, and, in the garden, succulents with red flowers.

Rear entrance. (Collection of the Elsie de Wolfe Foundation)

The European writer and illustrator Ludwig Bemelmans, who stayed at After All during the war and in 1955 wrote a fanciful book about his Beverly Hills experience with the Mendls, described the house as "the reincarnation of the scenes of a former life." For him it was "a little palace, exactly like the lovely silver and blue Amalienburg that stands in the park of Nymphenburg outside Munich."[6] Although historical references were hardly in evidence at After All, the spirit of old Europe was present in the house's rococo personality and strong undercurrent of whimsy.

The decorator also made much of the possibilities of inside meeting outside, which the California climate allowed her to do more expansively than in France or New York. At the rear of the house was an L-shaped veranda pierced with large, low arches that led to a garden of coconut palms, philodendrons, banana trees, masses of ivy, and a manicured green lawn. De Wolfe connected the house to the cool greenery outdoors by hanging reversible curtains on the outside of the arches: green canvas was used on the side of the curtains facing the garden, and green-and-white-striped cotton for the side facing the veranda. Striped curtains were installed at the entrance of the house, too, flanked by green ceramic pots filled with white Michaelmas daisies. Inside the veranda she positioned

Little garden house. (Collection of the Elsie de Wolfe Foundation)

View across to the L-shaped veranda. (Collection of the Elsie de Wolfe Foundation)

low, deep sofas covered with green, white, and yellow checked linen, placed Chinese ceramic lamps atop sturdy rattan tables, and scattered fluffy white rectangular rugs across the dark flagstone floor. White wrought-iron tables stood near woven-wicker chairs—their cushions matched the sofa material—and here and there stood white ceramic pots planted with dark green elephant's ears. The walls behind the sofas were mirrored to create an illusion of spaciousness as well as to reflect the garden beyond the arches.

Indoors, the life of the house was focussed on an enormous living room on the second floor. At one end was an onyx fireplace against a wall paved with mirror; on either side were nestled sofas covered in green-piped white damask and scattered with green pillows with humorous maxims embroidered in white. Matching banquettes were pushed against the white walls, as were black Regency-style side chairs and slipper chairs upholstered in de Wolfe's favorite fern-patterned chintz, leaving the center of the room open as if in anticipation of an after-dinner dance, following de Wolfe's vision of After All as a stage for entertaining. Large flower paintings by the Scottish artist William Ranken bloomed on the walls—one was hung above a console made of

Veranda. (Collection of the Elsie de Wolfe Foundation)

Living room looking toward the bar. (Collection of the Elsie de Wolfe Foundation)

gnarled grapevines topped with a sheet of glass—and surveying it all were statues of blackamoors.[7] It was an extravagant environment containing a high level of fantasy, and unlike de Wolfe's previous residences, After All was distinguished by its conspicuous lack of costly fabrics, museum-quality art, and precious antiques.

The most outstanding pieces of furniture in de Wolfe's California home were those made to order by her protégé Tony Duquette, a Michigan-born artist fond of transforming a variety of materials into rococo creations.[8] A store display artist who designed a table centerpiece that de Wolfe admired at a Hollywood dinner party, he would make numerous items for de

Wolfe, including complex candelabra studded with imitation emeralds and a black painted secretary ornamented with artificial jewels and leaves of crystal. These pieces typified the elaborate imagery at which Duquette excelled and which appealed enormously to de Wolfe at this stage in her career. The narrow upstairs hall of the house contained a chandelier created by Duquette, with a trompe l'oeil console painted on the wall below; he also created a flamboyant mural of overscale feathers, fern fronds, and leaves to frame the living room's grapevine console and Ranken paintings.

The interiors of After All indicated another major shift in de Wolfe's aesthetic vocabulary. Though

Living room fireplace. (Collection of the Elsie de Wolfe Foundation)

Living room banquette. (Collection of the Elsie de Wolfe Foundation)

Elsie de Wolfe and Blu-Blu, 1944.
(Collection of the Elsie de Wolfe Foundation)

artifacts became the objectification of their collector and of her taste and personality and, to some degree, became objects of intense affection, as much as the pets—pekingeses, chow chows, miniature poodles, and various birds—with which de Wolfe shared her homes. Bemelmans explained how de Wolfe interacted with her bibelots on a daily basis, rearranging them, talking to them, reinforcing her personal relationship with them. At a time when Villa Trianon was a significant distance away, these small, transportable decorative items acted as important substitutes and *aides-mémoires* for the very real treasures she had been forced to leave behind in Versailles. The fact that so many of them took the form of animals and birds only reinforced their animated nature for her.

Another room on the second floor leading off the living room was dubbed the withdrawing room and was used by the decorator to play gin rummy with guests after meals. It was a cozy space, with high-gloss, dark-green walls, a vaulted ceiling with a green-and-white trelliswork pattern pasted between its green-painted beams, and a large hooked rug patterned with magnolia leaves. Her familiar fern-patterned chintz was used for the full-length curtains and to upholster several chairs, and every book in this luxuriously colored, ultrafeminine room was bound in color-coordinated red, white, or green.

By the time she came to create her Beverly Hills home, de Wolfe had rejected the idea of a separate dining room. Instead, she constructed a multipurpose bar rather than a dedicated eating space. Rather than a conventional table and chairs, she created what amounted to a private nightclub. The room's feature was a tall bamboo bar with high stools, with small tables for four placed around the room as needed, utilizing a variety of mismatched chairs as the number of guests demanded, from bare folding metal chairs to white iron

in the early 1900s, she had endeavored to keep her rooms and those of her clients relatively restrained in terms of accessories. By the 1940s, de Wolfe had begun to mass tabletops with vases of flowers or animal figurines of glass, crystal, jade, and rose quartz. A glass cabinet at After All contained a cache of seashells, and she assembled a large amount of porcelain vegetables and similarly shaped serving pieces.[9] These collections, in addition to containing and expressing the beauty she continually sought in her life, also contributed the personal touch that de Wolfe thought essential to any domestic interior. She always had been an active acquirer, from the days when she had displayed historical shoes and dolls in the East 17th Street house. Selected by a single eye, her chosen

Second-floor hall, with chandelier designed by Tony Duquette. (Collection of the Elsie de Wolfe Foundation)

Desk designed by Tony Duquette in the living room. (Collection of the Elsie de Wolfe Foundation)

chairs pulled in fron the garden. The ceiling was tented with brown-and-white-striped canvas, and under one window was tucked a shallow leopard-print velvet banquette. Instead of a typical chandelier, de Wolfe hung a birdcage from the center of the ceiling above a large bamboo table where food often was set out buffet style; some photographs, however, show the table pushed against a wall, demonstrating the room's multifunctional character. The lighthearted scheme, so different from the formal elegance of de Wolfe's earlier dining rooms, was simultaneously contemporary and exotic. It was perfectly suited to Southern California's casual mode of entertaining.

Upstairs, the secretary in de Wolfe's bedroom was covered with decoupage bouquets of flowers, more evidence of the creativity of Duquette's work that suffused After All. As a writer in *House and Garden* explained, to create this piece of furniture, "Lady Mendl and her life-long secretary, Miss Hilda West, spent three months cutting up 17th and 18th-century prints."[10] Additional flowers were painted on two white Venetian chairs nearby, and the decorator's little bed was ornamented with similar bouquets and backed by a large mirror that caused the supine de Wolfe, according to Bemelmans, to resemble a "very modern Madonna set in a mirrored frame."[11] The fireplace was

Withdrawing room. (Collection of the Elsie de Wolfe Foundation)

Living room looking into the bar. (Collection of the Elsie de Wolfe Foundation)

Bar. (Collection of the Elsie de Wolfe Foundation)

encased in sheets of mirror as well. De Wolfe displayed feather and flower arrangements contained in shadow-box frames in her bedroom, also created by Duquette, and elsewhere in the house were charming pictures made of seashells by the artist-decorator Catherine d'Erlanger, the American-born aunt of one of de Wolfe's clients, Baron Leo d'Erlanger.

Bemelmans described in some detail the suite of rooms he occupied during his tenure at After All. It consisted of a bedroom, a small study, a dressing room, and a bath. De Wolfe's commitment to practicality revealed itself in the storage area in the dressing room, which avoided the need for anyone to bend down to use it. "I copied this room," she claimed, "in miniature from a haberdasher's shop in London."[12]

Even in this fanciful house, the practical requirements of storing and accessing items was still at the front of the decorator's mind, as necessary as when, during her acting career, a journalist marveled at how de Wolfe's gowns were maintained in the manner of a French department store. The challenge of the bathroom continued to engage her as well, especially the problem of the toilet, what de Wolfe called "the unspeakable." Even concealing it in an enamel-painted Louis XIV–style cane chair, or *chaise percée*, did not alleviate her anxieties.[13]

Bemelmans was less pleased with his hostess' redecoration of a small beach hut in which he regularly worked. "Suddenly I stood in front of what had been my shack, and it was now an extension of 'After All,'"

Elsie de Wolfe's bedroom. (Collection of the Elsie de Wolfe Foundation)

Black and White room. (Collection of the Elsie de Wolfe Foundation)

he wrote. "There was a pavilion where the rickety table had stood. The inside of the house was the latest in modern beach living. It was well thought out and sensible, and even beautiful. One wall of the bedroom was an immense mirror; the closet space, so important to Elsie, was perfect; the lighting fixtures were of material stretched over metal frames, the carpeting, woven raffia squares in sand color."[14]

Though de Wolfe was nearly 80 years old when she decorated After All, her ability to create exciting interiors had not dulled. By returning to the lessons learned during her work as a set designer, recognizing

the mid-century's epochal shift in lifestyle from historical formality to casual entertaining, and cannily using inexpensive materials—mirrors, paint, cotton canvas, novelty fabrics—to create a customized environment, de Wolfe once again established herself as a decorator of innovation and influence. However, when peace was declared in 1945, she was keen to return to Villa Trianon and attend to the restoration of rooms that had been damaged by occupying forces during the war. She moved back to Versailles in 1946, after four years in Beverly Hills, although she continued to spend winters in California until her death in 1950.

The decoupage bureau in de Wolfe's bedroom. (Collection of the Elsie de Wolfe Foundation)

Elsie de Wolfe's bedroom. (Collection of the Elsie de Wolfe Foundation)

Elsie de Wolfe Residence

Villa Trianon
Versailles, France

"My perfect Eden . . ."[1]

etween 1915 and 1950, the year of her death, Elsie de Wolfe continually reworked her vision of the interior of her most beloved home, Villa Trianon. "For twenty-seven years or more I have never stopped planning," she explained in 1935. Her work here was to continue unabated for the next 15 years. Even in 1940–1946, when she was not occupying the house, she was thinking about it, and she dedicated the last four years of her life to its second major restoration.[2] De Wolfe's devotion to the house was made explicit when she told her friend Ludwig Bemelmans that she sought "to lavish on that house all the infinite care a house wants that anything in this world that you love deserves."[3] For a period of more than 30 years, therefore, Villa Trianon served as the experimental base for many of de Wolfe's decorating ideas and as the place where her personal dreams and identity were most fully realized.

During World War I, the villa had been used by women stitching garments for the wounded and as a rendezvous point for senior military figures. One of the outbuildings had been converted into convalescent homes for officers, and the de Wolfe restored and decorated house of Charlotte Morton next door was pressed into service for enlisted soldiers. Anne Morgan and Bessy Marbury did not travel there very much after the war, the former because she became preoccupied with projects located elsewhere, and the latter due to the rebuilding

Opposite: A corner in the Villa Trianon, 1940. (André Ostier, collection of the Elsie de Wolfe Foundation)

Elsie de Wolfe by the pool in the garden, 1920s.
(Collection of the Elsie de Wolfe Foundation)

celebrity and her ability to provide him entrée into an international high society, she was intrigued by his fortune and hero-worship, Weiller granted the decorator permission to live in the villa for as long as she liked and, at de Wolfe's request, he continued to purchase items for it and allowed her to sell various furnishings at her whim. When de Wolfe died in 1950, Weiller left the villa intact, using it for weekend visits until 1981, when its contents were finally sold at a Paris auction.

A number of decorative transformations took place in the villa in the decade following the end of World War I. The first was the development, in 1919, of the first floor of the 1912 Morgan Wing into the Long Gallery. This project marked de Wolfe's move into a new phase of decorating, one that remained partially committed to 18th-century French style but that became increasingly contemporary as she acknowledged and was influenced by developments she saw around her in the French decorative arts.

A number of new themes entered into the postwar decoration of Villa Trianon at this time: an increased use of whimsical murals executed in a contemporary idiom, and the inclusion of animal skins and fabrics with animal-skin motifs. Though the latter reflected a minor aspect of 18th-century French decoration, when printed fabrics sometimes had leopard-spot motifs, it actually more importantly mirrored the work of several contemporary French decorative artists working in Paris, among them Maurice Dufrêne, Jean Dunand, and Emile-Jacques Ruhlmann. They were using animal skins in the mid-1920s as part of their growing interest in the exotic and in rare and sumptuous materials, such as ivory, tortoiseshell, lizard and shark skin, African woods, and lacquer. Although de Wolfe could never be described as an Art Deco designer, she made certain moves in the direction of this modern French style, which reached its apogée in

of her disrupted theatrical business and an increasing involvement in Democratic politics. De Wolfe's personal relationship with the house became stronger as her companions' presences there became less and less frequent. Morgan and de Wolfe eventually bought out Marbury's share. Later de Wolfe became the sole owner, but such were the fortunes of her decorating company and her financial situation at the time that she immediately sold it to a friend, Paul-Louis Weiller (1893–1993). He was an aviation pioneer and financier with strong social aspirations who reportedly owned more than a dozen homes, all of them decorated by de Wolfe. As he was influenced by de Wolfe's

Long Gallery. (After All, 1935)

William Ranken's painting of the Long Gallery, 1920s. (Collection of the Elsie de Wolfe Foundation)

Library, 1940s. (Collection of the Elsie de Wolfe Foundation)

Elsie de Wolfe and guests in the garden, late 1920s. (Collection of the Elsie de Wolfe Foundation)

1925 on the banks of the Seine in Paris, site of the Exposition des Arts Decoratifs.[4]

In the Long Gallery, de Wolfe deliberately contrasted old and new. As with the contemporary artistic world around her, she showed that her taste had been reformed in the new postwar climate. Leopard-spot velvet ottomans in the gallery, similar to those she used in Marbury's house at 13 Sutton Place, bore witness to her new interest in the modern, and the new style was especially apparent in her use of murals. She had worked with the painter Everett Shinn, among others, before the war, and she turned now to the artists Etienne Drian

(1885–1961) and Marcel Vertès (1904–89) to help update the decoration of Villa Trianon. Drian's reputation had been formed through his fashion drawings, published in *La Gazette du Bon Ton* between 1913 and 1915.[5] The murals he executed in the Long Gallery were, as de Wolfe explained in her autobiography, frescoes executed in sepia on a dull gold ground, depicting the stairs and terraces leading up to the Palace of Versailles. These overtly modern panels contrasted with the 18th-century chandeliers and the flower sprays of gilt bronze and enamel.

A Drian mural in the entrance hall depicted a parchment map showing directions to the villa with de

William Ranken's painting of the garden music pavilion, 1922. (Collection of the Elsie de Wolfe Foundation)

onto the *tapis vert.* Outside the gallery, de Wolfe created "a columned portico with an enormous mirror set in the wall, and a fountain banked with greens," an echo of her little window box and fountain at 122 East 17th Street.[7] When she returned to Versailles in 1946, after a six-year absence during which Nazis had inhabited the villa, she found bullet holes in the mirror, reportedly put there by American troops.[8]

Many paintings of the villa itself were executed by the artists Walter Gay (1856–1937) and William Ranken (1881–1941). The former lived with his wife, Matilda, in nearby Le Breau and had been a visitor to Villa Trianon from the early years of the century, producing pictures of it between 1906 and 1922. His 1910 painting of the salon hung in de Wolfe's private

The garden, 1930s. (Collection of the Elsie de Wolfe Foundation)

Wolfe, seated on a leopard-skin blanket next to a pet Pekingese dog, holding back a velvet curtain and greeting guests on their arrival. In addition, Marcel Vertès painted a mural on the ceiling of the library illustrating an enthusiastic de Wolfe leaping across the Atlantic. Later in the 1940s, the same artist also painted a portrait of de Wolfe. [6] (p. 278)

Long banquettes, positioned at the bottom of the frescoes, were made especially for the Long Gallery and were upholstered in ivory velvet. Little 18th-century chairs, covered with petit-point-embroidered fabric, were placed by the windows, which looked out

Painting of the garden, 1920s.
(Collection of the Elsie de Wolfe Foundation)

William Ranken's painting of Elsie de Wolfe's bedroom, 1922. (Collection of the Elsie de Wolfe Foundation)

sitting room on the second floor for a number of years.[9] In 1922, the Scottish-born Ranken created paintings of the music pavilion, the garden, and de Wolfe's bedroom and sitting room on the second floor.[10] Ranken, who had trained at the Slade in London, had been close to John Singer Sargent and moved in the same social circles as de Wolfe before the war. He had known Isabella Stewart Gardner and painted Cora Potter. He also produced a portrait of Elisabeth Marbury sitting in the library of her country house in Maine.

De Wolfe purchased Ranken's four paintings of the villa and hung them on the windowless corridor on the second floor. They provided an important record of the villa as it appeared in 1922. The picture of de Wolfe's boudoir, for example, depicted the way in which the green and pink colors of the vertically striped wallpaper echoed those of the rug on the floor and of the upholstery on little side chairs. The numerous prints on the wall and the single roses in vases and glass birds on the cabinet, captured by Ranken in his painting, were also familiar de Wolfe decorating strategies of the period. The watercolor painting of de Wolfe's bedroom depicted the light paneling, the yellow silk curtains, the Louis XVI bed, the prints on the wall, the mirrored door, and the pink of the bedcovers and the rug. A later photograph of the same room taken in 1982, after the refurbishment of 1946–49, indicated that relatively little change had taken place, although the number of prints on the wall had increased to include engravings of 18th-century balloon ascents and a Tiepolo drawing of the Madonna and Child.

Other changes made in the decade between 1918 and 1928 included the 1923 glazing of the terrace, which de Wolfe then furnished with "easy chairs and couches upholstered in bright chintz."[11] She also added a camp bed that had belonged to General Murat, Napoleon's brother-in-law. By 1936, she had covered the house wall and doors with mirrors reflecting the garden beyond. She also added curtains and a tent ceiling made from orange-red Venetian sailcloth and covered the furniture with leopard-skin chintz and orange sailcloth, plain Chinese tables of dark wood or black lacquer, and leopard-print area rugs.[12] A particularly curious accent, shown in a photograph of the room taken in 1936, was a rustic Mexican equipale chair made of raw cedar and tanned pigskin, which she placed next to the sailcloth sofa.

The first of the glamorous balls hosted by de Wolfe leading up to World War II began in 1930. It was held in the Ritz Hotel in Paris. Throughout the 1930s, Villa Trianon was also used as a site for lavish entertainments attended by the international fête set, including film star Norma Shearer, who was filming *Marie Antoinette* at Château de Versailles next door. An article published in *Vogue* in 1933 suggested to its readers that a weekend at Villa Trianon could provide a "fore-taste" of the summer and of the holidays.[13] De

William Ranken's painting of Elsie de Wolfe's boudoir, 1922. (Collection of the Elsie de Wolfe Foundation)

Wolfe's biographer, Jane S. Smith, has suggested that there was a commercial aspect to these events inasmuch as they brought de Wolfe decorating clients. Employing de Wolfe as a decorator, a taste adviser, and an assistant in purchasing antiques was seen as a means by which rich American businessmen and their wives could acquire invitations to Villa Trianon, which brought with them a considerable amount of social cachet.[14] It was in these years that de Wolfe added the role of professional hostess to that of interior decorator, and she devoted the same amount of attention to detail and energy to this area of her life as she did to her decorating projects.

The Circus Ball, the most visually dramatic of all the entertainments at Villa Trianon, was held on July 2,

Long Gallery, 1920s.
(Collection of the Elsie de Wolfe Foundation)

Long Gallery, 1940. (André Ostier, collection of the Elsie de Wolfe Foundation)

Seating designed by Stephane Boudin for the 1938 Circus Ball. (André Ostier, Collection of the Elsie de Wolfe Foundation)

Dance pavilion interior designed by Stephane Boudin for the 1938 Circus Ball. (André Ostier, the Elsie de Wolfe Foundation)

1938. Smith explained that "the house of Jansen, the premier furniture dealers in Paris and, since the turn of the century, a major decorating house, had an arrangement by which Elsie received a percentage of any business she steered their way."[15] This relationship with Jansen was crucial to the success of the Circus Ball, as de Wolfe used its head designer, Stephane Boudin, to create (most probably according to her wishes) an appropriate setting for it. Paul-Louis Weiller provided the funds for the event.

The most important long-term result of the Circus Ball was the decision to create a new wing to the villa in order to provide enough entertaining space for 700 guests. A green-and-white-striped dance pavilion was added; when its disappearing screen walls were opened, it was exposed to the garden on three sides. Boudin introduced Regency-style draperies that hung around the doorways leading onto the lawn. Semicircular seating units covered with white leather were also added. Above them were positioned lights in the form of blackamoors holding parasols.

The party was conceived on a level of extravagance that surpassed most of what had gone on at the villa hitherto. Coco Chanel (1883–1971), Elsa Schiaparelli (1893–1973), and the Duke and Duchess of Windsor were among the numerous illustrious guests who attended. A pair of artificial trees, their trunks painted white, was installed one on either side of the stairs that led from the Long Gallery to the dance pavilion, and a champagne bar, complete with a striped roof, was built around the trunk of a large tree in the garden. The whole effect in the new wing was completed by an abundance of pink and red roses arranged by the English floral expert Constance Spry (1886–1960), who brought them from England in three airplanes. Perhaps the

Entrance hall with the mural by Etienne Drian, 1940.
(André Ostier, collection of the Elsie de Wolfe Foundation)

most striking effect of all was the subtle lighting, provided by de Wolfe's favorite lighting expert, Rudolf Wendel, who installed an elaborate system, with the result that "night was turned into day."[16] After the event, the new wing remained a permanent feature of the villa and the dance floor was replaced by parquet flooring.

The party's decor was created by Boudin and provided a dramatic, theatrical setting for the main attraction: a circus-style performance by acrobats, jugglers, satin-clad tightrope walkers, clowns, and trained Shetland ponies made to perform by Lady Mendl herself. The following year saw a repeat event, but this time, to add a new level of extravagance, elephants were added to the list of performers.

A corner in the Villa Trianon, 1940.
(André Ostier, collection of the Elsie de Wolfe Foundation)

The luxurious balls of the late 1930s epitomized the role that Villa Trianon played within de Wolfe's fantasy life. Still a set designer in many ways, she was able to create an environment for performance, for herself, for her immediate friends, and for her entire social circle. The balls were held at a moment when de Wolfe's desire to elaborate the villa had reached its peak. She left for the United States in 1940, forced to flee France because of the invading German army, but not before she had made a photographic record of the villa's interiors. The Nazis took it over in the same year. The photographs of the house and the garden were taken by André Ostier and

numbered around 60 in total. They showed the numerous subtle changes that had been implemented at the villa during the period since the end of World War I. A photograph of de Wolfe's private boudoir, for example, revealed that the green and pink stripes had been exchanged for wood paneling. The cut-velvet upholstery of the salon's sofas had been substituted with a beige fabric dappled with dark stylized flowers, and a topiary elephant (presumably created for the party of the previous year) had been added to the garden. In the 1920s, other topiary had been planted and trained, including an extraordinary evergreen rooster more than six feet tall. At some point, too, the reflecting pool in front of the music

Mantelpiece in the Long Gallery, 1940. (André Ostier, collection of the Elsie de Wolfe Foundation)

Elsie de Wolfe's private sitting room, late 1940s. (Collection of the Elsie de Wolfe Foundation)

pavilion had been deepened to become a proper swimming pool.

In 1944, General Dwight D. Eisenhower and his troops occupied the villa following the departure of the Nazis. Two years later, de Wolfe returned to find her house looted and left to decay. Ludwig Bemelmans recorded the story of the return to France in his book *To the One I Love the Best*, describing the decorator's determination to restore the villa to its former glory. As he explained, "She saw neither broken window, nor wavy parquet floor, nor the unhappy elephant in the garden"—it had lost its billiard ball eyes.[17]

Although most of the villa's valuable contents had been put in storage, a number of small decorative items had inevitably disappeared. Bemelmans recounted how a golden unicorn, reportedly made by Cellini and

Elsie de Wolfe's bathroom, 1940. (André Ostier, Collectioni of the Elsie de Wolfe Foundation)

Sofa, 1940. (André Ostier, Collection of the Elsie de Wolfe Foundation)

one of de Wolfe's favorite objects, had been saved from the Germans by an enterprising maid. The decorator set about getting her precious furnishings out of storage, having them repaired or replaced and buying new items, among them an altarpiece, a tapestry for the hall, and a Blue Period Picasso for which she paid $25,000.

Despite the Nazi occupation, the main interior schemes were more or less intact. De Wolfe re-created the salon with most of its original items, including the 18th-century portraits by Carmontelle; the alcove, with its Louis XV armchair; the small octagonal sitting room situated next to a guest bedroom filled with chinoiserie; her private sitting room with its long corner sofa bedecked

with cushions embroidered with mottos; and the Marie-Antoinette bust that had been displayed in East 17th Street and transferred to the villa in 1927. De Wolfe restored the formal bedroom, with its four-poster Louis XVI bed, for special guests. She also revived her own bedroom, and her extravagant private bathroom—as much a living room as a bathroom—with its green chinoiserie wallpaper, collection of Chinese reverse paintings on glass, antique corner cabinet, marble basin, and a toilet disguised by a *chaise percée* and hidden by a lacquered screen. Later, after the house had become one of Weiller's weekend houses, some items from de Wolfe's Avenue d'Iéna apartment found their way here, including the mirrored zodiac center table from her bathroom, which Weiller placed at the center of Villa Trianon's salon.

By this time, de Wolfe had accumulated so many decorative items, prints, paintings, and furniture that the villa was full almost to overflowing. Gone was the simplicity and clarity of its early years, and in its place was a rich language of the interior, which brought together in one place all the themes that de Wolfe had developed through her working life and recalled the Victorian horror vacui of her early days at 122 East 17th Street. Her unique way of arriving at color schemes from decorative details; the personalization of interior spaces; the combination of antique with reproduction items; the mixture of discreet privacy with public grandeur; the lively inclusion of art in interiors, whether in the form of antique paintings or modern murals; the lack of a distinction between inside and outside; the need for modern comforts and conveniences, expressed in the villa by each bedroom having its own bathroom and by de Wolfe putting a telephone in her private bathroom—all these and more were present in the interior of this relatively small house, which for 45 years Elsie de Wolfe had thought of as her only real home.

Catalog of known Elsie de Wolfe projects

As with the majority of interior decorators, de Wolfe accepted projects large and small, from boudoir to mansion to clubhouse. The number of projects she oversaw is impossible to determine; her company's business records were disposed of after its demise in 1938. The projects listed here represent known commissions, both published and unpublished, executed by de Wolfe or her firm, variously known as Elsie de Wolfe & Co. and Elsie de Wolfe Inc.

1892–1911 / Offices at 122 East 17th Street, New York City

1897 / Sets and costumes for A Marriage of Convenience, Empire Theatre, New York City

> De Wolfe, who appeared as a maid in this production, oversaw the authenticity of the sets and costumes at the request of producer Charles Frohman.

1899–1902 / The Hermitage, rue de la Postrophe Hermitage, Versailles, France

> For three years, de Wolfe and Marbury rented a pavilion at the home of the estate of their friend Minnie, Marchioness of Anglesey and decorated it with antique purchases guided by the connoisseurship of Pierre de Nolhac, curator of the Château de Versailles.

1901 / Sets and costumes for The Way of the World.

> When overseeing the sets of *The Way of the World* in 1901, de Wolfe went so far as to underscore the authenticity of its society setting by enlisting prominent society women to appear as extras in the production. She also decorated the sets with the kind of furniture that would be used in a fine New York house, including an Italian-made tea table borrowed from the Versailles home of Lady Anglesey.

1902–1905 / Villa les Buissons, 69 Boulevard St. Antoine, Versailles, France

After the lease on the Anglesey *pavillon* ended, Marbury and de Wolfe rented Villa les Buissons, a larger house nearby, owned by the widow of Charles Morgan, a British artist. The decoration of its interiors is unknown.

1903 / Sets and costumes for Cynthia.

1905–1950 / Villa Trianon, 57 Boulevard St. Antoine, Versailles, France

1905–1906 / Emily and John R. McLean, Friendship, Tennallytown Road (later 3600 Wisconsin Avenue), Washington, DC

The decoration of an 'entertainment annex' at the country house of this District of Columbia couple was de Wolfe's first professional project, commissioned in 1905 and undertaken for the sum of $10,000. Friendship and its 75 surrounding acres had been purchased in 1898 by John Roll McLean (1848–1916). He had commissioned John Russell Pope to alter and enlarge the house into a Georgian revival mansion. A Democratic presidential candidate in the election of 1896, McLean was the publisher of *The Washington Post* and *The Cincinnati Enquirer.* His wife, Emily Beale (1854–1912), was an exclusive hostess who "never makes a call and rarely accepts an invitation of any kind." It was this sort of superior behaviour that led to her to be fictionalized as the egocentric debutante Virginia Dare in "Democracy," an 1880 novel by de Wolfe client Henry Adams. The building was "handed over without restriction or reserve" to de Wolfe and her work there was described as being "a symphony in pink, all in the style of the Seize Louis." The decorator would later work for the McLean's daughter-in-law, Evalyn Walsh McLean, the owner of the Hope diamond. It was an association that proved unsatisfactory; de Wolfe successfully sued the young socialite for non-payment of services.

1905–1906 / Opera box for J. Pierpont Morgan, The Metropolitan Opera, 147 West 39th Street, New York City

Soon after the Metropolitan Opera constructed a state-of-the-art stage for its first production of Wagner's *Parsifal*, Elsie de Wolfe redecorated the box of one of the opera's major stockholders, millionaire financier John Pierpont Morgan (1837–1913). Like all the boxes at the opera house, which was built in 1883, Morgan's parterre box (number 35) on the so-called Diamond Horseshoe was 7 feet wide by 13 feet deep and divided roughly in half, with seating for six at the front and an ante-room at the rear. Its decoration was 18th-century French in style. A writer in *The New York American*, on 19 January 1906, remarked that "with her artistic eye and deft fingers [she has] worked to obtain the best effects, for her client is a man of critical taste."

1905–1906 / Helen and Payne Whitney, 972 Fifth Avenue, New York City

Along with Jules Allard et fils, A.H. Davenport & Co., and Edward F. Caldwell & Company, de Wolfe was one of several decorators employed by the architect Stamford White (1853–1906) to create the interiors of his white-granite town house for the Whitneys. Payne Whitney

(1876–1927) was a banking heir whose father served as a Secretary of the Navy. His poet wife, Helen (née Hay, 1875–1944) was the only daughter of John Milton Hay (1838–1905), a U.S. ambassador to the Court of James', a United States Secretary of State and a close friend of de Wolfe's client Henry Adams. De Wolfe organised the manufacture and supply of numerous furnishings for the private quarters of the Whitney house, which was designed in 1902 and completed in 1908 after several setbacks, not least of which was White's murder at Madison Square Garden in 1906. The items the decorator supplied included a table for the Adam-style, octagonal breakfast room. It was "finished in pure white", she wrote to White, adding that it was "cosy and just right for four". She also procured or designed a chintz-hung canopy bed for Helen Whitney's bedroom. Additionally, de Wolfe was responsible for the decoration of a bathroom at 972 Fifth Avenue and would later work at Greentree, the Whitney estate near Manhasset, New York..

1905–1906 / Cora Brown–Potter, Maidenhead, England

Brown–Potter (née Mary Cora Urquhart) was an early mentor of de Wolfe, socially and professionally. Married to James Brown Potter (1853–1922), a banker whose uncle and great-uncle were Episcopal bishops of New York, the Louisiana-born beauty created an international scandal when she abandoned her husband in 1887 to become an actress; they divorced in 1900. After dazzling London theatregoers with her compelling beauty and minimal talent – "acting is no longer considered absolutely essential for success on the English stage," one observer wrote after witnessing one of the star's performances – Mrs.Brown–Potter, as she was known professionally, built a house on the River Thames, in Maidenhead, a picturesque town in Berkshire about 25 miles from London and popular as a weekend society destination. An article in the 20 May 1906 issue of *The Telegraph* described it as a "pretty cottage which ate thousands of pounds", adding of its interiors that "one can always recognise a de Wolfe room wherever one finds it" and praising the decor's "personal quality." Two undated early 20th-century photographs depict Potter lounging in a hammock outside a charming red-brick cottage with mullioned windows and leaning against a window seat in the same house, likely the Maidenhead residence. From the objects on view in the hand-colored photograph, the sitting-room was traditional but fresh, with windows simply dressed in pale-blue curtains edged with an embroidered Greek-key motif and plum-colored undercurtains. The window seat was upholstered in pale rose with a saffron yellow cushion, Georgian-style paneling was painted light blue, and an elegant gilt mirror and console was visible. Due to her disastrous management of the Savoy Theatre in London, Brown–Potter was forced to declare bankruptcy in 1905 and sell her Maidenhead residence and its contents. The actress retired from the stage in 1912, after which she turned to performing in Vaudeville, lecturing on the occult, and writing a beauty and health manual. De Wolfe later decorated a New York City apartment for the actress, with boldly striped green-and-white curtains held with plate-size rosettes of the same fabric.

c. 1905 / Painted iron bed, designed and patented by de Wolfe.

1905 / Brooks Hall, Barnard College, Broadway and 116th Street, New York City

1905–1907 / The Colony Club, 120–124 Madison Avenue, New York City

1906 / Florence and Walter Hamlin Dupee, 1015 Ocean Boulevard, Coronado, California

Once de Wolfe had completed "the task of remodelling and beautifying the interior of the Crocker mansion at Burlingame," a newspaper reported, the decorator travelled south to Coronado, "there to decorate the fine residence of Walter Dupee." Built in 1902 by the architects Irving J. Gill (1870–1936) and William Sterling Hebbard (1863–1930), the Dupee residence at Coronado, a summer-resort peninsula across the bay from San Diego, was a stucco-and-timber Tudor-style mansion overlooking the Pacific. The stockbroker son of a Chicago grain operator, Dupee was a champion polo player who, besides owning the Coronado house, had Edgemoor Farm, a Guernsey cattle ranch in Santee, California, a 40-room country house in Oconomowoc, Wisconsin, and a residence in Chicago. His wife was Agnes Florence Kennett, later Mrs. George Burnham. The Coronado house was probably the first introduction of future de Wolfe client, the duchess of Windsor, to the decorator's interiors. The duchess and Florence Dupee met in 1918, when the former was living in Coronado and married to her first husband, a naval officer, and she and Florence remained lifelong friends.

1907 / Clyde Fitch, 113 East 40th Street, New York City

Under de Wolfe's direction, Everett Shinn painted a piano for the playwright Clyde Fitch, with extravagant rococo-style decorations that were much admired. De Wolfe appeared in several of Fitch's acclaimed melodramas.

1907 / Clara Bloodgood, Hotel Lorraine, Fifth Avenue and East 45th Street, New York City

A society girl turned actress—she performed alongside de Wolfe in the 1901 Clyde Fitch production of *The Way of the World* and was managed by agent Elisabeth Marbury—Bloodgood (née Stevens, 1870–1907) ordered a dressing table for the apartment she shared with her third husband, a stockbroker, William Laimbeer (d. 1913). It probably was never delivered; reportedly beset with financial problems, Bloodgood committed suicide a few months after placing the order. She was previously married to William Moller Havemeyer of the sugar processing clan and banker John Bloodgood Jr.

c. 1907 / Henrietta and Benjamin S. Guinness, 8 Washington Square North, New York City

Daughter of a British baronet and wife of an Irish banker, Henrietta Guinness (née Williams-Bulkeley) and her husband (1868–1947) hired de Wolfe to decorate some, if not all of, her New York residence, an 1833 Greek Revival redbrick town house. The couple began renting the house around 1907 and lived there for approximately a decade. During their tenure, 8 Washington Square North was a center for Manhattan society's bohemian element, thanks to Henrietta Guinness' reputation as a theater patron and amateur artist. A visitor to her December 1913 exhibition of portraits at Knoedler Galleries in Manhattan gingerly called it "a courageous attempt to reach toward qualities not quite yet within the painter's grasp." De Wolfe described a portion of her work for the Guinnesses in May 1913 as "a little hallway wainscoted in white with a green trellis covering the wall space above." The trelliswork was also hung with della Robbia-style ceramic rondels, probably similar to those de Wolfe sold at her shop.

c. 1907 / Homewood, the residence of Elizabeth and George G. Haven, South Salem Road, Ridgefield, Connecticut

George Griswold Haven Jr. (1870–1925), president of the Connecticut Exchange National Bank, head of the Metropolitan Opera Real Estate Company, and son of a founder of *The New York Times,* had a 42-room Shingle-style summer house built for his young family at the end of the 19th century. About a decade later, two wings were added, one of which contained an 18th-century-style French ballroom created by de Wolfe. The ballroom was reportedly built for the 16th-birthday dance in honor of one of the Havens' two daughters—probably Leila Ingersoll Haven, who came out as a debutante in 1909. Haven's wife, Elizabeth Shaw Ingersoll, daughter of a Connecticut governor, died in 1923. Two years later, Haven committed suicide, five months after his second marriage to Dorothy James.

c. 1907 / Viola and Edward Truesdell Cockcroft, Lily Pond Lane, East Hampton, New York

De Wolfe decorated the dining room and loggia of the newlywed Cockcrofts' beach-sand stucco house, which had been designed by Harrie T. Lindeberg (1879–1959), whom she probably met when he worked in the office of McKim, Mead & White. She equipped the loggia, a suburban Parthenon ringed by thick, dramatically fluted Doric columns, with woven-willow furniture by Millet and Company, a New York City firm with factories in New Jersey. Between two columns that framed the French doors to the dining room, de Wolfe hung curtains to give the effect of a stage, similar to her work at After All three decades later. Indoors, she used painted French furniture and a screen decorated with a rococo pattern. De Wolfe may also have had input on the interior of the couple's New York town house, 59 East 77th Street, which also was designed by Lindeberg. Cockcroft was a wealthy landscape painter; his wife was Viola Augusta Tilden (née Baker). Their East Hampton house was later owned by James T. Lee (1888–1968), the maternal grandfather of Jacqueline Kennedy Onassis (1929–1994).

c. 1907 / Josephine W. Livermore, North Castle, New York

Located on Bryam Lake in Westchester County, about 50 miles north of New York City, the Livermore estate was the country house of Josephine Whitney Brooks (d. 1965), the widow of John R. Livermore (1872–1906), a wealthy lawyer. No photographs have been located of this commission, but de Wolfe got the job for obvious reasons: the client's mother-in-law, Baroness Raymond Seillière, formerly Mrs. Charles F. Livermore, was a long-time friend of both de Wolfe and de Wolfe's mother. In 1926, prior to her marriage to Channing W. Hare, Josephine Livermore sold the lakeside property to Frank L. Fuller of Liggett & Myers, the tobacco company. Given her longstanding relationship with the family, de Wolfe also may have advised on the decoration of Livermore's other homes, among them, 17 East 73rd Street and 7 East 65th Street, both in New York City, and Inchiquin, an estate on Bellevue Avenue in Newport, Rhode island.

1907 / Ethel and William H. Crocker, New Place, Burlingame, California

1907–08 / Lolita and J. Ogden Armour, Mellody Farm, Lake Forest, Illinois

1908 / T. Nixon Residence, Washington, D.C.

Describing one of the day rooms of the Nixon house in Washington, de Wolfe explained that it had been "left for the owners to bring in their own pictures and *objets d'art.*" She described it as a simple space with paneled walls and a fireplace with no mantel. The reception room was illustrated in *Good Housekeeping* (March 1913, p. 356). The clients may have been Lewis Nixon (1861–1940), a battleship builder who invented sonar, and his first wife (née Sally Lewis Wood, d. 1937).

1908 / Henry Adams, 1608 H Street, N.W., Washington, D.C.

De Wolfe stayed with Adams, a renowned historian, while she worked on the Nixon project in the summer of 1908 in Washington. On completing it she also redecorated an unidentified room in her host's house on H Street, N.W., across Lafayette Square from the White House. Adams (1838–1913) was a grandson and a great-grandson of two American presidents, and his majestic Romanesque revival house was one of a pair completed in 1885 for him and his best friend, John Hay, the father of de Wolfe client Helen Hay Whitney. The conjoined Hay–Adams houses were the work of architect Henry Hobson Richardson (1838 – 1886)).

c. 1908 / James Deering, 1430 Lake Shore Drive, Chicago, Illinois, and New York, New York

A vice president of International Harvester, which merged in 1902 with his family's Deering Harvesting Company, James Deering (1859–1925) approached de Wolfe when it was time to decorate portions of his New York and Chicago residences. To her eventual regret, she put an ambitious young associate, artist Paul Chalfin (1874–1959), in charge of installing a fountain in the Chicago house. Its architect was Arthur Heun, who also designed Mellody Farm, which de Wolfe was decorating at the same time for the J. Ogden Armours. Before long, Chalfin had usurped her role as Deering's style advisor, going on to oversee the construction and decoration of Vizcaya, a romantic Italianate palazzo that the millionaire bachelor built on a 180-acre site on Biscayne Bay near Miami. De Wolfe did provide a few items for the house but otherwise had no direct influence on its interiors.

1909 / The Lenox Library, Fifth Avenue and East 70th Street, New York City

An article in the *The New York Telegraph* of 15 May 1909 explained that, in addition to working on "clubs, hotels, private palaces, modest city homes, comfy country bungalows and lodges in all parts of the country" de Wolfe had created the decorations for a "wonderful fete" to be held 18–20 May at the Lenox Library for the benefit of Hope Farm, a 500-acre rural retreat and vocational training center for neglected and underprivileged children. In the yard behind the massive white limestone building designed by Richard Morris Hunt (1827–1895), the fete was held in a temporary neoclassical French garden of potted bay trees, faux-marble columns, and booths illuminated by 3,000 electric lights. There was also an open-air restaurant, a dance floor, shopping kiosks, and other entertainment venues for the charity event. Landscape architect Andrew Robeson. Sargent (1876–1918, who worked for de Wolfe client Mai Coe and whose sister-in-law Rita Lydig rented de Wolfe's East 55st Street house, was in charge of the overall design of the event, though de Wolfe's participation is frequently cited in contemporary articles. In 1912, the library was demolished by the Pittsburgh steel magnate Henry Clay Frick to make way for his new mansion.

1909 / The New Theatre, Central Park West and 62nd Street, New York City

The article in *The New York Telegraph* quoted above also mentioned that de Wolfe had worked on the sets and costumes of the opening production of the New Theatre, one of Elisabeth Marbury's business ventures. The theatre's first show, presented in November 1909, was Shakespeare's *Antony and Cleopatra*, though it seems more probable, given de Wolfe's tastes, that she oversaw the sets and costumes for Sir Richard Brinsley Sheridan's 18th-century farce *The School for Scandal*, staged a month later. Designed by the architects John Mervin Carrère (1858–1911) and Thomas Hastings (1860–1929), the New Theatre was a non-profit performance space known as the Millionaires' Theatre because of its rich backers. It closed in 1911, having staged ambitious new works by John Galsworthy (1867–1933), Edward Knoblock (1874–1945), Maurice Maeterlinck (1862–1949), and Henrik Ibsen (1828–1906) that proved too expensive to produce and too high-brow to attract a dedicated audience. The building was torn down in 1930 to make way for the Art Deco Century Apartments towers.

c. 1910 / Lillie and Frederick C. Havemeyer, 34 East 37th Street, New York City

De Wolfe illustrated Lillie Havemeyer's chinoiserie chintz bed in *The House in Good Taste* of 1913. Furnished for the first wife of Frederick Christian Havemeyer (1860–????), scion of the American Sugar Company fortune, the bedroom seems to have been decorated in a typical de Wolfe manner, with wood paneled walls covered with framed pictures and bedside tables with good lighting. The canopy bed very closely resembled that of Helen Whitney, next to which it was illustrated. First married and divorced from millionaire horseman William R. Travers (1861–1905), Lillie Havemeyer was a sister of Anne Vanderbilt and Emeline Olin and a sister-in-law of Daisy Harriman, all of them de Wolfe clients. The decorator also likely worked on Havemeyer's Paris house, formerly the home of Napoleon's stepdaughter, Hortense de Beauharnais, , as well as her New York town house, 16 Sutton Square, and her country house in Roslyn, New York; the latter two were designed by architect Mott B. Schmidt.

c. 1910–1911 Alice and William E. Iselin, 745 Fifth Avenue, New York City

In *The Delineator* of March 1912 de Wolfe described the dining room in the home she decorated for the William Iselins as a "very stately Georgian dining-room in a large city house." She continued, "This room is extremely simple, but it is the simplicity of elegance. The heavy marble molding of the mantel is treated without a shelf. The portrait is set in the wall, with Grinling Gibbons carvings above it." The decorator subsequently used the photograph of the Iselins' dining room in her 1913 book, *The House in Good Taste*, (p. 179), and in the text added that "It is extremely formal but there is about it none of the gloominess one associates with New York dining-rooms". William Emil Iselin (1848–1937), a dry goods merchant, was a member of an enterprising Swiss immigrant family who made millions in textiles, banking, and real estate at the end of the 19th century. His wife was Chemical Bank heiress Alice Rogers Jones (1850–1932), a cousin of the novelist Edith Wharton (1862–1937).

c. 1910 / Pauline and Ernest Iselin, New York City

De Wolfe's known contribution to the Iselin house was a bedroom whose plaster walls were painted to resemble 18th-century English pine paneling, with sober furniture of the same period and a folk-art hooked hearth rug. Heir to a private-banking fortune, Iselin (1872–1954) was an officer of numerous corporations; his wife (née Pauline Whittier, 1877–1946) was a social leader who was the president and founder of Generosity Thift Shop. The bedroom was likely at the Iselins' town house at 20 East 56th Street, which they bought in 1906 and lived in until approximately 1925.

c. 1910 / Charlotte Morton, Boulevard St. Antoine, Versailles, France

An article in *Vogue* magazine of 1914, on the subject of the Villa Trianon, mentioned that "through a break in the trees may be seen the roofs of the house of Mrs. Paul Morton, another American woman who has purchased an old French house. This house, also, was restored under the supervision of Miss de Wolfe." Born Charlotte Goodridge (1858–1938), de Wolfe's neighbor was the widow of Paul Morton (1857–1911), the Michigan-born, Nebraska-bred president of the Equitable Life Assurance Society, who had been Theodore Roosevelt's Secretary of the Navy; his brother, Joy Morton (1855–1934), was a founder and chairman of Morton Salt. The Paul Mortons' New York residence was 844 Fifth Avenue, which might have been a de Wolfe project, too. Interestingly, one of the couple's two daughters, Pauline Smith (1887–1955, later Mrs. Charles H. Sabin and Mrs. Dwight F. Davis) launched an interior decoration business around 1914, possibly inspired by de Wolfe's work for the family. She eventually consulted on the redecoration of the White House during the Truman Administration, though was more famous as a Republican Party leader and founder of the Women's Organization for National Prohibition Reform. (Vogue March 1914, p. 46)

1910 / Elsie de Wolfe and Elizabeth Marbury, 131 East 71st Street, New York City

1910 / 103 East 35th Street, New York City

The offices records of the architect Ogden Codman Jr. list unspecified work on this address for de Wolfe and Marbury. Nothing about the project is known.

1910 / Mary and Charles W. Harkness, Mirador, Madison Avenue, Madison, New Jersey

1910 / The Pacific-Union Club, 1000 California Street, San Francisco, California

An unidentified article of January 1910 reported that Elsie de Wolfe's "latest success" was in winning the job of furnishing the new Nob Hill headquarters of the Pacific-Union Club, an august gentlemen's social organization. To obtain this, the writer explained, she had had to "compete against most of the interior decorators in this country, many of them men." Built in 1886 as the home of silver-mining magnate James C. Flood (1826 – 1889), the majestic brownstone building survived the devastating San Francisco earthquake of 1906 and was remodelled and enlarged as the club's headquarters by architect Willis Jefferson Polk (1867–1924). It opened in January 1911.

1910–1911 / Anne Morgan, 219 Madison Avenue, New York City

1911 / Elsie de Wolfe and Elizabeth Marbury, 123 East 55th Street, New York City

c. 1911 / Ethel Barrymore, New York City

According to the September 1911 issue of *The Delineator*, de Wolfe "has had a beautiful time decorating Ethel Barrymore's apartment." The actress (née Ethel Blythe, 1879–1959) had been de Wolfe's understudy in *The Bauble Shop* in the early 1890s and continued to cross paths with de Wolfe, with whom she shared a manager and a dressmaker. In 1909, Barrymore married Russell Griswold Colt (1882–1959), son of the president of U.S. Rubber Co. Though it is possible that de Wolfe decorated Barrymore's apartment at 4 West 40th Street, the same building where de Wolfe established her first office, it is more likely that she decorated a later flat, shared by the actress and her new husband.

c. 1912 / Bertha and Potter Palmer, 1350 North Lake Shore Drive, Chicago, Illinois

Around this time, de Wolfe designed at least one chair and presumably executed other decorating projects for the home of the queen of Chicago society, Bertha Palmer (née Bertha Matilde Honoré, 1850–1918). Known for her philanthropic endeavors, she was also the president of the board of lady managers of the World's Columbian Exposition. Her husband, Potter Palmer (1826–1902), amassed a reported $25 million fortune in real estate, hotels, and retail pursuits; her sister was married to a son of Ulysses S. Grant.

c. 1912 / Laura and Edwin S. Bayer, 32 East 70th Street, New York City

Given de Wolfe's frequent association with the artist Everett Shinn in the creation and installation of custom-painted paneling for French-style dressing rooms, it seems probable that the decorator was involved in a boudoir that Shinn painted for Laura Stanton Bayer (née Kayser, later Countess Antoine Sala, d. 1961), heir to the Julius Kayser & Co. silk hosiery and lingerie fortune, valued at a reputed $100 million. Part of a neo-French classical limestone town house designed by the architects Taylor & Levi and completed in 1912, the Louis XVI-style boudoir was an small octagonal room with raised panels that Nancy McClelland described as decorated with "the pastoral scenes, the blue ribbons, the musical trophies, and the soft colourings [sic] that make a classically feminine and seductive background." Each panel was topped with a trompe l'oeil parted drapery of "old French blue," while the windows were hung with matching blue silk taffeta curtains, each topped with a pelmet copied from the trompe l'oeil versions. The furnishings were of a type long associated with de Wolfe, including a chaise longue upholstered in toile de Jouy, an elegant white-painted Louis XVI armchair in a fabric dappled with sprigs of flowers, and wall-to-wall plush carpeting, likely in pale blue. From the ceiling hung a small, electrified chandelier ornamented with colorful porcelain flowers, probably Sèvres. Bayer's first husband, who died in 1929, was the treasurer and later president of Julius Kayser & Company, and was a noted collector of Gothic art. Her second husband, whom she married in 1931, was a Franco-American nobleman who was a longtime friend of de Wolfe's.

1912 / Ruth and W. Bayard Thayer, 84 Beacon Street, Boston, Massachusetts

Though de Wolfe's work for banker William Bayard Thayer (1862–1916) and his wife, the former Ruth Simpkins (1865–1941) appears largely undocumented, photographs of the couple's hall appears in *The House in Good Taste* (1913), an inclusion that certainly indicates the decorator's association with the project. The Georgian revival red brick mansion was designed for the Thayers by Ogden Codman Jr. (1863–1951), who worked on de Wolfe's house on East 17th Street in New York City as well as the remodelling of 131 East 71st Street. In the wood-paneled Thayer library stood one of the little kidney tables—produced in oak, walnut or mahogany—that de Wolfe designed and often produced for clients. The decorator described the room as being "very beautiful . . . [and] full of suggestion." Thayer was a grandson of a prominent Boston clergyman and a descendant of Dutch patroons. His wife, "a conspicuous figure in society of Boston, Newport, Washington, and New York," was a prize-winning grower of roses, camellias, and Chinese lilies. According to the couple's grandchildren, de Wolfe also advised on the decoration of the Thayers' country house, Hawthorne Hill, 679 George Hill Road, Lancaster, Massachusetts. Codman's office records indicate that he also contributed to that house's interior decoration.

1912 / Amanda and Jay P. Graves, Waikiki, 12415 Fairwood Drive, Spokane, Washington

1912 / The Women's Industrial Exhibition, Grand Central Palace, 480 Lexington Avenue, New York City, New York

A successful independent career woman, Elsie de Wolfe was invited to participate in the third Women's Industrial Exhibition—the first two having been held in London and Glasgow in 1910 and 1911 respectively—a female-exhibitors-only fair which demonstrated "the many ways Women [sic] can earn a living." It was held at the Grand Central Palace from 14 March - 23 March 1912, and de Wolfe contributed a model apartment that contained, as she recalled in *After All,* a "modern kitchen, demonstrating many of the time- and labor-saving devices which have only recently come into general use." Constructed alongside Grand Central Terminal, the Grand Central Palace was an exhibition hall, built in 1911–12 by the terminal's co-architects Warren & Wetmore.

1912 / Eva and James Warren Lane, Suffolk House, Boney Lane, St. James, New York

De Wolfe created sumptuous interiors for the Long Island home of Lane (1865–1927) and his wife (née Eva Metcalf Bliss, 1867 – 1922). Lane's father-in-law, Eliphalet Williams Bliss (1836–1903), a manufacturer of torpedoes, had previously used Arthur Little (1852–1925) of the Boston architectural firm Little & Browne for two of his New York residences, so it was only natural that the Lanes employed him in 1912 to relocate and remodel their country house, which dated from around 1860. Ten years later, de Wolfe would decorate the Lanes' house at 49 East 52nd Street in New York City, which was partly remodelled by Ogden Codman Jr. The former guest house of de Wolfe client Anne Vanderbilt, it was located in a nineteenth-century Warren & Wetmore-designed mansion. It would later become an apartment building, the graduate school of the Juilliard School of Music, and after extensive modernist remodelling, the studios of the Columbia Broadcasting System, a.k.a. CBS.

1912–13 / Florence Baldwin, 25 Quai Voltaire, Paris, France

A controversial New England beauty who spent most of her adult life in France and Italy, Florence Baldwin (1859-1918) hired de Wolfe after she acquired an apartment in a 17th-century *hotel particulier* on the left bank of the Seine. They may have met through their mutual friends, the esthete Count Robert de Montesquiou (1885–1921) and the art expert Bernard Berenson (1865–1959), but Baldwin's scandalous reputation surely preceded her. In 1892, her husband, Edward Parker Deacon went to prison for shooting and killing her French lover. By the time de Wolfe began the Quai Voltaire project, her client was the mistress of a Roman prince. The second-floor apartment, where Baldwin lived from 1912 onwards, was admiringly described by Berenson's wife, Mary, as a "little jewel."

c. 1913 / Elizabeth and John Whipple Slater, Hopedene, Cliff Avenue, Newport, Rhode Island

Presumably during a major redecoration in 1913, de Wolfe decorated an enclosed porch at Hopedene. It was the summer house of Slater (1852–1924), a cotton manufacturer and real-estate investor, and his wife (née Elizabeth Hope Gammell, 1854–1944), an heiress to the Brown & Ives mercantile fortune, built on textile manufacturing and East Indies shipping. Ogden Codman decorated much of the Georgian revival house in 1902–03, which had been designed by Peabody and Stearns.

c. 1913 / Florence and J. Borden Harriman, 35 East 49th Street, New York City

In the April 1913 issue of *Good Housekeeping*, de Wolfe included an illustration of Florence "Daisy" Harriman's bedroom, which she described as exhibiting "dignity and repose." Closets, concealed by mirrors, flanked a Louis XVI mantel, and light fixtures were positioned on either side of a carved mirror. The five-story house was unfinished when the couple purchased it in the fall of 1904, the year Daisy Harriman became president of the Colony Club, and it is very possible that de Wolfe was brought in to plan its completion as well as the decoration. Harriman (née Florence Jaffray Hurst, 1870–1967) was a leading figure in national civic, charitable, and political circles and served as U. S. Minister to Norway during World War II. In 1889, she married banker Jefferson Borden Harriman (1864–1914), a railroad heir and brother of de Wolfe clients Anne Vanderbilt, Emeline Olin, and Lillie Havemeyer.

1913 / Grace and Ormond G. Smith, Shoremond, Center Island Road, Oyster Bay, New York

1913 / Castle House, 26 East 46th Street, New York City

1913–14 / The Vacation Association Headquarters, 38th West 39th Street, and 35-37 West 38th Street, New York City

1914 / Magnolia and George Sealy, Open Gates, 2424 Broadway, Galveston, Texas

1914–15 / Adelaide and Henry Clay Frick, 1 East 70th Street, New York City

1914–15 / The Strand Theatre Roof Garden, Broadway and West 47th Street, New York City

1915 / Julia and Lydig Hoyt, New York City

De Wolfe executed decorations for Hoyt and his first wife (née Julia Wainwright Robbins, 1897–1955), a socialite and popular amateur actress he had married the previous year. And when de Wolfe held the grand opening of her showroom at 2 West 45th Street in 1915, Julia Hoyt served as co-hostess, along with Anne Morgan and Bessy Marbury. Once proclaimed a peerless example of American beauty by the French artist Paul Helleu, she later became a stage and silent-film actress and married movie actor Louis Calhern and studio executive Aquila C. Giles.

1915 / Sets and costumes for "Nobody Home" and "Very Good Eddie," The Princess Theatre, 104 East 39th Street, New York City

1915–16 / Louise and Rudolph M. Weyerhaeuser, 266 Summit Avenue, St. Paul, Minnesota

Rudolph Michael Weyerhaeuser (1868–1946) was an heir to the timber fortune founded by his father, Frederick Weyerhaeuser (d. 1914). In 1896, he married Louise Bertha Lindeke (1870–1952). Little is known about de Wolfe's interiors for the looming red-brick Queen Anne-style house that the couple inherited upon the senior Weyerhaeuser's death—they also owned an estate in Cloteau, Minnesota, on the Mississippi River—but Louise Weyerhaeuser's diaries indicate that the renovation was extensive enough for the family to move to rented quarters until its completion. De Wolfe described Louise Weyerhaeuser's surprise when she bid her client farewell after only visiting the house for a few hours. "My work begins at the office," she explained. "I have seen your house; now I have to think about it." This recollection, expressed in the decorator's autobiography, seems to be an exaggeration. Weyerhaeuser's diaries indicate that in 1915, on the day of de Wolfe's visit to 266 Summit Avenue, she escorted the decorator to a ladies' luncheon held in her honor at the Missouri Club before seeing her off to New York. In addition, Weyerhaeuser's diaries report that a de Wolfe associate known only as Mr. Petry (Petrie?) oversaw the project, which included the installation of French-style boiseries.

1915–1937 / Automobiles

Throughout her long career, Elsie de Wolfe's name was used as a barometer of good taste in consumer advertising, and she enthusiastically promoted products ranging from Lucky Strike cigarettes to haute couture. Frequently, her name was linked with the latest automobiles. Soon after she was reported examining the Peugeots and Lancias on display at a 1915 foreign automobile exposition in New York City, for example, de Wolfe , "the leading authority in design and decoration, famous for her unerring good taste," had become an advisor to the Locomobile Company. An advertisement for the American luxury car company stated that "her influence will extend to the decorative treatment of Closed Car Interior." In 1922, she was the star of an advertising campaign for the Willys-Knight Great Six four-door sedan—the car had been conceived, she claimed, by "someone with a true sense of the fitness of things"—and in 1937, advertisements touted de Wolfe as the style consultant for the 1937 Chrysler Imperial, a car she called "a refreshing new note in beauty and style … [that] will prove intensely interesting to women."

c. 1916 / Jane and John Philip Sousa

Reference to the fact that America's March King, the composer John Philip Sousa (1854–1932), was one of de Wolfe's celebrity clients was made in a 1916 newspaper clipping: "John Philip Sousa, who has been decorated by the King of England, and redecorated by Elsie de Wolfe, is to be further honoured by being made a lieutenant in the United States Marines." Which of his residences she decorated is not specified, though it probably was the house Sousa and his wife (née Jane van Middlesworth Bellis, d. 1944), bought in 1914, Wilbank, a handsome Mediterranean-style villa overlooking Hempstead Harbor in Port Washington, New York.

1916 / A Pantomime Rehearsal, Plaza Hotel, New York City

For a war benefit to raise funds, in part, for the American Women's Ambulance Hospital at Versailles, France—housed in Villa Trianon—de Wolfe appeared as Lady Muriel Beauclerc in a one-act musical comedy by British composer Edward Jones. It was, *The New York Times* noted, her first stage appearance "after an absence of eleven years" and she received "a rousing ovation." De Wolfe also oversaw the set and the costumes.

1919 / Virginia and Daniel C. Jackling, Hotel St. Francis, 335 Powell Street, San Francisco, California

The decoration of the penthouse apartment of Daniel Cowan Jackling (1869–1956), a pioneer of open-pit mining and the founder of the Utah Copper Company, was undertaken by Elsie de Wolfe Inc. under the supervision of the decorator's sister-in-law Winifred de Wolfe (1871–1957). Jackling, a widower, had recently married San Francisco socialite Virginia Jolliffe (1879–1957), and the newlyweds established themselves on the top floor of the St. Francis, a leading hotel overlooking Union Square. The wide hall leading to the living room was dominated by a huge tapestry (probably one of many the Jacklings bought from J. E. French and Company) and a tall Chinese screen (likely from the fabled stock of Asian artifacts at Gump's, another of the couple's favorite emporia). The living room, praised for its "ease and comfort," had the air of an English country house, with oak paneling, a molded plaster ceiling, and needlework chairs.

c. 1920 / Rue Leroux, Paris, France

Soon after the end of World War I, de Wolfe reportedly rented a town house on rue Leroux.. The precise address of this de Wolfe project is unknown. It is possible that de Wolfe actually lived at 10 rue Leroux, the Paris residence of Anne Vanderbilt.

c. 1920 / Johanne and Joseph Graham Crane

Crane (1885-1954) was a grandson and great-nephew of the founders of the National Cash Register Company of Dayton, Ohio; his wife, the former Johanne Marie Andreasen (died 1954), was Danish. It is not known which of the Cranes' residences de Wolfe decorated; the couple had homes in Dayton, New York City, and Manhasset, New York.

1920–28 / Nell and Thomas H. Cunningham, 103 Warren Street, Glens Falls, New York

1920s–1949 / Paul-Louis Weiller, France

Over a period of nearly 30 years, de Wolfe reportedly worked on as many as 16 residences belonging to Weiller (1893–1993), a Jewish industrialist who was the director of Gnome-Rhône, the French aircraft-engine manufacturer. Weiller met de Wolfe during World War I, when he was a young aviator and she was nursing wounded soldiers. They quickly became co-dependent—he, the generous patron, and she, a crucial society conduit. For decades, de Wolfe decorated and re-decorated Le Noviciat, Weiller's villa in Versailles, where he lived with his Greek wife, Aliki Diplarakos (1912–2002, later Lady Russell). Combining 18th-century elegance with modern convenience, Le Noviciat was characterised by what one magazine called "period accuracy and warm livability." From 1949 to 1953, Weiller rented the duke and duchess of Windsor a house he owned at 85 rue de La Faisanderie in Paris; its de Wolfe-designed interiors included a shell-encrusted bathroom.

1921 / Elisabeth Marbury, 13 Sutton Place, New York City

1921 / Anne Vanderbilt, 1 Sutton Place, New York City

1922 / Anne Morgan, 3 Sutton Place, New York City

c. 1922 / Sun porch, client and location unknown

Published in the June 1922 issue of *Arts & Decoration*, though doubtless completed much earlier, this glassed-in sun porch featured blue-green trellis-covered walls inset with full-length mirrors and topped with openwork medallions depicting "Native birds in natural colorings." The floor was paved with glazed square tiles, probably terra cotta, and the modest, highly-polished furniture included numerous colonial-style ladder back chairs with woven rush seats and painted decorations.

1924 / Condé Nast, 1040 Park Avenue, New York City

c. 1924 / John McMullin, New York City

The living room of John McMullin, an editor at *Vogue*, featured several of the decorator's hallmarks of this period, including a velvet-textured carpet of artificial leopard laid on a floor of black-and-white linoleum squares, a leopard-print velvet throw, and a lean tuxedo-style sofa upholstered in beige damask.

c. 1925 / Marjorie and George B. Hedges, Jericho Turnpike, Westbury, New York

Only one photograph appears to exist of the interiors of the house on the Hedges' Long Island estate, in which de Wolfe or a member of her firm decorated a dressing room between 1920 and 1925. Nancy McClelland decorated the dining room in Jacobean fashion around the same time. A narrow space, the dressing room was dominated by an outsize American Colonial-style corner cupboard displaying antique ceramic bowls and candlesticks. It had bright flowered chintz curtains, a matching skirted dressing table, and a graphic hooked area rug patterned with leaves and flowers. Marjorie Hedges (née Burnes, d. 1952) was an Illinois real-estate heiress once hailed as "the most beautiful woman in America." From 1907 to 1911, she was the second wife of Chicago stockbroker Sidney C. Love (1873–1952). She married Hedges, a lawyer, in 1920. The contents of the Hedges house were sold at Meredith, a New York auctioneer, in 1953.

c. 1925 / Ella Dodge, Long Island, New York

The former Rachel Ella Lynch (1874–1964) was the second wife and widow of sportsman and steel heir William Earl Dodge III, the son of de Wolfe client Emeline Harriman Olin.

c. 1925 / Frances and Zalmon G. Simmons Jr., Rambleside, Clapboard Ridge Road, Greenwich, Connecticut

1926 / Rita H. de Alba Lydig, 123 East 55th Street, New York City

A fabled aesthete of Cuban and Spanish background and author of the melodramatic society novel *Tragic Mansions*, Lydig (née Rita Hernandez de Alba de Acosta, 1879-1929) began renting de Wolfe's former residence in 1926, for which the decorator or her firm provided unspecified furnishings and accessories. Formerly married to the industrialist W.E.D. Stokes Sr. and Maj. Philip Lydig, the beauteous socialite filed for bankruptcy in 1927. Among a list of creditors that included French couturiers, English decorators, a Boston jeweler, and a New York automobile dealership was "Elsie de Wolfe & Co.," which she owed $12,732. The contents of the house, which included rare antiques selected by Stanford White, were sold at auction to settle her debts.

1927 / J. Walter Thompson, 420 Lexington Avenue, New York City

In 1927, the J. Walter Thompson advertising agency moved from 224 Madison Avenue into the new Graybar Building on Lexington Avenue. The offices were designed by Carrère & Hastings. Helen Lansdowne Resor (1886–1964), a pioneering female copywriter who ran the company with her husband, Stanley Resor (1879–1963), commissioned prominent tastemakers of the day—including industrial designer Norman Bel Geddes (1893–1958) and the master blacksmith Samuel Yellin (1885–1940)—to remodel the interior spaces of their new location. Geddes, for instance, created a two-story space that was a combination auditorium and conference room, a vertiginous modern room with gray walls, turquoise curtains and upholstery and brass wall details. The executive offices on the 11th floor, however, were decorated by Elsie de Wolfe, Inc. with a combination of antiques and modern furniture to create personalized spaces geared to the tastes of the individual employee.

1929–30 / Sir Charles and Lady Mendl, 10 Avenue d'Iéna, Paris, France

c. 1930 / Fritz Mannheimer, Villa Monte Cristo, Vaucresson, France

A banker who placed de Wolfe's fortune in English investments, Fritz Mannheimer (1890–1941), a German Jewish financier who became a Dutch citizen in 1936, was the director of the Amsterdam bank Mendelssohn & Co. An international currency manipulator nicknamed "the king of flying capital," Mannheimer maintained a luxurious de Wolfe-decorated home, Villa

Monte Cristo, in Vaucresson, about three miles from Versailles. However they were introduced, client and decorator surely found much to mutually admire, given her appreciation for all things 18th-century French and Mannheimer's impressive cache of drawings and paintings by ancien-régime artists such as Fragonard, Watteau, and Chardin. It is conceivable that de Wolfe may have advised on the decoration of his Dutch residences too: a house at Hobbemastraat 20 in Amsterdam and another country place, Villa Protsky. Eight months before Mannheimer died suddenly in Vaucresson, he married a young Brazilian, Marie Annette Reiss. Not only was his demise unexpected, it was suspiciously timed. The day after his death, the Dutch newspaper *Handelsblad* announced that Mendelssohn & Co. had collapsed, and soon it was common knowledge that much of its director's art collection, and presumably the furnishings he obtained from de Wolfe, had been bought on credit extended by the bank. Whether de Wolfe's investments were affected is unknown. Much of Mannheimer's art ended up being bought by Adolf Hitler but was returned to the Netherlands and France after the war.

c. 1930 / Edwina and Leo d'Erlanger, Upper Grosvenor Street, London, England

With the exceptions of working on residences for Wallis Simpson and a house for the actress Cora Brown-Potter, little is known of de Wolfe's work in the United Kingdom. Evidence that the decorator may have had other work in England comes from her correspondence in the inter-war years with the English textile designer–retailer, Elspeth Little. One of her few known English projects was the house of one of the city's most dashing couples— Baron Leo F.A. d'Erlanger, son of a prominent German Jewish banking clan, and his bride, Edwina Prue (1907–1994), an American ballroom dancer he met on a London train platform and married in 1929.

1930 / Mainbocher, 12 Avenue George V, Paris, France

Magazine editor Main Rousseau Bocher (1891–1976) opened a Paris couture business under the name Mainbocher, and one of his major investors was de Wolfe. The salon's mirrored chimney-pieces and furniture upholstered in animal hides were reminiscent of de Wolfe's décors at Villa Trianon and 10 Avenue d'Iéna, strong evidence of the decorator's guiding hand..

1930–31 / Reba and J. Robert Rubin, 993 Fifth Avenue, New York City

One of the most soigné spaces created by Elsie de Wolfe Inc. was a duplex apartment for J. Robert Rubin (1882–1958), senior counsel and executive vice president of the Hollywood film studio Metro-Goldwyn-Mayer, and his wife, the former Reba Hitchcock (d. 1971). Punctuated by mirror-backed vitrines displaying antique Asian ceramics, the oval breakfast room was a chinoiserie fantasy of cream lacquer walls with incised decorations of flowers and bamboo executed by Robert Pichenot, an engraver and artist whose illustrations were the staple of the early 20th-century French fashion magazine *Journal des Dames et des Modes.* The master bedroom was formally French but with a contemporary, characteristically de Wolfe, twist: every corner, cornice, baseboard, door, and window surround was outlined with broad flat bands of etched and carved mirror. The half-tester bed was hung with sapphire-blue satin, meticulously quilted in the manner of 18th-century Provençal quilts, and triangular sconces of blue and colorless mirrored glass— arguably the work of French designer Serge Roche—hung on ivory-white walls. Like many de

Wolfe schemes of this period, and appropriate for a film-industry icon whose triumphs including buying the rights to the novel *Grand Hotel* and turning it into a film for Greta Garbo, the decor used period and modern furnishings, rich fabrics (satin, silk, chenille) and a smoky color scheme enlivened with reflective glass. The apartment was located in a 16-story building built opposite the Metropolitan Museum of Art in 1929-1930. The Rubins began renting the duplex in 1930 from its owner, movie mogul Jesse L. Lasky (1880–1958), a founder of Famous Players-Lasky.

1932–33 / Frances Clyne, 6 East 56th Street, New York City

Famed in her youth as America's best-dressed actress, de Wolfe continued to maintain strong personal links with the international fashion industry throughout her life, both as an eager private client, a canny promoter of up-and-coming talent, and an inspired creator of retail fashion settings. In a five-story townhouse leased by the society dressmaker Frances Clyne (1879– 1944), Elsie de Wolfe Inc., created stylish retail spaces that combined 18th-century French furniture with some simple, geometric, modern chairs and sofa and an abundance of mirrors. It was an appropriately chic setting for Clyne's blue-chip clients, like the exiled Queen Victoria Eugenia of Spain (1887–1969), who made headlines when she stopped by the recently decorated shop and bought three outfits.

1934 / Dining room, The Fine Arts Exposition, Rockefeller Center Forum, New York City

Elsie de Wolfe Inc. was one of 58 exhibitors who participated in the first Fine Arts Exposition, a three-week show held at the Rockefeller Center Forum from November 3 to December 1, 1934, and organized by the Antique & Decorative Arts League. The firm's contribution was an oval dining room with pale gray walls, silver lamé curtains, and a flamboyant purple, white, and gray floor in a radiating pattern of scalloped, graduated rectangles and squares that recalled the work of contemporary French designer Emilio Terry. The floor was reportedly "mosaic" but a surviving photograph suggests high-polished inlaid linoleum. The room's mirror-and-gray-lacquer dining table, mirrored fireplace surround, and plaster-and-mirror obelisks were by the French modernist designer Serge Roche; at the center of the table stood de Wolfe's favored centrepiece, a crystal ship in full sail. The room was lighted by Rudolf Pierre Wendel (1902–1955), the German-born American lighting expert famed for garden illumination that uncannily replicated moonlight. Wendel, who crafted the after-dark landscape lighting for Villa Trianon as well as for high-society clients like Singer sewing-machine heiress Marguerite "Daisy" Fellowes (1887–1962), also designed lighting for the Chicago Century of Progress Exposition of 1933 and the New York 1939 World's Fair.

1934 / The Elsie de Wolfe Suite, Essex House Hotel, 160 Central Park South, New York City

1934 / The Café Lounge and Bar, The Savoy-Plaza Hotel, Fifth Avenue and 59th Street, New York City

1935 / Wallis and Ernest A. Simpson, 5 Bryanston Court, London, England

1935 / Frances and Nate B. Spigold, , 12 East 77th Street, New York City

The dining room of the Spigold house was executed by Eleanor Cosden (née Neves, 1887–1963), a longtime Syrie Maugham client who became an associate at Elsie de Wolfe Inc. after financial misfortunes struck her husband, Oklahoma oil man Joshua Seney Cosden, Sr. (1881-1940). Under the nom-de-couture Madame Frances, Frances Spigold was a fashion designer patronized by film stars such as Mary Pickford, Barbara LaMarr, and Leatrice Joy. She also was an early employer of Travis Banton (1894–1958), who designed the Madame Frances gown Pickford wore at her 1919 marriage to Douglas Fairbanks, Sr. Spigold's husband (1886–1959) was a vice president with Columbia, the Hollywood motion-picture studio, and a noted collector of French impressionist paintings and modern American art.

1935 / Hope Hampton and Jules Brulatour, 1145 Park Avenue, New York City

1935–36 / Veronica and Gary Cooper, Brentwood Heights, California

The crisply dramatic rooms that de Wolfe created for film star Gary Cooper (1901–1961) soon after his 1933 marriage to the New York socialite Veronica "Rocky" Balfe (1914–2000, later Mrs. John Marquis Converse) possessed an appropriately camera-ready style. De Wolfe's familiar mirrored screens made another appearance, and as in the apartment of J. Robert Rubins, there was a mirrored fireplace with a mirrored hearth, this one a massive neo-medieval example by Serge Roche; Roche also was the source of the mirror-paved console tables flanking it. Designed by the New York City architects Harvey Stevenson (1895–1984) and Eastman Studds (1905–1972), in association with Roland E. Coate, Sr. (1890–1958), the house was a low-slung adaptation of a traditional Bermuda cottage, and its broad, spare rooms and wide doorways and windows gave it an open-plan feeling. De Wolfe responded to these spatial qualities by decorating the Coopers' home with a graphic restraint that complemented the architecture's airy modernity. The living room was furnished with a pair of tailored tuxedo sofas clad in acid green damask, a stark white carpet spread across a floor of black linoleum, wing chairs with exaggerated scrolling arms, and two large Mexican-style starburst mirrors, another Roche creation. The adjoining dining room was a surprisingly elegant take on the era's Asian-tropical decorative themes, the Chinese Chippendale-style chairs of natural bamboo and glossy black leather standing on a coarse-fringed yellow carpet. The wide-mouthed fireplace was framed in natural bamboo laid in a bold herringbone pattern and surmounted by a colorful contemporary Japanese print wrapped by a bamboo-and-mirror frame. In contrast the newlywed Coopers' bedroom was a striking combination of femininity and masculinity: walls painted dusty pink, with deep brown wall-to-wall carpeting, and a sumptuous sleigh bed upholstered in crushed white velvet, its seams lined with fanciful bobble fringe in the manner of British interior decorator Syrie Maugham. The fireplace and door and window surrounds of the bedroom also were outlined with wide strips of mirror.

1936 / King Edward VIII of England, Fort Belvedere, Windsor Great Park, Berkshire, England

De Wolfe advised on the decoration of three unspecified rooms at the king's country retreat. The scope of the work or whether any of it was executed remains unknown. However, it is known that de Wolfe produced three models or maquettes for the king's consideration.

1936 / Wallis Simpson, 16 Cumberland Terrace, London, England

1936 / Pedac Galleries, Christmas dining table, New York City

Participating in a showcase of designers at Pedac Galleries, Elsie de Wolfe Inc. presented a Christmas dining table entitled "Frankincense and Myrrh." The centrepiece was described as "two bronze heads in Eastern headdress flanking a pile of gold and silver glass balls."

1936 / Ina Claire, The Pierre, 21 East 61st Street, New York City

De Wolfe's involvement with the best-dressed Broadway star Ina Claire (1893–1985) included the sets for *Ode to Liberty,* a 1934 comedy, as well as the interiors of a suite that the actress maintained at The Pierre hotel around the same time. It is uncertain whether de Wolfe oversaw either of these projects personally but the elements utilized are part of her established vocabulary of the period. The living room of Claire's small apartment, for example, contained a mirrored coffee table, a six-panelled mirrored screen and six mirrored flower pots, all of which appeared in other contemporary de Wolfe schemes. Simple 18th-century French furniture pieces were juxtaposed with modern side chairs upholstered with leopard-spot velvet. A large, overstuffed chair was covered in feather-pattern chintz to provide a whimsical note that underscored de Wolfe's reliance on novelty fabrics printed with animal-skin patterns or fern fronds.

1937 / Grosfield House, 320 East 47th Street, New York City

Five years after the firm's founder severed her ties with the company, Elsie de Wolfe Inc. participated in an exhibition of model rooms illustrating trends in decoration at Grosfield House, the showroom of an American furniture manufacturer known for designs in Lucite. The de Wolfe display was a living room and bedroom. According to a contemporary report, "Modernizing the Venetian style, she has adorned the hearth wall of the living room with a white plaster scroll and leaf ornamentation." The closet was framed by "antique mirror glass" and in the bedroom were "twin beds cleverly united by damask-covered headboard and have an elaborately quilted spread in an old-gold fabric." The neo-Louis XV dressing table was set before a wall of antique mirror glass panels.

1938 / The Duke and Duchess of Windsor, Château de La Croë, Cap d'Antibes, France, and 37 Boulevard Suchet, Paris, France

1938 / Natoma Estates Inc. and Boak & Paris, Architects

Elsie de Wolfe Inc. decorated portions of a 20-story apartment building at Riverside Drive and West 82nd Street in New York City. The firm also displayed a loveseat with a slipcover of blue material patterned with "fluffy white leaf pattern" at an exhibition at Pedac Galleries in New York. The company also decorated the set for a program by the actress-singer Cecilia Loftus. Shortly after this, Elsie de Wolfe Inc. went out of business, its remaining stock of furniture and accessories sold at a four-day auction in November 1938.

1940 / The Lady Mendl Suite, St. Regis Hotel, 2 East 55th Street, New York City, New York

1942 / Sir Charles and Lady Mendl, After All, 1018 Benedict Canyon Drive, Beverly Hills, California

1944 / The Lady Mendl Suite, Rooms 317-325, The Plaza Hotel, Fifth Avenue, New York City

Notes

Introduction

1. Elsie de Wolfe, *The Standard and Vanity Fair* (June 9, 1905), n.p.

2. De Wolfe, *The House in Good Taste* (New York: Century, 1913), 12.

3. Although 1865 is generally accepted as the year of de Wolfe's birth, she constantly lied about her age, a fact that is evidenced by dramatic inconsistencies that appear in Ellis Island immigration records of de Wolfe's translatlantic crossings and New York City federal census forms.

4. De Wolfe, *The House in Good Taste*, 5.

5. Ibid.

6. De Wolfe, "Stray Leaves from My Book of Life: A Little Autobiography and Some Fleeting Thoughts by a Famous Woman of the American Stage," *Metropolitan Magazine* XIV (1901), 809.

7. De Wolfe, *After All* (New York: Harper and Brothers, 1935), 2.

8. Ibid.

9. Ibid., 8.

10. De Wolfe, *The House in Good Taste*, 27.

11. Anonymous article, *The Telegraph*, May 20, 1906, Robinson-Locke Collection of Theatre Scrapbooks, New York Public Library (series 3, vol. 373), 13.

12. De Wolfe's biographer, Jane S. Smith, gives the date as 1887; Marbury, in her memoirs, gave the year of their meeting as 1884.

13. In his memoirs, the art dealer Joseph Duveen recalled his astonishment when a rich client, Arabella Huntington, initially refused to purchase an outstanding portrait of the 18th-century English actress Sarah Siddons because Huntington (curiously, a former kept woman) equated the celebrated thespian's career with loose morals.

14. Kim Marra, "A Lesbian Marriage of Cultural Consequence: Elisabeth Marbury and Elsie de Wolfe, 1886–1933," in Robert A. Schanke and Kim Marra, eds., *Passing Performances: Queer Readings of Leading Players in American Theater History* (Ann Arbor: The University of Michigan Press, 1998), 116.

15. "While she was never a great actress she had a distinction and a diction which were admirably suited to the parts she played. . .. Her talent was indisputable but she gave no evidence of genius." Elisabeth Marbury, *My Crystal Ball* (Boni and Liveright, 1923), Chapter X.

16. De Wolfe, *After All*, 31.

17. Jane S. Smith, *Elsie de Wolfe: A Life in the High Style: The Elegant Life and Remarkable Career of Elsie de Wolfe, Lady Mendl* (New York: Atheneum, 1982), 245.

18. Edith Wharton and Ogden Codman Jr., *The Decoration of Houses* (New York and London: W. W. Norton and Company, 1978 [reprint]).

19. Cecil Beaton, *The Glass of Fashion* (London: Weidenfeld and Nicholson, 1954), 206.

20. "Her flair in detecting the real from the imitation was extraordinary. Her sense of proportion was unerring. She might make a mistake in many things, but she was physically incapable of a mistake in the matter of taste." Marbury, Chapter X.

21. T. H. Robsjohn-Gibbings, *Goodbye Mr. Chippendale* (New York: Alfred A. Knopf, 1944), 25.

122 East 17th Street

1. De Wolfe, *After All*, 85.

2. Daughter of a prominent New York lawyer, Marbury (1856–1933) represented the dramatic works of many important American and European writers, among them George Bernard Shaw, Victorien Sardou, and Oscar Wilde, and established the modern royalty system. She also was a breeder of champion French bulldogs and English mastiffs. She was a leader of the Democratic Party and played an important role in Franklin Delano Roosevelt's political ascent.

3. De Wolfe, "Our Lady of the Decorations I: The Old Washington Irving House in New York as It Is Today," *The Delineator* 78 (October 1911), 214.

4. Margherita Arlina Hamm, *Eminent Actors in Their Homes: Personal*

Descriptions and Interviews (New York: James Pott & Company, 1902), 56.

5. Kathleen D. McCarthy, *Women's Culture: American Philanthropy and Art, 1830–1930* (Chicago: The University of Chicago Press, 1991), 76–77.

6. Even when the house was built, this view would have been impossible to enjoy. More than half a dozen city blocks separated it from the East River, not to mention a plethora of town houses and other buildings. In *The House in Good Taste*, de Wolfe stated that she missed seeing the river from her old dining room window. It was a picturesque exaggeration; the dining room window actually faced north, onto a row of brownstone houses. In 1911, the house became the Washington Irving Tea Room; from 1917 until 1920, the house was the site of a photography studio run by Jane and Clarence White. (www.ci.nyc.ny.us)

7. The 1910 federal census of New York City noted that Marbury and de Wolfe had a Swedish-born cook and footman, an English-born waitress, and two German-born ladies' maids.

8. De Wolfe, "Our Lady of the Decorations: I," 214.

9. De Wolfe, *After All*, 85.

10. Wharton and Codman, *The Decoration of Houses*.

11. Various press cuttings in scrapbook in Robinson-Locke Collection of Theatre Scrapbooks, vol. 151; Elsie de Wolfe, vols. 1 and 152; and Elsie de Wolfe, vol. 2, in New York Public Library, including ones from *The Morning Telegraph* (March 9, 1907) and *Broadway Magazine* (n.d.), n.p.

12. Pauline C. Metcalf, ed., *Ogden Codman and the Decoration of Houses* (Boston: The Boston Atheneum/Godine, 1988), 21.

13. De Wolfe, "Our Lady of the Decorations: I," 215.

14. De Wolfe, *The House in Good Taste*, 37.

15. Undated article, Robinson-Locke Collection of Theatre Scrapbooks, New York Public Library (series 3, vol. 373).

16. Ibid.

17. De Wolfe, "Our Lady of the Decorations I," 215.

18. Hamm, *Eminent Actors*, 59.

THE COLONY CLUB

1. Mrs. J. Borden Harriman, *From Pinafores to Petticoats* (New York: Henry Holt and Company, 1923), 79.

2. De Wolfe, *After All*, 47.

3. Newspaper cutting, October 21, 1905, Robinson-Locke Collection of Theatre Scrapbooks, New York Public Library (series 3, vol. 373), 13.

4. McLean, a former Republican candidate for president, was married to Emily T. Beale, a socialite who was fictionalized as Virginia Dare in Henry Adams's novel *Democracy*.

5. Newspaper article, March 11, 1906, Robinson-Locke Collection of Theatre Scrapbooks, New York Public Library (series 3, vol. 373), 12.

6. Florence Jaffray Hurst was the daughter of Francis W. Hurst, a retired British army officer. She married Harriman in 1889. He died in 1914.

7. Harriman, 72.

8. In fact, there was a wine room on the ground floor of the Colony Club, and an early photograph of the trelliswork tea room clearly shows ashtrays on every table. For some time, however, the club did not have a liquor license because of its proximity to Madison Square Church. In any case, insisted Bessy Marbury, chairman of the club's board of governors, little imbibing was done on the premises. "Women are too vain to do that. They want to remain slender, and liquor produces fat," she said. "No Liquor License for Women's Club," *The New York Times* (April 6, 1907), 6.

9. Dunbar (1874–1953) was an essayist and biographer. Her husband was the poet Ridgely Torrence.

10. Olivia Howard Dunbar, "The Newest Woman's Club," *Putnam's Monthly* (May 1907), 196.

11. Ibid., 76.

12. De Wolfe also called it the winter garden. It opened on January 30, 1908. "Colony Club's Roof Garden," *The New York Times* (January 29, 1908), 7.

13. Letter from de Wolfe to Irvin, December 27, 1905. McKim, Mead & White Archive (New York: Collections of The New-York Historical Society).

14. Letter from McKim, Mead & White office to Colony Club house committee of November 17, 1906. McKim, Mead & White Archive (New York: Collections of The New-York Historical Society).

15. White had an affair with Evelyn Nesbit, a model and showgirl, before she married the Pittsburgh millionaire Harry K. Thaw. Her husband took revenge on White by murdering him, although at trial Thaw pleaded insanity.

16. Letter from de Wolfe to McKim, Mead & White office, July 1906. McKim, Mead & White Archive (New York: Collections of The New-York Historical Society).

17. De Wolfe, *The House in Good Taste*, 96.

18. The chef was an Englishwoman, Sophia Nailer, who had previously served as cook in the households of millionaires William C. Whitney and Clarence Mackay, as well as W. Bourke Cochran, an Irish-born orator and Democratic politician who was a close friend of Bessy Marbury. Specialties of the kitchen included chicken croquettes with peas, shad roe with tomatoes, mock turtle soup, and cold eggs in aspic.

19. De Wolfe, "Our House Interiors XIII: The Art of Treillage," *Good Housekeeping* (May 1913), 642.

20. "Colony Club Finds Midsummer Pleasures in the City," *The New York Times* (July 7, 1907), X5.

21. Around 1915, Paul Chalfin, de Wolfe's one-time associate, and F. Burrell Hoffman Jr., an architect, added a stucco-clad concrete tea house lined with green trelliswork to the gardens of Vizcaya, the Miami palazzo of industrialist James Deering.

22. De Wolfe, "Our House Interiors XIII: The Art of Treillage," 642.

23. Marlborough chairs—comfortable upholstered armchairs made in Marlborough, Massachusetts—emulated English 18th-century models. In the United States they were called Colonial or Federal-style chairs.

24. Only the pool at the men-only University Club was believed larger.

25. Various forms of hydrotherapy, the last originating in Bad Nauheim, Germany, involved water being poured from a bucket or from a hose.

26. "Women's New Club, the Colony, Opened," *The New York Times* (March 12, 1907), 9.

27. In 1899, de Wolfe exhibited a show of Shinn's pastels, including portraits of herself and Marbury, at 122 East 17th Street; she then commissioned him to execute a double portrait of her and Marbury. Shinn had a show of his work at the Colony Club in 1910.

28. The artist's papers in the Archives of American Art contain several notes and letters from de Wolfe that encourage Shinn to take inspiration from the works of Giovanni Battista Pergolesi, Piat Sauvage, and Elisabeth Vigée-Lebrun when executing painted furniture and wall decorations for her; she also arranged for him to study the 18th-century painted French furniture and architectural relics at the Cooper Institute.

29. An article in *The New York Times* explained that this second winter garden would be used as a tea room or after-dinner lounge.

30. Arriving in America after a trip to Europe with Marbury, de Wolfe described the stoves as "modeled after the style of Lucca della Robbia" and "bound to make a sensation . . . . I believe they will revolutionize heating in New York." "New French Plays to Be Seen Here," *The New York Times,* (October 21, 1907), 7.

31. De Wolfe referred to the enclosed area as a sun porch.

32. "Colony Club Finds Midsummer Pleasures in the City," *The New York Times* (July 7, 1907), X5.

33. "It is a great tribute to the successful management . . . that in a little more than six years it has actually outgrown its luxurious headquarters." "The Colony Club to Move Uptown," *The New York Times* (December 13, 1913), 1.

34. William Adams Delano (1874–1960) and Chester H. Aldrich (1871–1940) set up an architecture practice in New York in 1903.

35. In 1917, Genevieve Garvan Brady, wife of the financier and philanthropist Nicholas F. Brady, bought the building for $400,000 in order to donate it to the Red Cross. Today it is the American Academy of Dramatic Arts. Few of the de Wolfe fittings survive.

ETHEL AND WILLIAM H. CROCKER

1. De Wolfe, *After All,* 67. Burlingame is now Hillsborough, and since 1955, the Crocker house has been the Burlingame Country Club.

2. Ibid.

3. Ibid.

4. Undated, untitled article, Press Cuttings file, Theatre Collection, New York Public Library.

5. Crocker grandson Charles de Limur quoted in Michael Svanevik and Shirley Burgett, "Matters Historical," *Palo Alto Daily News* (July 5, 2004), 15.

6. De Wolfe, *After All,* 68.

7. www.gracecathedral.org.

8. "Nob Hill Residents Mean to Rebuild," *The New York Times* (May 19, 1906), 6.

9. Porter Garnett, *Stately Homes of California* (Boston: Little, Brown, and Company, 1915), 9.

10. Ibid.

11. Ibid., 10.

12. Ibid.

13. De Wolfe, *The House in Good Taste,* 213.

14. Ibid.

BROOKS HALL

1. Article in *The New York American* (January 19, 1906), Robinson-Locke Collection of Theatre Scrapbooks, New York Public Library (series 3, vol. 373), 12.

2. For example, in a letter dated May 28, 1907, written by de Wolfe to Osborn, the decorator explained that "the office on the first floor is to [be] filled similar to the office at the Colony Club" (Barnard College Archives).

3. The editor of a well-regarded collection of George Washington's letters, Osborn (née Lucretia Thatcher Perry, 1858–1930) was a crusader for women's rights, the Republican Party, and environmental causes. In 1913, as the chairman of the Women's

Auxiliary of the New York Zoological Society, she led a movement to ban the aigrette, a fashionable ladies' head ornament made of feathers from egrets and birds of paradise. She was married to Henry Fairfield Osborn, president of the American Museum of Natural History.

4. Marian C. White, *A History of Barnard College* (New York: Columbia University Press, 1954), 3.

5. Ibid., 13.

6. Ibid., 20.

7. A graduate of Smith College and an activist for the welfare of Cuban children orphaned by the Spanish-American War, Gill (1860–1926) resigned her Barnard post in 1908, soon after a student she had expelled was allowed to return to the college over her objections. She eventually joined the faculty of Berea College in Kentucky.

8. Married to businessman-turned-painter Col. Abraham Archibald Anderson, Elizabeth Milbank Anderson (1850–1921) was heiress to a $10 million fortune amassed by her father, Jeremiah Milbank, a banker who was a founder of Milbank Tweed as well as Borden Condensed Milk Company. She ended up donating more than $2 million to Barnard College and also funded disparate philanthropic endeavors including children's health, ancient Egyptian studies, and the American Field Service in France during World War I.

9. J. Dawson, *Residential Life at Barnard College: Precedents and Prototypes* (unpublished essay submitted to Barnard College, May 1, 1995), 27.

10. Christopher Gray, "Architecture of Barnard, in the Shadow of Columbia," *The New York Times* (December 7, 2003),

11. *Barnard Bulletin* (vol. XII, no. 1, Wednesday, September 25, 1907), 1.

12. Ibid., 53.

13. Quoted in Dawson, *Residential Life at Barnard College*, 30.

14. Letter from de Wolfe to Gill, May 25, 1907 (Barnard College Archives).

15. Ibid., undated (Barnard College Archives).

16. Ibid., May 28, 1907 (Barnard College Archives).

17. Ibid.

18. *Barnard Bulletin*, 1.

19. Ibid., 53.

20. Brooks Hall was the site of the first meeting of Alpha Epsilon Phi, a non-disciminatory sorority founded by a group of largely Jewish students soon after the hall opened. The dormitory also made headlines in 1908 when Kang Tong Pih, daughter of an earl who was a close advisor to the Emperor of China, arrived to live in what was described as "the most expensive suite" in the building. "Chinese Noblewoman Here," *The New York Times* (October 18, 1908), 20.

21. Andrew S. Dolkart, *Housing the Columbia Community* (www.beatl.barnard.columbia.edu/cuhistory/archives/housing.htm), 6.

22. De Wolfe, *The House in Good Taste*, 248.

23. Dawson, 29.

24. Ibid.

25. Ibid.

26. Ibid., 32.

LOLITA AND J. OGDEN ARMOUR

1. Ruby Ross Goodnow, "The Story of Elsie de Wolfe," *Good Housekeeping* 56 (June 1913), 762.

2. The Potter Palmer chair is illustrated in de Wolfe, "Our House Interiors X: A Light, Gay Dining-Room," *Good Housekeeping* (February 1913), 357.

3. De Wolfe, *After All*, 68.

4. Ibid.

5. Ibid.

6. The first mention was in *The Chicago Tribune*, June 26, 1955, although she was credited with only the upstairs rooms.

7. Heun was born in 1864 and died in 1946. Peter B. Wight, "Mellody Farm: The Country Home of J. Ogden Armour Esq., Lake Forest, Ill.," *The Architectural Record* (vol. 29, no. 2, February 1916), 5–102.

8. *Harper's Bazaar* (August 1918), 35.

9. Obituary in *The Chicago Tribune*, February 7, 1953.

10. Ibid.

11. M. Carroll, "The Legacy of Mellody Farm: A Slice of How the 'Other Half' Lived," in *The Chicago Tribune* (August 26, 1984), 7.

12. "Mellody Farm (Armour Estate)," a series of unpublished notes about the Armour house taken down in 1932, from the archives of *Fortune* magazine.

13. Wight, "Mellody Farm," 102.

14. De Wolfe, *The House in Good Taste*, 280.

15. De Wolfe, *After All*, 69. The green-and-white velvet sofas may have been a later alteration, based on contemporary photographs of the winter garden.

16. Ibid.

17. *Harper's Bazaar* (August 1918), 35.

SHOW HOUSE, 131 EAST 71ST STREET

1. De Wolfe, "After All," *Ladies' Home Journal* (February 1935), 34.

2. By 1915, she still owned the house, carrying a mortgage of $25,000. She finally sold it in 1921, completely furnished.

3. *The New York Times* (March 23, 1910).

4. The scope of and reason for this project are unclear. Perhaps de Wolfe and Marbury planned to rent and renovate this house before finding the town house on East 55th Street.

5. Metcalf, *Ogden Codman*, 32.

6. Ibid., 21.

7. De Wolfe also would send Chalfin (1875–1959) to Chicago to install a wall fountain in farm-equipment millionaire James Deering's house, which eventually resulted in him being hired to oversee the construction and decoration of Deering's mansion in Miami, Vizcaya. De Wolfe played only a minor role at Vizcaya, which was as important in establishing Chalfin's reputation as the Frick house had been to de Wolfe's. Though she doubtless would have preferred to have had greater input in this multimillion-dollar project, in the end she only supplied a few fabrics, an English console, and a French dressing table. Chalfin also worked as a designer for the silent-film studio Famous Players–Lasky and as a curator of Japanese art at the Museum of Fine Arts in Boston.

8. *The New York Times* (April 16, 1902).

9. De Wolfe, "Transforming a Small City House," *The Delineator* (February 1912), 132.

10. Letter from Codman to de Wolfe, July 26, 1910 (Society for the Preservation of New England Antiquities), quoted in Metcalf. The use of the word "more" would indicate that de Wolfe had another idea for the floor that did not pass muster with her collaborator.

11. De Wolfe, *The House in Good Taste*, 129.

12. Wharton and Codman, *The Decoration of Houses*, 120–21.

13. De Wolfe, "Transforming a Small City House," 132.

14. Ibid.

15. Ibid.

16. Ibid.

17. "The rooms are heirs of all the ages . . . whether . . . of the Samurai [sic] or French Kings [sic]." *The New York Times* (January 15, 1911), X9.

18. De Wolfe, "Transforming a Small City House," 132.

19. Ibid.

20. *The New York Times* (January 15, 1911), X9.

21. De Wolfe, "Transforming a Small City House," 132.

22. A newspaper account of the opening noted that de Wolfe greeted welcomed visitors in the drawing room while two assistants — one presumably Paul Chalfin - led tours of the house.

23. De Wolfe, "Transforming a Small City House, 132.

24. Ibid. The jars and vases would eventually be displayed atop the trumeau mirror in de Wolfe and Marbury's house on East 55th Street.

25. De Wolfe, *The House in Good Taste*, 80. One visitor to the house described this space as "a man's sleeping room." *The New York Times* (January 15, 1911), X9

26. *The New York Times* (January 15, 1911), X9.

27. De Wolfe, *After All*, 125.

28. *The New York Times* (January 15, 1911), X9.

123 EAST 55TH STREET

1. De Wolfe, *After All*, 129.

2. Ibid., 126.

3. H. M. Yeomans, "A Remodeled City House," *American Homes and Gardens* (December 1913), 42.

4. Ibid.

5. "The Real Estate Field," *The New York Times* (March 30, 1911), 16. After de Wolfe and Marbury's lease ended, the house was sold to the photographer Baron de Meyer, whose portraits of de Wolfe often appeared in *Vogue*. The house was later rented by Rita Lydig, a society beauty and longtime client of both de Wolfe and Stanford White.

6. De Wolfe, "My Own House," *Harper's Bazaar* (July 1913), 17.

7. De Wolfe, *The House in Good Taste*, 318.

8. Ibid., 44.

9. By 1920, according to the New York City federal census of that year, at 123 East 55th Street, de Wolfe and Marbury employed a Swiss butler and private maid, a German private maid, a Swedish cook, and a Norwegian servant.

10. De Wolfe, *The House in Good Taste*, 48.

11. Ibid.

12. Ibid.

13. Ibid.

14. De Wolfe, *After All*, 128.

15. In her diaries, Matilda Gay, a longtime friend and wife of the artist Walter Gay, admiringly called 123 East 55th Street "a little Versailles in New York." Rieder, 119.

16. Classified advertisement, *The New York Times* (April 15, 1914), 21.

17. She also devoted several pages to the importance of private sitting rooms and discussed men's need for a similar refuge to replace the more popular idea of the den, which she described, negatively, as "an airless cubby-hole."

18. Yeomans, 45.

19. De Wolfe, *The House in Good Taste,* 169.

20. Undated journal entry, Wood Archives

21. *The New York Times* (January 25, 1903), 27.

22. Ibid. Marbury certainly was a de facto resident of East 55th Street but a newspaper article reported that she also on occasion had "lived in a hotel or in the Colony Club." "Miss Marbury Wins Customs Duty Suit," *The New York Times* (February 16, 1918), 12. Curiously, the 1912 New York City telephone directory listed her as living at 105 East 40th Street and de Wolfe at East 55th Street.

23. De Wolfe, *After All,* 129.

24. Yeomans, 42.

MARY AND CHARLES W. HARKNESS

1. *Madison Eagle* (June 15, 1917).

2. De Wolfe, *The House in Good Taste,* 149 and 256.

3. J. W. Rae Sr. and J. W. Rae Jr., *Morristown's Forgotten Past: "The Gilded Age"* (Morristown, New Jersey: John W. Rae, 1979), 6.

4. *Madison Eagle* (June 15, 1917).

5. Ibid. (June 25, 1909).

6. De Wolfe, *The House in Good Taste,* 157.

7. De Wolfe, *The House in Good Taste,* 148.

8. *Madison Eagle* (June 15, 1917).

ANNE MORGAN'S ROOMS

1. "Walls Do Not a Prison Make," *Harper's Bazaar* (February 1912), 59.

2. Frederick Allen Lewis, *Ladies and Not-So-Gentle Women: Elisabeth Marbury, Anne Morgan, Elsie de Wolfe, Anne Vanderbilt, and Their Times* (New York: Viking, 2000), 166. Codman eventually would marry one of his clients, a rich widow, and J. Pierpoint Morgan's biographer makes it clear that Anne Morgan and Bessy Marbury probably became lovers around 1904. Jean Strouse, *Morgan: American Financier* (New York: Random House, 1999).

3. Ibid., 55.

4. Ibid.

5. "Lady into Dynamo," *The New Yorker* (October 22, 1927), 23.

6. "Walls Do Not a Prison Make," 59.

7. Ibid.

8. "A Little Portfolio of Good Interiors," *House and Garden* (January 1917), 35. The *Harper's Bazaar* article of 1912 described the sofa and one armchair as upholstered in chenille damask, not cut velvet.

9. De Wolfe, *The House in Good Taste,* 256.

10. Rollin van N. Hadley, *Elsie de Wolfe and Isabella Stewart Gardner in Fenway Court* (Boston: Isabella Stewart Gardner Museum, 1981), 40.

11. De Wolfe, "Period Furniture," *The Delineator* (March 1912), 214.

12. De Wolfe, *The House in Good Taste,* 162.

13. Ibid., 164.

14. Ibid.

15. Ibid., 219.

16. Ibid., 222–23.

17. Ibid., 230.

AMANDA AND JAY P. GRAVES

1. Graves's career is described in John Fahey, *Shaping Spokane: Jay P. Graves and His Times* (Seattle and London: University of Washington Press, 1994).

2. *Spokane Daily Chronicle* (November 3, 1920).

3. *Spokesman-Review* (May 14, 1911).

4. Ibid.

5. Fahey, *Shaping Spokane,* 91.

6. *Spokesman-Review* (May 14, 1911).

7. Fahey, *Shaping Spokane,* 92.

8. De Wolfe, *The House in Good Taste,* 230.

VILLA TRIANON

1. Ludwig Bemelmans, *To the One I Love the Best: Episodes from the life of Lady Mendl (Elsie de Wolfe).* (New York: The Viking Press, 1955), 21.

2. Goodnow, 762.

3. Ibid.

4. De Wolfe, "Castles in Touraine," *Cosmopolitan* (February 1891).

5. Smith,, 44.

6. Ibid., 81.

7. Born in Georgia, Mary (Minna) Livingstone King married twice

into the English aristocracy, first to a member of the Wodehouse family and second to the 4th Marquess of Anglesey.

8. De Wolfe, *After All*, 159.

9. Wharton and Codman, 1.

10. De Wolfe, *After All*, 150–51.

11. Ruby Ross Goodnow, "The Villa Trianon," *Vogue* (March 15, 1914), 54.

12. Ibid.

13. Known for his work at Vaux-le-Vicomte and Château de Courances, Achille Duchêne(1866-1947) alsoworked at Blenheim Palace for Gladys Deacon, the wife of the 9th Duke of Marlborough and a daughter of Florence Baldwin, an American client of de Wolfe.

14. De Wolfe, *After All*, 166. See also Goodnow, "The Villa Trianon," 54. Gontaut-Biron's American widow, Martha Leishman, would become chatelaine of Minna Anglesey's Versailles house after she married insurance millionaire James Hazen Hyde. An ardent Francophile, Hyde bought the house from Lady Anglesey around 1914.

15. De Wolfe, "Our Lady of the Decorations: Villa Trianon," *The Delineator* (May 1913), 416.

16. De Wolfe, *After All*, 160.

17. Ibid., 161.

18. De Wolfe, "Our Lady of the Decorations," 416.

19. Ibid.

20. Marbury, Chapter XXVIII.

21. Steven M. L. Aronson, "Gérald Van Der Kemp: Versailles," *Interview* (February 1979).

GRACE AND ORMOND G. SMITH

1. *The New York Times* (April 18, 1933).

2. Some sources give the size of the property as 65 acres.

3. "A Million-Dollar Country Home Being Erected On North Shore of Long Island for Ormond G. Smith," The New York Times (January 12, 1913), X18.

4. "Artistic Country Residence on Long Island's North Shore," *The New York Times* (February 25, 1912), XX2.

5. H. de Witt Fessenden, "The Country House of Ormond G. Smith, Esq., Oyster Bay, L.I.," *The Architectural Record* 40 (August 1916), 116.

6. Ibid., 116–17. See also Eileen Harris, *The Genius of Robert Adam: His Interiors* (New Haven: Yale University Press, 2001), 285.

7. Ibid., 117.

8. Ibid.

9. De Wolfe, *The House in Good Taste*, 275 and 319.

10. Fessenden, 117.

11. De Wolfe, *The House in Good Taste*, 283..

12. Fessenden, 117.

13. Ibid.

14. Ibid.

15. Ibid.

16. "Long Island Realty Has Record Year," *The New York Times* (April 4, 1920), RE2. See also Real Estate Field," *The New York Times* (November 20, 1919), 25. By 1945, Shoremonde, or what was left of it, was valued at only $285,000. "Oyster Bay Estate of 65 Acres Bought," *The New York Times* (July 21, 1945), 21.

17. "Mrs. W.K. Vanderbilt Sells County House, 'Stepping Stones,' to Ormond G. Smith," *The New York Times* (January 19, 1921), 1.

18. According to *Long Island Country Houses and Their Architects: 1860-1940* (New York: Society for the Preservation of Long Island Antiquities/W.W. Norton & Company, 1997), Shoremonde was demolished in the 1940s, after it was given to John N. Willys's first wife in their divorce settlement. However, evidence suggests that the house survived and was sold again, in 1945, to Marcel A. Palmaro, a Monaco-born investment banker who was the principality's consul general in the United States.

PROJECTS FOR FRIENDS

1. The Fourth Annual Report of the Vacation Committee of the Women's Department (New York and New Jersey Section of the National Civic Federation, 1914), 5.

2. The Third Annual Report of the Vacation Committee of the Women's Department (Metropolitan Section for New York and New Jersey of the National Civic Federation, 1914), 5.

3. Lewis, *Ladies and Not-So-Gentle Women*, 294.

4. Ibid.

5. Ibid.

6. Smith, 169.

7. "Stages in the Building of a Castle," *Vogue* (June 1, 1915), 51.

8. Ibid.

9. Smith, *e*, 155.

10. Press cutting in file in the Theatre Collection of the Museum of the City of New York, undated.

11. Advertisement, *The New York Times* (July 16, 1914).

12. Smith, 180.

13. Untitled article (December 5, 1913), Robinson Locke Collection of Theatre Scrapbooks, New York Public Library (series 3, vol. 373), 52.

14. Rebecca W. Strum, *Elisabeth Marbury, 1856–1933: Her Life and Work* (New York University, unpublished Ph.D. thesis, Department of Performance Studies, 1989).

15. Ibid., 178–79.

16. Ibid., 179.

17. Ibid., 201.

18. Ibid., 205 and 207.

19. Ibid., 214.

20. Untitled article in *Strand* (October 1915), Robinson-Locke Collection of Theatre Scrapbooks, New York Public Library (series 3, vol. 373), 53.

21. Ibid.

DE WOLFE SHOWROOMS

1. Untitled newspaper article (1914), Robinson-Locke Collection of Theatre Scrapbooks, New York Public Library (series 3, vol. 373), 18.

2. Untitled article, *The New York Telegraph* (May 15, 1909), Robinson-Locke Collection of Theatre Scrapbooks, New York Public Library, 18.

3. De Wolfe's sister-in-law was born Winifred Kimball (1871–1957). She was a granddaughter of the Mormon patriarch Heber Kimball and the mother of silent film actress and designer Natacha Rambova (née Winifred Shaughnessy, later Mrs. Rudolph Valentino). Winifred Kimball married Edgar Sands de Wolfe as his second wife in 1907. After their divorce, she married Richard Hudnut, the perfume and cosmetics magnate.

4. A letter from de Wolfe to Shinn, May 19, 1906, made reference to his "sending [an] overmantel" to Strand, which could have been a New York City furnishing source or the popular magazine of the same name (Everett Shinn Collection, Archives of American Art, New York City).

5. Letter from de Wolfe to Stanford White, March 29 1906, McKim, Mead & White Archive in the Collections of The New-York Historical Society, New York.

6. Formerly the home of William de Forest Manice, an importer, 4 West 40th Street was divided into apartments after his death in 1903 and subsequently converted into a six-story mixed-use building. In addition to de Wolfe's office, it was home to the apartments of Ethel Barrymore and her brothers, Lionel and John. The building also held the studio of Elizabeth Eaton Burton, a decorative artist, and the studio of Herman Patrick Tappe, a society milliner. Another tenant was the Ford School of Expression, an academy specializing in "Elocution, Physical Training, Dancing, Fencing." *The New York Times* (November 11, 1907), 9.

7. Letter from de Wolfe to Frick, undated (Helen Clay Frick Foundation Archives, New York).

8. Letter from Kneissel to Frick, April 24, 1915 (Helen Clay Frick Foundation Archives, New York).

9. Letter from de Wolfe to Frick, June 19, 1915 (Helen Clay Frick Foundation Archives, New York).

10. *Arts and Decoration* (November 1921), 49. Cammeyer was a luxury shoe company that had its showroom on the premises, as well. The building still stands, opposite the highly social St. Thomas Episcopal Church, and was clearly in a very visible location.

11. In her 50th year, pictures of de Wolfe appeared in both *Vogue* (June 1, 1915) and *Town and Country* (May 10, 1915).

12. "As a Decorator Decorates Her Own Salons," *Vogue* (September 1, 1915), 44—45.

13. Ibid., 44.

14. Ibid., 45.

15. De Wolfe, *After All*, 199.

16. Ibid., 200.

17. *The New York Times* (May 1, 1937) declared that Elsie de Wolfe Inc. had liabilities of $45,856 and assets of $171,587. The president of the firm at that time was Wolf J. Overhamm.

18. *The New York Times* (November 20, 1938).

ADELAIDE AND HENRY CLAY FRICK

1. H. C. Frick, in letter to Miss G. V. Butler, August 14, 1914 (Helen Clay Frick Foundation Archives, New York).

2. M. F. S. Sanger, *The Henry Clay Frick Houses: Architecture, Interiors, Landscapes in the Golden Era* (New York: The Monacelli Press, 2001), 16.

3. Ibid., 27.

4. Ibid., 86–87.

5. Undated letter from the Ritz Hotel, from de Wolfe to Frick (Helen Clay Frick Foundation Archives, New York).

6. Sanger, *The Henry Clay Frick Houses*, 137.

7. Ibid., 142.

8. These objects were part of the Wallace Collection, based in London. They had been left to Sir John Murray Scott and, after his death, to his mistress, Lady Sackville. She in turn had made a deal with the art dealer Jacques Seligman that he could buy it from her if the contested will went in her favor.

9. Letter from de Wolfe to Frick, January 27, 1914 (Helen Clay Frick Foundation Archives, New York).

10. Letter from Frick to de Wolfe, March 19, 1914 (Helen Clay Frick Foundation Archives, New York).

11. In 1912 de Wolfe created interiors for Suffolk House, located in Boney Lane, Smithtown, on Long Island, New York. It was the summer home of the James Warren Lanes.

12. Letter from de Wolfe to Frick, March 20, 1914 (Helen Clay Frick Foundation Archives, New York), quoted in Edgar Munhall, "Elsie de Wolfe: The American Pioneer Who Vanquished Victorian Gloom," in *Architectural Digest* (January 2000), 149–239.

13. Ibid., September 2, 1915 (Helen Clay Frick Foundation Archives, New York).

14. Ibid., May 26, 1914 (Helen Clay Frick Foundation Archives, New York).

15. Ibid.

16. Ibid., undated, Friday, Hotel du Rhin (Helen Clay Frick Foundation Archives, New York).

17. Ibid., May 28, 1914 (Helen Clay Frick Foundation Archives, New York).

18. Letter from Frick to de Wolfe, December 1914 (Helen Clay Frick Foundation Archives, New York).

19. Letter from de Wolfe to Frick, June 5, 1914 (Helen Clay Frick Foundation Archives, New York).

20. Ibid., June 18, 1914 (Helen Clay Frick Foundation Archives, New York).

21. Attached as "private and confidential" to a letter from de Wolfe to Frick, June 14, 1914 (Helen Clay Frick Foundation Archives, New York).

22. Letter from Frick to Butler, August 14, 1914 (Helen Clay Frick Foundation Archives, New York).

23. Sanger, *The Henry Clay Frick Houses*, 203.

MAGNOLIA AND GEORGE SEALY

1. Stated by the daughter of Magnolia and George Sealy, Margaret Sealy Burton, in an unpublished history of the house (Galveston and Texas History Center, Rosenberg Library, Galveston, Texas).

2. E. H. Gustafson, "The Open Gates: The George Sealy House in Galveston," in *Antiques* (September 1975), 513.

3. Ibid.

4. Ibid., 508.

5. See note 1.

6. Gustafson, 513. Vernis Martin refers to a finish for furniture created in around 1720 by the Martin family, who invented a technique of painting items lightly in oil and covering the work with a layer of clear varnish (www.hammondmuseum.org).

7. B. L. Brooks, "Clarity, Contrast and Simplicity: Changes in American Interiors, 1880–1930," in Foy and Marling, *The Arts and the American Home, 1890–1930* (Knoxville: University of Tennessee Press, 1994), 32.

MAI AND WILLIAM R. COE

1. Planting Fields Inventory, no. 02-FG (April 2, 1991), 11.

2. Ibid.

3. R. Van Houghton, "Mrs. William R. Coe's Hand-Made Tea House," in *Town and Country* (July 1, 1916), 20.

4. General Ledger #1, 1912–18 (Planting Fields Foundation Archive, Planting Fields Foundation, Oyster Bay, New York).

5. Brochure on Coe Hall (Planting Fields Foundation, Oyster Bay, New York).

6. Letter from Walker and Gillette to W. R. Coe, May 21, 1920 (Planting Fields Foundation Archive, Oyster Bay, New York).

7. Giles Edgerton, "Modern Murals Done in French Spirit of Decoration," *Arts and Decoration* (November 1924), 28.

ELISABETH MARBURY

1. *The New York Times* (January 23, 1921).

2. Mark Alan Hewitt, *The Architecture of Mott B. Schmidt* (New York: Rizzoli, 1991), 3.

3. Ibid., 4.

4. *Gossip* (November 13, 1921), in Smith, 209.

5. Hewitt, 161.

6. Lewis, 360. Though Marbury's purchase of the house and the submission of Schmidt's remodeling plans were announced in *The New York Times* on January 15, 1921 (page 23), the approved remodeling design was dated April 11, 1921 (Hewitt, 161).

7. The distinctive bow windows were removed by a later owner and replaced by conventional double-hung windows.

8. The anemone painting, which hung in the second-floor stair hall amid 18th-century sketches and watercolors, strongly recalls the work of French society painter Bernard Boutet de Monvel, whose work was popular in the 1920s and 1930s.

9. The house was sold to the Hollywood film star Miriam Hopkins. Marbury's farm in Maine was sold to the cosmetics entrepreneur Elizabeth Arden, who had become close to Marbury in her last years. She turned it into the first Maine Chance health spa.

ANNE VANDERBILT

I. Anne Harriman was married three times. Her first husband was Samuel Stevens Sands Jr.; they married in 1880, and he died in 1888. Her second was Lewis Morris Rutherfurd, Jr.; they married in 1890, and he died in 1901. She married William Kissam Vanderbilt Sr. in 1903.

2. Circumstantial evidence suggests that the relationship between Morgan and Vanderbilt was more than platonic. A reporter sent by *The New York Times* to cover Vanderbilt's funeral delicately noted the "conspicuous absence" of Morgan, who was traveling in France.

3. Vanderbilt's sister Emeline Olin and her second husband, Stephen H. Olin, became Sutton Place residents soon after, moving next door to 3 Sutton Place. They would soon sell the house to Anne Morgan. Another of Vanderbilt's sisters, Lillie Havemeyer, would become a resident of the Sutton Place area as well, and she hired Mott B. Schmidt to design her house there as well as her country house in Roslyn, N.Y.

4. The lot was 100 feet long by 20 feet wide. *The New York Times*, (January 19, 1921), I.

5. The doorway in question is only reputedly by Wren. "Two Notable Houses on Sutton Place, New York," *The Architectural Forum* (August 1924), 49. The plan for Vanderbilt's house was dated March 2, 1921 (Hewitt, 161).

6. Schmidt, who also designed Anne Morgan's house next door, at 3 Sutton Place, reportedly ensured that its exterior harmonized with the architecture of Vanderbilt's house, which had recently been completed.

7. Off the dining room was a small riverfront terrace whose iron flower boxes, lamp posts, and fountains were adorned with playful modernist monkeys mounted on narrow pedestals, The designer of all these objects was artist Renée Prahar (1880-1962). *The New York Times* (February 9, 1922), 15.

8. Caroline Duer, "Painted Doors of Privacy." *House & Garden* (April 1922), 65.

9. A few years later, Cox executed similarly flamboyant chinoiserie murals for the dining room of Atlanta socialites Mae and James Goodrum.

10. Nancy McClelland, *The Practical Book of Decorative Wal-Treatments* (New York, Philadelphia, and London: J. B. Lippincott Company, 1926), 89.

11. Subsequent owners of the house include financier Charles Merrill (for whom Mott B. Schmidt would alter the house in 1943),; financier Richard Jenrette; Steuben Glass president Arthur A. Houghton, Jr., and condiment heiress Drue Heinz. The last redecorated its rooms with the help of the Italian designer Renzo Mongiardino, among others.

12. It is now the Hudson Hotel.

ANNE MORGAN

I. Hewitt, 8.

2. "Anne Morgan Plans a Bigger New Home," *The New York Times* (November 27, 1921), 5. The plans for the house, located in Schmidt's archives in the Avery Architecture Library at Columbia University, New York City, New York, are dated December 27 1921 (Hewitt, 161).

3. According to an article in *The Chicago Tribune* (August 17, 1955), the processional paper was removed as a "cost of $1,000" when the house changed owners after Morgan's death. It was then valued at $9,500.

4. De Wolfe, *The House in Good Taste*, 224.

5. Lewis, 422. Circumstantial evidence suggests that the two women were more than friends.

6. Morgan, who died in 1951, spent much of her remaining life traveling between France and a country house in Mount Kisco, N.Y., which she shared for many years with Anne Vanderbilt. In her absences, the Sutton Place house was leased to several individuals, including Arthur Amory Houghton, Jr., the president of Steuben Glass, and the banking heiress Ailsa Mellon and her husband, David K.E. Bruce, the future U.S. ambassador to the Court of St. James's. Houghton eventually bought 3 Sutton Place and had it altered by Mott B. Schmidt in 1952 (Hewitt, 164). Today it the official home of the Secretary General of the United Nations.

CONDÉ NAST

I. Edna Woolman Chase and Ilka Chase, *Always in Vogue* (London: Gollancz, 1954), 61.

2. Ibid.

3. Ibid., 55.

4. Ibid.

5. *Vogue* (June 1, 1915), 65.

6. *Vanity Fair* (March 1914, December 1917, July 1919).

7. Chase and Chase, 123.

8. Ibid., 173.

9. *Vogue* (August 1, 1928), 44–47.

10. Ruby Ross Wood, unpublished journals (Ruby Ross Wood Archives, Bangor, Maine).

11. McClelland, 95.

12. Ibid.

13. Ibid.

14. Chase and Chase, 174.

15. Ibid.

16. Ibid.

17. Ibid., 175.

NELL PRUYN CUNNINGHAM

1. Today it is a museum, The Hyde Collection. The Pruyn sisters' homes now are all part of The Hyde Collection complex; Nell Cunningham's house is the administrative building, with many of the furnishings supplied by the de Wolfe studio presently in storage.

2. Payment-received notice from Elsie de Wolfe Inc. to Mrs. L. F. Hyde, December 16, 1920 (The Hyde Collection Archives, Glens Falls, New York).

3. Letter from Blanche Judge to Miss N. K. Pruyn, March 25, 1924 (The Hyde Collection Archives, Glens Falls, New York).

4. Other employees of the de Wolfe studio in the interwar period included Albert Frank and Jessie Earnshaw (1890–1965), both of whom established independent decorating businesses after the demise of Elsie de Wolfe Inc. The latter was married to Philadelphia clubman Warner Gibbs Earnshaw Sr.; she went on to design a collection of modernized French Empire–style furniture for Grosfield House, a New York furniture company. Another de Wolfe staff decorator was Eleanor Cosden, the second wife of an Oklahoma oil millionaire.

5. Letter from Bachman to Pruyn, April 29, 1921 (The Hyde Collection Archives, Glens Falls, New York).

6. Ibid., June 4, 1921 (The Hyde Collection Archives, Glens Falls, New York).

7. Letter from Schmidt to Cunningham, February 16, 1925 (The Hyde Collection Archives, Glens Falls, New York). Elena B. Schmidt went on to become a successful decorator, counting among her achievements the decor and furnishings of the Rockefeller Center's Rainbow Room, created in 1934. Obituary of Elena Schmidt, *The New York Times* (June 30, 1955).

8. Letter from Schmidt to Hyde, January 28, 1929 (The Hyde Collection Archives, Glens Falls, New York).

9. Bill from Elsie de Wolfe Inc. to Pruyn, February 15, 1921 (The Hyde Collection Archives, Glens Falls, New York).

10. Letter to Schmidt from Cunningham, February 19, 1925 (The Hyde Collection Archives, Glens Falls, New York).

11. Bill from Elsie de Wolfe Inc. to Pruyn, December 13, 1920 (The Hyde Collection Archives, Glens Falls, New York). Born Netta Deweze Frazee Scudder (1869–1940), the Indiana-born artist was well known for her Renaissance-style sculptures, usually of playful children or animals. She was greatly admired by Stanford White, who used her work in his clients' homes and gardens.

12. "Serious Illness of Mrs. Mary Pruyn," *The New York Times* (June 24, 1884) 1. Also "Obituary Notes," *The New York Times* (February 12, 1885), 2.

FRANCES AND ZALMON G. SIMMONS JR.

1. Smith, 236.

2. Norman Bel Geddes, *Horizons* (Boston: Little, Brown, and Company, 1932), 236–37.

3. "Apartments in Demand," *The New York Times* (March 10, 1923), 22.

4. Best known for his more than 100 revival-style schools for the New York City Board of Education, (Harold) Eric Kebbon (1890–1964) also designed the Franklin Delano Roosevelt Library & Museum in Hyde Park, New York, as well as a summer house for Zalmon Simmons Jr.'s son Gilbert on Fishers Island, New York. In partnership with Edward Durrell Stone, Richard Boring Snow, Philip L. Goodwin, and Morris Ketchum Jr., Kebbon co-designed Food Court South for the Food Zone of the 1939 World's Fair.

5. Lowthorpe School was devoted to the professional training of women in English-style gardening.

6. Unfinished pine-paneled rooms were actually quite rare in 18th-century England, the wood being considered too inferior to be left unpainted. It is likely that the Simmonses's study incorporated paneling that had been stripped raw in response to a trend launched more than a decade earlier by de Wolfe ghostwriter-turned-decorator Ruby Ross Goodnow (later Wood). An authentic Georgian pine room that Goodnow exhibited in 1916 at John Wanamaker in New York City, reputedly the first seen in America, caused a stir in decorating circles across the country and launched a corresponding frenzy of chemical stripping.

7. The history and descriptions of Rambleside and its interiors was accessed in the William E. Finch Jr. Archives in the Historical Society of the Town of Greenwich. Information is also available in *The Great Estates: Greenwich, Connecticut, 1880–1930* (Canaan, NH: The Junior League of Greenwich, 1986) and *Greenwich in Pictures* (Greenwich, CT: The Greenwich Press, 1929).

10 AVENUE D'IÉNA

1. On the orders of the late prince's daughter, the psychoanalyst Marie Bonaparte (Princess George of Greece), the mansion was converted into apartments and sold, in 1928, to the Suez Company. The library became the headquarters of the French Geographic Society, an apt utilization given the prince's nickname, the Prince of Science. For years, his fortune supported geographical and ethnographical research.

2. De Wolfe, *After All*, 226.

3. De Wolfe, *The House in Good Taste*, 5.

4. De Wolfe, *After All*, 226.

5. Clipping entitled "Lady Mendl's Paris Apartment," magazine

unknown, circa 1932. Collection of R. Louis Bofferding, New York City.

6. Château de Courcelles, then long abandoned, became an international cause célèbre in 1926, when it was reportedly sold to an unidentified American millionaire, who intended to reconstruct it on Long Island. (In actuality, he only bought some major architectural features.) De Wolfe likely obtained its walnut boiserie from the Paris dealer H. S. de Souhami.

7. The coach was probably James Upjohn (1722–95), an English clock- and watchmaker and goldsmith who worked in Clerkenwell.

8. De Wolfe, *After All*, 227.

9. Ibid., 228.

10. Oswald Mosley, *My Life* (London: Thomas Nelson & Sons, 1968), 83.

11. De Wolfe soon replaced the antique chimneypiece with a sleek mirrored version and the likely uncomfortable zebra skin upholstery with a white material, perhaps cotton canvas, accented with loose zebra cushions.

12. Ordered in December 1929, it was delivered four months later. The table was recently (2004) being sold by Delorenzo, a New York City gallery.

13. Decades later, the secretary was found at a tag sale in New York City.

HOPE HAMPTON AND JULES BRULATOUR

1. "Bloodgood Suicide Laid to Anxiety," *The New York Times*, (December 7, 1907), 5.

2. The artist Everett Shinn, to whom de Wolfe subcontracted the project, recalled the completed piano as "a sort of Frenchy thing." Aline B. Lochheim, "Last of the 'Eight' Looks Back." *The New York Times* (November 2, 1952), X9.

3. Smith, 245.

4. *The New York Times* (January 29, 1939).

5. Brulatour became wealthy through his investment in, and quick sale of, undeveloped motion picture film. On his death in 1946, he left an estate of more than $2.1 million.

6. Hewitt would photograph the house in various decorative incarnations from 1935 until 1943.

7. L. Ray, "Achieving Eighteenth-Century Luxury with Modern Comfort," *Arts and Decoration* (January 1938), 35.

8. Ibid.

9. Ibid.

10. Ibid.

11. Ibid.

12. In spring and summer, the windows, bed, and other upholstered furniture were dressed entirely in flowered chintz.

THE DUKE AND DUCHESS OF WINDSOR

1. McMullin died in 1944, aged 55. He was the Paris editor of *Vogue* until 1940, as well as a syndicated columnist on men's fashion. In some accounts of the Mendls' life, McMullin is incorrectly described as their adopted son.

2. Though neither she nor de Wolfe ever mentioned the connection, Simpson's first brush with one of the decorator's interiors came in 1918, when she was living in Coronado, California, and was a frequent guest at the home of de Wolfe client Florence Dupee.

3. Elsie de Wolfe (Lady Mendl), *Elsie de Wolfe's Recipes for Successful Dining* (New York and London: D. Appleton-Century Company, 1935).

4. Greg King, *The Duchess of Windsor: The Uncommon Life of Wallis Simpson* (New York: Citadel Press, 1999), 126.

5. Untitled newspaper clipping (undated), in "Photos of de Wolfe" file in archive of the Museum of the City of New York.

6. The Cholly Knickerbocker society column was a feature of *The New York Journal-American*. At the time of the Windsor–de Wolfe mention, it was written by Maury Paul (d. 1942), the paper's society editor.

7. Untitled newspaper cutting dated July 8, 1936, in "Photos of de Wolfe" file in archive of the Museum of the City of New York.

8. "Mrs. Simpson Rents House," *The New York Times* (October 4, 1936), N4. Another article in *The New York Times* several weeks later states that Simpson had rented the house for a year. In any event, Edward VIII abdicated in December, and Simpson fled to France, cutting short her lease.

9. Described by *The New York Times* as "an actress of beauty and promise" in her youth, the former Eileen Kearney (born c. 1892) was better known for her marital history. Her first husband was Charles B. Dillingham (1868–1934), a theatrical and movie producer who was the partner of de Wolfe's mentor Charles Frohman, and she was married twice to Capt. Julian B. L. Allen (1899–1967), an American banker. During her 1913–1924 marriage to Dillingham, Allen worked closely with members of the de Wolfe–Marbury–Vanderbilt circle on war-relief activities. In 1920, she and Dillingham also purchased a house at 153 East 63rd Street from Anne Vanderbilt, which suggests they may have been de Wolfe clients as well.

10. Cecil Beaton, *Cecil Beaton's Scrapbook* (London: B.T. Batsford Ltd., 1937), 27.

11. Article in *The Telegraph*, dated April 8, 1937, in File NWE2, nc 13,222, Robinson-Locke Collection of Theatre Scrapbooks, New York Public Library.

12. De Wolfe, "Modern Regency: A New Interpretation of an Old Period," *Arts and Decoration* (May 1937), 34–36 and 48.

13. Ibid., 34.

14. Ibid., 48.

15. In 1938, however, they did spent a few months at a rented house in Versailles, Château de la Maye, and so were de Wolfe's neighbors for a brief period.

16. Windsors May Take Villa," *The New York Times* (April 20, 1938), 11. A two-year lease was signed April 22, 1938, "Duchess of Windsor Gets Gold Bathtub in Villa," *The New York Times* (April 23, 1938), 6.

17. As of 2004, the house is an abandoned ruin, much damaged by fire.

18. Sir Pomeroy Burton (1868–1947), was an American-born journalist, a one-time executive on the *The New York World,* and later general manager of *The London Daily Mail* (*The New York Times,* Oct. 16, 1947).

19. P. H. Philip, "First Windsor Anniversary," *The New York Times* (May 29, 1938), 39.

20. For Boudin's association, see Suzy Menkes, *The Windsor Style* (London: Grafton Books, 1987), 82. According to the duchess, her first weeks at La Croë were spent amid "an avalanche of crates, linen baskets, furniture, trunks of clothing, bales of draperies, [and] chests of silver" (Menkes, 76).

21. King, 305.

22. *The New York Times* (April 23, 1938).

23. McMullin, undated, part of lot 1791, described in Sotheby's catalogue for Property from the Collection of the Duke and Duchess of Windsor (New York, 1997), 8.

24. The president of Jansen, the eminent French decorating company, and later a decorator of the Kennedy White house, Boudin was intimately involved in La Croë's interiors, as well as the rooms of Boulevard Suchet and later Windsor homes. Since de Wolfe no longer had her own decorating establishment, it is likely that many of La Croë's furnishings passed through Jansen's workrooms, being reupholstered, refinished or, in the case of curtains and cushions, created there.

25. Among these items were numerous antiques, most important being the George III library table at which the then King of Great Britain and Emperor of India signed the Instrument of Abdication on December 10, 1936.

26. *The New York Times* (January 24, 1939).

27. King, 309.

28. The tabletop was eventually changed to polished mahogany when it became apparent that the glare reflected off the mirrored top was distracting.

29. King, 311.

30. Untitled newspaper cutting (1939), Clippings File, Robinson Locke Collection of Theatre Scrapbooks, New York Public Library, New York.

New York Hotels

1. "Ina Claire Lives Here," *House and Garden* (October 1936), 50.

2. Serge Platonovitch Obolensky Neledinsky-Meletzky (1890–1978) was a Russian prince born to a family close to the Romanov czars. His first wife, Princess Catherine Bariatinsky, in fact, was an illegitimate daughter of Alexander II of Russia. Obolensky married in 1924, as his second wife, Alice Astor, the daughter of Ava Astor, a founder of the Colony Club. They were divorced in 1932, though Obolensky went on to work for the Astor family's real-estate company, which included the St. Regis Hotel. Serge Obolensky, *One Man in His Time* (New York: McDowell, Obolensky, 1958).

3. People who owned de Wolfe–decorated homes also recognized the value in publicizing her association with their properties. A real-estate advertisement in *The New York Times* (May 24, 1925, WI) emphasized the desirability of a furnished 12-room apartment available for summer rental by identifying de Wolfe as its decorator.

4. Rogers (née Mary Benjamin, 1879–1956) was the former wife of Standard Oil millionaire Col. Henry Huddleston Rogers, mistress of the French society painter Bernard Boutet de Monvel, and mother of socialite and jewelry designer Millicent Rogers. She exhibited her paintings frequently in New York and California and was the subject of admiring reviews that praised her works' "warmth and personal charm," "French spirit," and "individual lyric quality." Howard Devree, "A Reviewer's Notes: Recent Sculpture by de Creeft–Bohrod, Serger, Mrs. Rogers and George Chann," *The New York Times* (November 21, 1943), X7.

5. Obolensky, 399. Obolensky can be credited with fueling this movement. In addition to de Wolfe's suite, other rooms in hotels he managed featured spaces decorated by Cecil Beaton, Charles de Beistegui, and other international arbiters of taste.

6. Curtis Gathje, *At The Plaza: An Illustrated History of the World's Most Famous Hotels* (New York: St. Martin's Press, 2000), 89.

7. Smith, 311.

After All

1. Bemelmans, 19.

2. Smith, 300.

3. De Wolfe, *After All.*

4. Ibid., 301.

5. One of her protégés, the decorator James Amster, took de Wolfe's advice and installed a large sheet of mirrored glass on

the rear wall of his midtown Manhattan garden. Eventually, a thick frame of ivy grew around it, providing the illusion of a door to another garden.

6. Bemelmans, 7.

7. Ranken was a de Wolfe favorite, having painted a portrait of Bessy Marbury as well as views of Villa Trianon. As for black-amoor statues, these exotic representations of costumed Africans, often in 18th-century fancy dress, were highly popular in the 1920s and 1930s, favored by international tastemakers like Charles de Beistegui, Diana Vreeland, and Elsa Schiaparelli.

8. Duquette (1914–1999) later shared a Tony Award with Adrian for costumes designed for the 1961 Broadway production of *Camelot*. He also designed interiors and objects for J. Paul Getty, the Duke and Duchess of Windsor, and Doris Duke, as well as a segment of the 1961 film *The Four Horsemen of the Apocalypse*.

9. Bemelmans, 43.

10. "A Woman of Taste," *House and Garden* (April 1950), 108. Given that de Wolfe suffered from arthritis, it seems likely that her secretary did the work.

11. Bemelmans, 61.

12. Ibid., 19.

13. Ibid., 20.

14. Ibid., 145.

VILLA TRIANON

1. Bemelmans, 92.

2. De Wolfe, *After All*, 201.

3. Bemelmans, 92.

4. Martin Battersby, *The Decorative Twenties* (New York: Walker and Company, 1969).

5. Ibid., 51.

6. Marcel Vertès, who had left his native Hungary in 1918, was a chronicler of Parisian nightlife of the 1920s and had established a reputation for himself by creating images for illustrated magazines. In addition to the murals for Villa Trianon and his portrait of de Wolfe, he painted a mural for de Wolfe's suite in the Plaza Hotel and executed books illustrations for the heiress-novelist Daisy Fellowes and advertising art for the couturier Elsa Schiaparelli.

7. De Wolfe, *After All*, 203.

8. Bemelmans, 202.

9. Rieder, 119.

10. Smith, 217.

11. De Wolfe, *After All*, 203.

12. *House and Garden* (November 1936), 46.

13. French *Vogue* (August 1933), 50.

14. Smith, 237.

15. Ibid.

16. British *Vogue* (August 24, 1938), 30.

17. Bemelmans, 204.

Bibliography

BOOKS

Beaton, Cecil. *The Glass of Fashion.* London: Weidenfeld and Nicolson, 1954.

Bemelmans, Ludwig. *To the One I Love the Best.* New York: Viking, 1955.

Betsky, Aaron. *Queer Space: Architecture and Same-Sex Desire.* New York: William Morrow and Company, 1997.

Brooks, Bradley C. "Clarity, Contrast, and Simplicity: Changes in American Interiors." In Jessica H. Foy and
    Karal Ann Marling, eds., *The Arts and the American Home.* Knoxville: The University of Tennessee Press, 1994.

Campbell, Nina, and Caroline Seebohm. *Elsie de Wolfe: A Decorative Life.* New York: Panache Press, 1992.

Castle, Irene. *Castles in the Air.* New York: Doubleday, 1958.

Castle, Vernon, and Irene Castle. *Modern Dancing.* New York: Harper and Brothers, 1914.

Chase, Edna Woolman, and Ilka Chase. *Always in Vogue.* New York: Doubleday, 1954.

Cox, Anne F. *The History of the Colony Club, 1903–1984.* New York: Private Press, 1984.

DeShazo, Edith. *Everett Shinn, 1876–1953: A Figure of His Time.* New York: Clarkson N. Potter, 1974.

de Wolfe, Elsie. *After All.* New York: Harper and Brothers, 1935.

———. *The House in Good Taste.* New York: The Century Company, 1913.

————(Lady Mendl). *Elsie de Wolfe's Recipes for Successful Dining.* New York: D. Appleton-Century, 1934.

Doumato, Lamia. *Candace Wheeler and Elsie de Wolfe (Decorators): A Bibliography.* Monticello, IL: Vance Bibliographies, 1989.

Fahey, John. *Shaping Spokane: Jay P. Graves and His Times.* Seattle: University of Washington Press, 1994.

Flanner, Janet. *An American in Paris: Profile of an Interlude Between Two Wars.* New York: Simon and Schuster, 1940.

————. *Paris Was Yesterday, 1925–1939.* New York: Viking, 1972.

Garnett, Porter. *The Stately Homes of California.* Boston: Little, Brown, and Company, 1915.

Hamm, Margherita Arlina. *Eminent Actors in Their Homes.* New York: James Pott and Co., 1902.

Hampton, Mark. *Legendary Decorators of the Twentieth Century.* New York: Doubleday, 1992.

Hewitt, Mark Alan. *The Architecture of Mott B. Schmidt.* New York: Rizzoli, 1991.

King, Greg. *The Duchess of Windsor: The Uncommon Life of Wallis Simpson.* New York: Citadel Press, 1999.

Lewis, Alfred A. *Ladies and Not-So-Gentle Women: Elisabeth Marbury, Anne Morgan, Elsie de Wolfe, Anne Vanderbilt, and Their Times.* New York: Viking, 2000.

Lowe, David Garrad. *Stanford White's New York.* New York: Watson-Guptill Publications, 1999.

Lynes, Russell. *The Tastemakers: The Shaping of American Popular Taste.* New York: Dover Publications, Inc., 1949.

MacKay, Robert B., Anthony K. Baker, and Carol A. Traynor, eds. *Long Island Country Houses and Their Architects.* Long Island: Society for the Preservation of Long Island Antiquities, in association with W. W. Norton and Company, 1997.

Marbury, Elisabeth. *My Crystal Ball: Reminiscences.* New York: Boni and Liveright, 1923.

Marra, Kim. "A Lesbian Marriage of Cultural Consequence: Elisabeth Marbury and Elsie de Wolfe, 1886–1933." In Robert A. Schanke and Kim Marra, eds., *Passing*

Performances: Queer Readings of Leading Players in American Theater History. Ann Arbor: University of Michigan Press, 1998.

Matthews, Henry C. *Kirtland Cutter, Architect in the Land of Promise.* Seattle: University of Washington Press, 1998.

McClelland, N. *The Practical Book of Wall Treatments.* Philadelphia: J. B. Lippincott Co., 1926.

Metcalf, Pauline C., ed. *Ogden Codman and the Decoration of Houses.* Boston: Atheneum and David R. Godine, 1988.

Morgan, Anne. *The American Girl: Her Education. Her Responsibility, Her Recreation, Her Future.* New York: Harper and Brothers, 1915.

Obolensky, Serge. *One Man in His Time.* New York: McDowell, Oblensky, 1958.

Rieder, William. *A Charmed Couple: The Art and Life of Walter and Matilda Gay.* New York: Harry N. Abrams, 2000.

Robsjohn-Gibbings, T. H. *Goodbye, Mr. Chippendale.* New York: Alfred A. Knopf, 1944.

Sanger, Martha Frick Symington. *The Henry Clay Frick Houses: Architecture, Interiors, Landscapes in the Golden Era.* New York: The Monacelli Press, 2001.

Smith, Jane S. *Elsie de Wolfe, A Life in the High Style: The Elegant Life and Remarkable Career of Elsie de Wolfe, Lady Mendl.* New York: Atheneum, 1982.

Sparke, Penny. "Elsie de Wolfe and Her Female Clients, 1905–1915: Gender, Class and the Professional Interior Decorator." In Brenda Martin and Penny Sparke, eds., *Women's Places: Architecture and Design, 1860–1960.* London and New York: Routledge, 2003.

Tapert, Annette, and Diana Edkins. *The Power of Style: The Women Who Defined the Art of Living Well.* New York: Crown Publishers, 1994.

Taves, Isabella. *Successful Women and How They Attained Success.* New York: E. P. Dutton, 1943.

The Great Estates: Greenwich, Connecticut, 1880–1930. Canaan, NH: Published for the Junior League of Greenwich by Phoenix Publishing, 1986.

Wharton, Edith, and Ogden Codman Jr. *The Decoration of Houses.* New York: Charles Scribner's Sons, 1897.

White, Marian C. *A History of Barnard College.* New York: University of Columbia Press, 1954.

ARTICLES

"Actress Is Decorator." In *Spokane Review,* May 31, 1909.

Armstrong, W. "Silhouettes: Miss Elsie de Wolfe." In *Leslie's Weekly,* January 16, 1902.

"The Art of Decorating a House Charmingly Displayed in a Fifth Avenue Home." In *New York Times,* January 15, 1915.

"As a Decorator Decorates Her Own Salons." In *Vogue*, September 1, 1915.

Baldwin, W. "Who's Afraid of Elsie de Wolfe?" In *Vogue*, June 1963.

"Commandant Paul-Louis Weiller's Villa." In *House and Garden*, June 1949.

de Wolfe, Elsie. "After All." In *Ladies' Home Journal*, October 1934–May 1935.

―――. "The American Woman as Decorator." In *International Architect*, December 1931.

―――. "Chateaux in Touraine." In *Cosmopolitan*, February 1891.

―――. "Individuality in Stage Settings." In *Strand Magazine*, October 1915.

―――. "Modern Regency: A New Interpretation of an Old Period." In *House and Garden*, September 1936.

―――. "My Own House." In *Harper's Bazaar*, July 1913.

―――. "The Old Washington Irving House in New York as It Is Today." In *The Delineator*, October 1911.

―――. "Our House Interiors I: The Development of the Modern House." In *Good Housekeeping*, May 1912.

―――. "Our House Interiors II: The Treatment of Walls." In *Good Housekeeping*, June 1912.

―――. "Our House Interiors III: The Effective Use of Color." In *Good Housekeeping*, July 1912.

―――. "Our House Interiors IV: The Treatment of Windows." In *Good Housekeeping*, August 1912.

―――. "Our House Interiors V: The Small Apartment." In *Good Housekeeping*, September 1912.

―――. "Our House Interiors VI: Halls and Staircases." In *Good Housekeeping*, October 1912.

―――. "Our House Interiors VII: Reproduction Versus Antiques." In *Good Housekeeping*, November 1912.

―――. "Our House Interiors VIII: The Problem of Artificial Light." In *Good Housekeeping*, December 1912.

―――. "Our House Interiors IX: The Equipment of the Bedroom." In *Good Housekeeping*, January 1913.

―――. "Our House Interiors X: A Light, Gay Dining Room." In *Good Housekeeping*, February 1913.

―――. "Our House Interiors XI: The Living Room." In *Good Housekeeping*, March 1913.

―――. "Our House Interiors XII: Closets and Dressing Rooms." In *Good Housekeeping*, April 1913.

———. "Our House Interiors XIII: The Art of Treillage." In *Good Housekeeping,* May 1913.

———. "Our House Interiors XIV: A Little Talk on Clocks." In *Good Housekeeping,* June 1913.

———. "Period Furniture." In *The Delineator,* March 1912.

———. "Recipes for Successful Dining." In *Ladies' Home Journal,* August 1934.

———. "The Revival of Chintz." In *The Delineator,* June 1912.

———. "A Romance of Old Shoes." In *Cosmopolitan,* April 1892.

———. "The Story of the Colony Club." In *The Delineator,* November 1911.

———. "Stray Leaves from My Book of Life." In *Metropolitan Magazine* XIV, 1901.

———. "Transforming a Small City House." In *The Delineator,* February 1912.

———. "Villa Trianon." In *The Delineator,* May 1912.

Duquette, T. "Elsie de Wolfe: The Decorator's Villa Trianon in Versailles." In *Architectural Digest,* September 1996.

———. "Historic Interiors: Lady Mendl—Her Beloved Villa Trianon." In *Architectural Digest,* June 1982.

Dunbar, O. H. "The Newest Woman's Club." In *Putman's Monthly,* May 1907.

"Elisabeth Marbury." In *Harper's Bazaar,* December 9, 1899.

"Elsie de Wolfe Circa 1901: The Dynamics Of Prescriptive Feminine Performance in American Theatre and Society." In *Theatre Survey,* May 1994.

Emery, S. R. "Elsie de Wolfe: The Legend Lives On." In *Interior Design,* August 1982.

Fessenden, H. de Witt. "The Country House of Ormond G. Smith Esq." In *The Architectural Record,* August 1916.

"Freedom in Interior Decoration As Expressed by Elsie De Wolfe in an Interview with Hildegarde Hawthorne." In *Touchstone* 8, February 1921.

Geran, M. "Women in Design." In *Interior Design,* February 1980.

Goodnow, Ruby Ross. "Our Lady of the Decorations." In *The Delineator,* September 1911.

———. "The Story of Elsie de Wolfe." In *Good Housekeeping* June 1913.

————. "The Villa Trianon." In *Vogue,* March 1, 1914.

Gustafson, E. H. "The Open Gates: The George Sealy House in Galveston." In *Antiques,* September 1975.

Hadley, R. van N. "Elsie de Wolfe and Isabella Stewart Gardner." In *Fenway Court 1981.* Boston: Isabella Stewart Gardner Museum, 1982.

"Houses of Miss Anne Morgan and Mrs. W. K. Vanderbilt." In *American Architect and Architecture,* February 13, 1924.

"Ina Claire Lives Here." In *House and Garden,* October 1936.

"Lady Mendl at Home." In *House and Garden,* May 1941.

"Lady Mendl Dies in France at 84." In *New York Times,* July 13, 1950.

"Long Island Lineage." In *Architectural Digest,* August 1999.

McMullin, Johnnie. "Arabian Nights in Paris." In *Vogue,* August 15, 1939.

————. "A House Party in Tunisia: As Seen by Him." In *Vogue,* August 15, 1931.

————. "Lady Mendl's Fête at Versailles." In *Vogue,* August 15, 1938.

————. "Palm Beach, 1934." In *Vogue,* February 1, 1934.

————. "The Paris Season: As Seen by Him." In *Vogue,* August 31, 1929.

————. "We Went to India." In *Vogue,* July 15, 1938.

McNeil, P. "Designing Women: Gender, Sexuality and the Interior Decorator." In *Art History Journal* 17 (December 1994), 631–57.

McQuade, W. "Miss de Wolfe Who Decorated." In *Architectural Forum,* March 1966.

Meenan, M. "Who's Afraid of Elsie de Wolfe?" In *Town and Country,* July 1979.

"Miss de Wolfe's Exquisite Gowns." In *Harper's Bazaar,* February 3, 1900.

Moats, A-L. "The Elsie Legend." In *Harper's Bazaar,* May 1949.

"Mr. Deeds Comes Home." In *House and Garden,* September 1936.

"The Multi-Millionaires of Chicago I: J. Ogden Armour." In *Chicago Tribune*, June 2, 1907.

Munhall, E. "Elsie de Wolfe: The American Decorator Who Vanquished Victorian Gloom." In *Architectural Digest*, January 2000.

"The New York Apartment of Conde Nast Esq." In *Vogue*, August 1, 1928.

Owens, M. "Echoes of Elsie." In *Metropolitan Home*, November 1992.

Pendleton, I. "A House and Garden Built in Four Months." In *Landscape Architecture*, April 1949.

Platt, F. "Elsie de Wolfe: The Chintz Lady." In *Art and Antiques*, September/October 1980.

"Portrait." In *Architectural Forum*, October 1936.

"Portrait." In *Interiors*, April 1951.

"Profiles: Lady into Dynamo." In *The New Yorker*. October 22, 1927.

Ray, L. "Achieving Eighteenth-Century Luxury with Modern Comfort." In *Arts and Decoration*, January 1938.

"Re-do for the Plaza: Bring the Outdoors In." In *Architectural Forum*, February 1946.

Richardson, N. "Elsie de Wolfe." In *House and Garden*, April 1982.

"Scrapbooks of Style." In *House Beautiful*, May 1997.

Sorensen, H. "American in Paris: The Villa Trianon, Lady Mendl's House in Versailles." In *Connoisseur*, November 1981.

Sparke, Penny. "The 'Ideal' and the 'Real' Interior in Elsie de Wolfe's *The House in Good Taste* of 1913." In *Journal of Design History* 16, no.1, 63–76.

"Stages in the Building of a Castle." In *Vogue*, June 1, 1915.

"Temperance Roof Garden Open: Women Experiment in New York." In *Minneapolis Journal*, January 5, 1915.

"Two Notable Houses on Sutton Place, New York: The Houses of Mrs. W. K. Vanderbilt and Miss Anne Morgan, Mott B. Schmidt, Architect." In *The Architectural Forum*, August 1924.

"Two Rooms Decorated by Elsie de Wolfe." In *House and Garden*, August 1934.

"Walls Do Not a Prison Make." In *Harper's Bazaar*, February 1916.

"What Every Woman Wants to Know: Miss Elsie de Wolfe Tells of Her Adventures in House Decorating—How She Re-made the Villa Trianon." In the *New York Times,* February 1, 1914.

Wight, Peter B. "Mellody Farm: The Country Home of J. Ogden Armour Esq." In *The Architectural Record,* February 1916.

"Woman of Taste." In *House and Garden,* April 1950.

Van Houghton, R. "Mrs. William Coe's Hand-Made Tea House." In *Town and Country,* July 1, 1916.

Yeomans, H. M. "A Remodelled City House." In *American Homes and Gardens* (December 1913), 422–25 and 441.

ARCHIVES/PRIMARY SOURCES

The Barnard College Archives, Wollmann Library, New York.

The Byron Collection, the Museum of the City of New York, New York.

Clippings files in the Theatre Collection, the New York Public Library for the Performing Arts, Lincoln Center, New York.

The Colony Club Papers in the McKim, Mead and White Archive, Collections of the New York Historical Society, New York.

The Everett Shinn Collection, Archives of American Art, Smithsonian Institution.

The Helen Clay Frick Foundation Archives, the Frick Collection and Frick Art Reference Library, New York.

The Hyde Collection Archive, Glen Falls, New York.

The Isabella Stewart Gardner papers, 1760–1956, Isabella Stewart Gardner Museum, Boston, Massachusetts / Archives of American Art, Smithsonian Institution.

The Local History Department Archive, the Joint Free Public Library of Morristown and Morris Township, Morristown, New Jersey.

The Mattie Edwards Hewitt and Richard A. Smith Photographic Collection, New York Historical Society, New York.

The Northwest Museum of Arts and Culture Archive, Spokane, Washington.

The Ogden Codman Drawings in the Avery Architectural Drawings Collection, the Avery Architectural and
Fine Arts Library of Columbia University, New York.

The Planting Fields Foundation Archive, Oyster Bay, New York.

The Samuel Gottscho Archives, the Avery Architectural and Fine Art Library, Columbia University, New York.

Scrapbooks from the Robinson Locke Collection, 1870–1920, in the Billy Rose Theatre Collection at the
New York Public Library for the Performing Arts, Lincoln Center, New York.

Strum, Rebecca W. *Elisabeth Marbury, 1856–1933: Her Life and Work.* New York University, unpublished Ph.D. thesis,
1989.

The Theatre Collection of the Museum of the City of New York.

The Vizcaya Museum and Gardens Archive, Miami, Florida.

The William E. Finch Jr. Archives, the Historical Society of the Town of Greenwich, Connecticut.

Index

My sincere thanks go to all the people who made researching and writing this book both easier than it might otherwise have been and, above all, pleasurable. Among those who either assisted me in accessing material or who gave me general support along the way were Jeremy Aynsley; Mary Beth Betts; Edith S. Bingham; Susan Bishop (the Hyde Collection, Glen Falls); Thea Bloomfeldt (Northwest Museum of Arts and Culture, Spokane); Andrew Bolton (the Costume Institute at the Metropolitan Museum of Art); Amy Braitsch (Historical Society of the Town of Greenwich); Christopher Breward; Quintin Colville; Nancy Compau (Spokane Public Library); Ellen M. Cone Busch (Planting Fields Foundation); Erin M. Coe (the Hyde Collection, Glen Falls); Helene Corlett (Madison Public Library); Lydia Cresswell-Jones (Sotheby's); John Culme; Lou DiGennaro (the Avery Library); Elana Donovan; Regina J. Drucker; Emma Ferry; Amy Folk (Oyster Bay Historical Society); Richard Foster (New York Public Library); Alice T. Friedman; Susan Galassi (the Frick Collection); Katherine M. Gerlough (the Frick Collection); Donald Glassman (Barnard College Archives); Paul Glassman (New York School of Interior Design); Martin Hale (the Colony Club); Robert Ham QC; Holly Hinman (New York Historical Society); Hartmut Hofacker; Maureen Hourigan; Debra Marsh Hunt (Crystal Springs Uplands School); Marty Jacobs (Museum of the City of New York); Maybeth Kavanagh (New York Historical Society); Trevor Keeble; Christine Kim (the Frick Collection); Deborah King (Chicago Historical Society); Pat Kirkham; Valerie Komor; Tom Lisanti (New York Public Library); Trina Lopez (California Historical Society); Julie A. Ludwig (Helen Clay Frick Foundation Archives); Grace Lees Maffei; Nik Maffei; Kim Marra; Rita Howard S. Marks; McAyeal (Lake Forest Academy); Catherine McDermott; Michele A. McDonald (Vizcaya Museum and Gardens); Susie McKellar; Angela A. Mattia (Museum of the City of New York); Martha May (Burlingame Historical Society); Mary Meehan (Lake Forest Academy); Gillian Naylor; Viviana Narotzky; Sara Nichols; Liz O'Brien; Alexandra Palmer; Susan E. Perry (the Art Institute of Chicago); Julia Anne Peterlin (the Rosenberg Library, Texas); Carol Peterson (San Mateo County Historical Association); Mary A. Prendergast; Sharon Prendergast (Foley Library, Spokane); Kate Riley (Oyster Bay Historical Society); Sandy Schreier; Jane S. Smith; Jason Stein; Michael Stier (Condé Nast); Mrs. Francis Thorne (the Colony Club); David and Jane Tolson; Philip Vergeylen; Paul Waite; Rayette Wilder (Northwest Museum of Arts and Culture, Spokane); Jamie Wolf; Janay Wong; Peggy Zeigler (California Historical Society).

The Arts and Humanities Research Board made possible the final stages of the research and the acquisition of many of the photographs through the award of a small research grant. Special thanks go to Tony Jones at the School of the Art Institute of Chicago and Susan Soros at the Bard Graduate Center for Studies in the Decorative Arts, Design and Culture in New York for accommodation in those two expensive cities. Above all, the research could not have been completed without the kind help and support of Mitchell Owens, the source of much information and the editor of the text, and Hutton Wilkinson, the chairman of the Elsie de Wolfe Foundation. The book could not have been produced without the vision and skills of Barry Cenower and the editing and production skills of Angela Buckley and Richard Johnson.

Finally, as ever, my most heartfelt thanks go to my family—my husband, John, and daughters Molly, Nancy, and Celia—who, having heard it so many times over the last few years, will, I am sure, never forget the name "Elsie de Wolfe."

Colophon

This book is set in Centaur, a font based on a roman type by Nicolas Jenson (Venice, 1469). The roman capitals were designed as a titling font by Bruce Rogers for the Metropolitan Museum (1912–1914). Subsequently lowercase letters were added, and the font was released by Monotype in 1929. The italic, called Arrighi, was designed by Frederic Warde in 1925 and is based on Ludovico Arrighi's chancery font (Venice, 1520). The typeface is named after the publication it was first used in, Maurice de Guérin's *The Centaur* (printed in an edition of 660 copies at the Press of the Wooly Whale). The display type is Shelley Script Allegro, a font designed by Matthew Carter in 1972.

Book design by Jeanne Abboud
Printed and bound by C & C Offset Printing Company, Ltd.

Luce de Goge